ISAIAH *for* I

CONTENTS

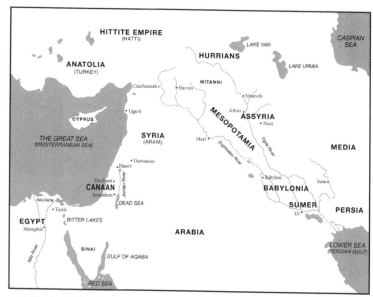

© Karla Bohmbach

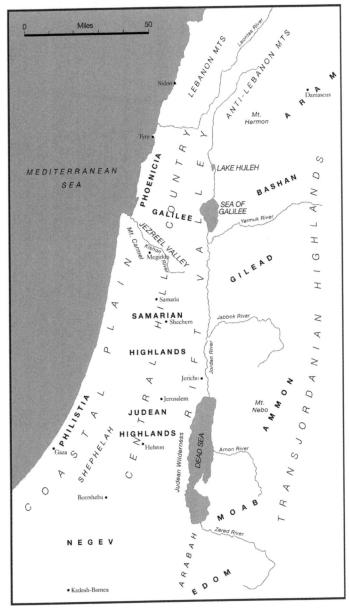

© Karla Bohmbach

ACKNOWLEDGMENTS

The translation at the beginning of each chapter (and in other biblical quotations) is my own. I have stuck closer to the Hebrew than modern translations often do when they are designed for reading in church so that you can see more precisely what the text says. Thus although I prefer to use gender-inclusive language, I have let the translation stay gendered if inclusivizing it would obscure whether the text was using singular or plural—in other words, the translation often uses "he" where in my own writing I would say "they" or "he or she." Sometimes I have added words to make the meaning clear, and I have put these words in square brackets. At the end of the book is a glossary of some terms that recur in the text, such as geographical, historical, and theological expressions. In each chapter (though not in the introduction or in the Scripture selections) these terms are highlighted in **bold** the first time they occur.

The stories that follow the translation often concern my friends or my family. While none are made up, they are sometimes heavily disguised in order to be fair to people. Sometimes I have disguised them so well that when I came to read the stories again, I was not sure at first whom I was describing. My first wife, Ann, appears in a number of them. Two years before I started writing this book, she died after negotiating with multiple sclerosis for forty-three years. Our shared dealings with her illness and disability over these years contribute significantly to what I write in ways that you may be able to see in the context of my commentary and also in ways that are less obvious.

Not long before I started writing this book, I fell in love with and married Kathleen Scott, and I am grateful for my new life with her and for her insightful comments on the manuscript. Her insights have been so carefully articulated and are so illuminating that she practically deserves to be credited as coauthor. I am also grateful to Matt Sousa for reading through the manuscript and pointing out things I needed to correct or clarify, and to Tom Bennett for checking the proofs.

INTRODUCTION

As far as Jesus and the New Testament writers were concerned, the Jewish Scriptures that Christians call the "Old Testament" *were* the Scriptures. In saying that, I cut corners a bit, as the New Testament never gives us a list of these Scriptures, but the body of writings that the Jewish people accept is as near as we can get to identifying the collection that Jesus and the New Testament writers would have worked with. The church also came to accept some extra books such as Maccabees and Ecclesiasticus that were traditionally called the "Apocrypha," the books that were "hidden away"—a name that came to imply "spurious." They're now often known as the "Deuterocanonical Writings," which is more cumbersome but less pejorative; it simply indicates that these books have less authority than the Torah, the Prophets, and the Writings. The precise list of them varies among different churches. For the purposes of this series that seeks to expound the "Old Testament for Everyone," by the "Old Testament" we mean the Scriptures accepted by the Jewish community, though in the Jewish Bible they come in a different order, as the Torah, the Prophets, and the Writings.

They were not "old" in the sense of antiquated or out-of-date; I sometimes like to refer to them as the First Testament rather than the Old Testament to make that point. For Jesus and the New Testament writers, they were a living resource for understanding God, God's ways in the world, and God's ways with us. They were "useful for teaching, for reproof, for correction, and for training in righteousness, so that the person who belongs to God can be proficient, equipped for every good work" (2 Timothy 3:16–17). They were for everyone, in fact. So it's strange that Christians don't read them very much. My aim in these volumes is to help you do so.

My hesitation is that you may read me instead of the Scriptures. Don't fall into that trap. I like the fact that this series includes much of the biblical text. Don't skip over it. In the end, that's the bit that matters.

An Outline of the Old Testament

The Christian Old Testament puts the books in the Jewish Bible in a distinctive order:

Genesis to Kings: A story that runs from the creation of the world to the exile of Judahites to Babylon

Chronicles to Esther: A second version of this story, continuing it into the years after the exile

Job, Psalms, Proverbs, Ecclesiastes, Song of Songs: Some poetic books

Isaiah to Malachi: The teaching of some prophets

Here is an outline of the history that lies at the books' background. (I give no dates for events in Genesis, which involves too much guesswork.)

1200s	Moses, the exodus, Joshua
1100s	The "judges"
1000s	King Saul, King David
900s	King Solomon; the nation splits into two, Ephraim and Judah
800s	Elijah, Elisha
700s	Amos, Hosea, Isaiah, Micah; Assyria the superpower; the fall of Ephraim
600s	Jeremiah, King Josiah; Babylon the superpower
500s	Ezekiel; the fall of Judah; Persia the superpower; Judahites free to return home
400s	Ezra, Nehemiah
300s	Greece the superpower
200s	Syria and Egypt, the regional powers pulling Judah one way or the other
100s	Judah's rebellion against Syrian power and gain of independence
000s	Rome the superpower

Isaiah

Isaiah is the first of the great prophetic books, though Isaiah was not the first of the great prophets. The first to have a book named after him was Amos. Neither did prophets such as Amos and Isaiah fulfill their ministries by writing books. Prophets fulfilled their ministry by showing up in a public place such as the temple courtyards in Jerusalem and declaiming to anyone who would listen and also to the people who didn't wish to listen. You can get an idea from reading the book of Jeremiah, which includes a number of stories about Jeremiah doing so, or from reading the Gospels, which portray the prophet Jesus doing so. Isaiah 8 and Jeremiah 36 include accounts of how these prophets came to have some of their messages written down, and it wouldn't be surprising if the actual books of Isaiah and Jeremiah ultimately go back to these acts of writing down.

The fact that the material in a book such as Isaiah goes back to prophetic preaching explains the way the book doesn't unfold in a systematic way like a normal book. It's a collection of separate messages that have been strung together. Often the same themes recur, as they do in Jesus' parables, because the same themes recurred in the prophet's preaching. There's a story about a Christian preacher whose people accused him of always repeating the same message; when they took notice of that one, he responded, he would preach another.

But the fact that the book is a compilation of prophetic messages doesn't mean it has no structure. At a macro level, it's rather clearly arranged.

Isaiah 1–12: Messages about Judah and Jerusalem, with references to King Ahaz

Isaiah 13–23: Messages about the nations around, with a reference King Ahaz

Isaiah 24–27: Messages about the destiny of the world around, with no reference to specific kings

Isaiah 28–39: Messages about Judah and Jerusalem, with references to King Hezekiah

Isaiah 40–55: Messages about Judah and Jerusalem, with references to King Cyrus

Isaiah 56–66: Messages about Judah and Jerusalem, with no reference to specific kings

One feature emerging from this outline is that at the macro level the book is arranged chronologically. Ahaz was king of Judah about 736 to 715. Hezekiah was king about 715 to 686. The last part of Isaiah 28—39 looks forward to the fall of Jerusalem and the exile of its leadership to Babylon, which happened in 587. Cyrus was the king of Persia who took over the Babylonian empire in 539 and allowed the Judahites in Babylon to go back home and rebuild the temple. The last chapters of the book make sense when understood in relation to the community in Judah after that event.

One implication of that outline is as follows. While Isaiah 39 speaks of the exile as something to happen in the future, the messages in Isaiah 40–55 speak of it as something that happened quite a while ago. The future they refer to is that promise that God is about to make it possible for people to return to Jerusalem. The implication is that the Isaiah of chapters 1–39 isn't the prophet whose preaching appears in chapters 40–55 or chapters 56–66. The book called Isaiah is a compilation of the messages of several prophets. Something of this sort may well be true of most of the prophetic books. It doesn't mean they're random compilations; one can see links between chapters 40–66 and chapters 1–39. As the outline above indicates, the last part of the book concerns itself with Judah and Jerusalem as much as the first part does. The most distinctive link between the parts is the description of God as "the holy one of Israel." That title, or a variant, comes twenty-eight times in Isaiah (only six times in the whole of the rest of the Old Testament), half in chapters 1–39 and half in chapters 40–66. The whole of the book called Isaiah is a message about the holy one of Israel.

Although the book's macro-structure divides it up neatly, there's also some mixing of prophecies within the major sections. For instance, the opening chapter is a compilation of prophecies that look as if they come from different contexts and have been brought together to form an introduction to the book as a whole. From time to time we will draw attention to other points where something of this kind happens, but generally it's hard to be sure whether it is so.

ISAIAH 1:1-20

I'm Fed Up to the Teeth with Your Worship

¹ The vision of Isaiah ben Amoz which he saw concerning Judah and Jerusalem in the days of Uzziah, Jotham, Ahaz, and Hezekiah, kings of Judah.

²   Listen, heavens, and give ear, earth,
      because Yahweh has spoken.
  I raised children and brought them up,
      but they— they rebelled against me.
³   An ox acknowledges its owner,
      a donkey its master's manger.
  Israel doesn't acknowledge,
      my people doesn't take any notice.
⁴   Hey, offending nation,
      a people heavy with waywardness!
  Offspring of evil people, decadent children,
      they've abandoned Yahweh.
  They've disdained Israel's holy one,
      they've become estranged, backwards.
⁵   Why will you be beaten more,
      continue rebelling?
  The whole head [has come] to sickness,
      the whole heart is faint.
⁶   From the sole of the foot to the head,
      there's no soundness in it.
  Bruise, blotch, fresh wound—
      they haven't been pressed out,
  they haven't been bandaged,
      it hasn't been softened with oil.
⁷   Your country is a waste,
      your cities are burned with fire.
  Your land—in front of your eyes
      foreigners are consuming it,
      a desolation, quite overthrown by foreigners,
⁸   and Ms. Zion is left
      like a hut in a vineyard,
  like a night shelter in a melon field,
      like a city besieged.

5

9   Had Yahweh Armies not left us a survivor,
     we'd have been like Sodom,
     we'd have resembled Gomorrah.

10   Listen to Yahweh's word,
     rulers of Sodom!
   Give ear to our God's teaching,
     people of Gomorrah!
11   What use to me is the abundance of your sacrifices?
     (Yahweh says).
   I'm full of burnt offerings of rams
     and the fat of well-fed animals.
   In the blood of bulls and lambs and goats
     I do not delight.
12   When you come to appear [before] my face,
     who sought this from your hands?
   Trampling my courtyards—
13   you will do it no more,
     bringing a meaningless offering.
   Incense is an outrage to me, new moon and Sabbath,
     the summoning of convocation;
     I cannot bear wickedness and assembly.
14   Your new moons and set occasions
     my whole being repudiates.
   They've become a burden to me
     that I'm weary of carrying.
15   And when you spread out your hands,
     I shall lift up my eyes from you.
   Even when you offer many a prayer,
     there'll be no listening on my part.
   Your hands are full of blood—
16   wash, get clean.
   Put away the evil of your actions
     from in front of my eyes.
   Stop doing evil,
17   learn doing good.
   Seek the exercise of authority,
     put the oppressor right.
   Exercise authority for the orphan,
     contend for the widow.

¹⁸ Come on, let's argue it out
    (Yahweh says).
  If your offenses are like scarlet,
    they are to be white like snow.
  If they are red like crimson,
    they are to be like wool.
¹⁹ If you're willing and you listen,
    you will consume the country's good things.
²⁰ But if you refuse and rebel,
    you'll be consumed by the sword;
    because Yahweh's mouth has spoken.

We just came home from our Palm Sunday service at church, a great occasion. As usual we began by distributing palm crosses; I can never take for granted that in California we can make our palm crosses from palm branches on trees that grow in the church grounds. We reenacted the events of the first Palm Sunday as we processed around the church grounds and back into the street to the church's main entrance, singing the Palm Sunday hymn "All Glory, Laud, and Honor." Even more moving was the dramatized reading of the account in Mark's Gospel of the last week in Jesus' life, with members of the congregation taking different parts but all of us joining in those terrible, repeated words, "Crucify him!" More than one person commented on how this brought them near to tears, while someone who shared in the leading of the service with me said afterward, "Well, that was a well-done service."

Then I came home and read of God asking the people of Judah what use their worship was to him. The problem was not that it was only outward sacrifices—he refers to their prayers. He doesn't suggest that they worshiped only externally and not in their hearts. It looks as if they meant every hallelujah. The problem was the disparity between what they meant in their hearts as they worshiped and what they did in their lives outside the context of worship. He likens them to the rulers and people of Sodom and Gomorrah, because they're about as responsive to Yahweh as those two cities were. When they lift their hands to God in prayer, all God can see is the blood on these hands. They need to clean themselves up. The community needs to cease to be the kind of city where people can be ill-treated and oppressed and can lose their lives for reasons that are nothing to do with them.

It's because they have failed to be that kind of community that they have experienced the chastisement from **Yahweh Armies** that the first paragraph describes. Isaiah 1 is a collection of Isaiah's messages from different contexts, brought together to introduce his ministry as a whole. The trouble that the first main paragraph describes didn't come at the beginning of this ministry but near the end; the description here serves to introduce the account of his ministry as a whole. You want to know where Isaiah's ministry led, how the story ends? Well, here's the answer. Then the second main paragraph takes you back to look at why it ended that way.

It ended that way because of how the **Judahites** had related to their heavenly Father. They're not little children but teenage children or young adults who are part of an extended family living together in a village. Father is still the authority figure. He sets the moral standards. But they have stopped taking any notice of him. So he has disciplined them. And they have ended up like an individual son who's been thrashed yet who is asking for more punishment. The literal picture is one that will be painted by chapters 37–38, which describe how the **Assyrians** invade Judah and all but crush it. They take all the cities in Judah except for Jerusalem itself, which is left like the lonely hut that sits in the middle of a vineyard or a melon field as a shelter for people keeping watch over the produce. Judah is almost as devastated as Sodom and Gomorrah, down in the Jordan valley, which is quite appropriate, given that they have behaved like Sodom and Gomorrah.

We should go back for a moment to the actual opening of the book. It describes the chapters that are to follow as a vision. They weren't something Isaiah thought up. They are a vision "concerning Judah and Jerusalem." That phrase usually refers to the community in Judah after the **exile**, and it thus invites readers in that later context to see that Isaiah's message relates to them and not just to the people of Isaiah's day. This introduction sets Isaiah's own ministry in the context of four kings' reigns. It was common for a king to nominate his successor (usually one of his sons) and make him co-king well before he died, a practice that should ensure smooth succession. Things were more complicated for Uzziah because he contracted the skin ailment commonly called leprosy, which meant he couldn't fulfill many public functions. So quite early in his reign he made his son Jotham co-king; actually Jotham likely died before his father. Uzziah's grandson Ahaz then succeeded Jotham as co-king. For practical purposes the kings who matter in Isaiah 1–39 are Ahaz and then Hezekiah. A key feature of their reigns is the political pressure on Judah arising from the development and aspirations of the Assyrian empire, which raise one sort of issue for Ahaz and a different sort for Hezekiah. Mentioning the kings at the beginning of the book draws our attention to the need to understand Isaiah's message in the context of the events of the day. What God has to say to people relates to where they are in their lives. Further, it comes to a particular prophet, Isaiah ben Amoz (not the Amos who appears in the book of Amos, whose name is spelled differently). It doesn't fall from heaven without human mediation. It comes through a human being who is himself an important part of his message. His very name makes the point: Isaiah means "Yahweh is deliverance."

ISAIAH 1:21–2:5

Second-Degree Manslaughter

1:21 Aagh! The trustworthy town
    has become an immoral woman.
It was full of the exercise of authority,
    faithfulness dwelt in it, but now murderers.
22 Your silver has become slag,
    your drink is diluted with water.
23 Your officers are rebels, the associates of thieves;
    every one of them loves a bribe, chases gifts.
They don't exercise authority for the orphan;
    the widow's cause doesn't come to them.
24 Therefore the declaration of the Lord Yahweh Armies,
    the mighty one of Israel, is:

9

"Aah, I will get relief from my adversaries,
   take redress from my enemies,
25   turn my hand against you.
I will smelt your slag as with lye,
   remove all your contamination.
26 I will restore your authorities as of old,
   your counselors as at the beginning.
Afterward you will be called faithful city,
   trustworthy town."
27 Zion will find redemption through the exercise of authority,
   and the people in it who turn, through faithfulness.
28 But [there will be] a crushing of rebels and offenders, all
   together,
   and the people who abandon Yahweh will be finished.
29 Because they will be shamed on account of the oaks that
   you desired;
   you will be disgraced on account of the gardens that you
   chose.
30 Because you will be like an oak wilting of foliage,
   like a garden for which there's no water.
31 The strong person will become tinder,
   his work a spark.
The two of them will burn all together,
   and there will be no one quenching.
2:1 The word that Isaiah ben Amoz saw concerning Judah and
   Jerusalem.

2 It will come about at the end of the time:
The mountain of Yahweh's house
   will have become established,
at the peak of the mountains,
   and it will be higher than the hills.
All the nations will stream to it;
3   many peoples will come and say,
"Come on, let's go up to Yahweh's mountain,
   to the house of Jacob's God,
so he may teach us of his ways
   and we may walk in his paths."
Because teaching will go out from Zion,
   Yahweh's word from Jerusalem.

⁴ He will exercise authority among the nations
    and issue reproof for many peoples.
  They will beat their swords into hoes
    and their spears into pruning hooks.
  Nation will not take up sword against nation;
    they will no more learn war.
⁵ Jacob's household, come on,
    let's walk by Yahweh's light.

The other Sunday, halfway on our five-minute drive to church there was a huge police presence off to the left of our street, with police cars and barriers and police officers apparently searching waste land and dumpsters. Some aspects of what happened are still disputed, but the story is approximately as follows: About midnight two teenagers had broken into a car and stolen a backpack with a laptop, and a man had called the police. To encourage a quick response he told them the youths were armed. The police came, chased the youths, and shot and killed one when they thought he was reaching for the gun that he didn't in fact have. The man who called the police has been charged with second-degree manslaughter.

You can be guilty in regard to someone's death whether or not you personally killed the person. In Jerusalem it was the position of the city as a whole, and so perhaps it is for my city. In Jerusalem it may have meant that there were people who were put to death on trumped-up charges like Naboth, whose story appears in 1 Kings 21. There will also have been widows and orphans such as are mentioned in this passage who were deprived of the land that had belonged to their families and/or not offered support by people who could have helped them. They were thus also guilty of second-degree manslaughter; failing to ensure that people such as refugees have adequate food kills them slowly, but it kills them surely.

The problem lies in whether **authority** is exercised in the city in a **faithful** way. Second Samuel 8 relates how David saw to the faithful exercise of authority in the city; those days are long gone. **Zion** has become like someone who is sexually unfaithful or like precious metal contaminated by slag or like watered-down liquor. Literally, the problem lies with the

11

administration, the people who ought to see to the faithful exercise of authority but are actually a hotbed of corruption and who implement policies that will ensure they themselves can do well rather than that serve the needs of the vulnerable.

So **Yahweh Armies** will crack down on them. Yet the aim won't be merely punishment but restoration, the turning of the city back into what it was supposed to be, so that authority is once again exercised with faithfulness. Admittedly this action won't necessarily benefit the administration. As is often the case, the announcement of what Yahweh intends to do presents people with a choice. Rebels and offenders and people who abandon Yahweh will be finished. People who return to Yahweh will enjoy the restoration Yahweh brings about.

The first paragraph began by describing the city as an immoral woman, which usually suggests religious unfaithfulness. Toward its end, it returns to that theme in speaking of oaks and gardens. The language presupposes practices belonging to the traditional religion of the land, one that seeks to reach out to God by means of nature—the allusion is too brief to be sure what precise kind of religious observances they are. Whereas the earlier part of the chapter referred to proper worship of Yahweh that was not accompanied by proper community life, here the problem lies in other forms of worship, offered outside the temple. Here, such worship that ignores the specifics of how Yahweh has been involved with Israel over the centuries accompanies a style of life that also ignores how Yahweh has been involved with Israel over the centuries.

So Jerusalem will be purged and restored to what it's supposed to be. That vision goes beyond its mere internal life, lived in isolation from the world around. It could hardly be otherwise. Israel always knew that Yahweh was not concerned only with Israel. Yahweh was, after all, the only real God, the God of the whole world. The psalms that people sang in the temple in Jerusalem frequently reminded people of that fact as they urged all the nations to acknowledge **Yahweh**, not least because of what he had done in Israel.

But the nations' recognition of Yahweh was not a present reality. The vision in the second paragraph promises that the moment will come when it becomes so. It also appears in

Micah 4; Micah was a contemporary of Isaiah. We don't know which of these prophets delivered it first or whether it came from another prophet and was adapted into their books. Most prophetic books likely collect words from God that were given by prophets other than the one whose name appears at the beginning.

The vision will come about "at the end of the time," literally "at the end of the days." The expression makes a link with the time in which Judah lives; it doesn't imply merely "in the future" nor "at the end of days." The end of the epoch in which Judah is involved will see these events. The mountain where the temple sits will be exalted above the mountains around. The image is figurative; the point is that it will be exalted in the eyes of the nations and will attract them. The implication isn't merely that it's geographically impressive but that there's something to be learned there. Maybe we should make a link with that earlier promise of restoration, because that was to involve the exercise of proper authority or government in Jerusalem, so that the idea is that the nations recognize their need of the proper exercise of authority and come to seek it. Specifically, it means their letting Yahweh be the one who sorts out their disputes and thus stops them warring with one another so that they gain a substantial peace dividend.

This vision has not been fulfilled yet. It gives Christians and Jews a promise on whose basis to pray. The immediate challenge to Israel was that the people itself should live in light of Yahweh's concern for the faithful exercise of authority and let Yahweh be the one who guides it, and to prove that this commitment brings it peace. Such a commitment might even be the means of Jerusalem being exalted in the world's eyes. But we should not turn the promise into a mere exhortation to accept a responsibility for bringing about peace. It's a promise.

ISAIAH 2:6–22

The Destiny of All That Is Humanly Impressive

2:6 Because you have abandoned your people,
    Jacob's household.

13

Because they are full from the east,
　　yes, of diviners like the Philistines,
　　and they abound in children of foreigners.
7　Their country is full of silver and gold;
　　there's no end to their treasures.
Their country is full of horses;
　　there's no end to their chariots.
8　Their country is full of idols;
　　they bow down to the work of their hands,
　　to what their fingers made.
9　So humanity bows down, the individual falls down
　　(may you not carry them!).
10　Go into the cleft,
　　bury yourself in the dirt,
before the fearfulness of Yahweh,
　　from the dreadfulness of his majesty!
11　Lofty human looks have fallen down,
　　the exaltedness of individuals has bowed down.
Yahweh alone will be on high
　　on that day.
12　Because Yahweh Armies has a day
　　against all majesty and exaltedness,
against all that is high—
　　and it will fall down,
13　against all the cedars of Lebanon, exalted and high,
　　and all the oaks of Bashan,
14　against all the exalted mountains,
　　against all the high hills,
15　against every lofty tower,
　　against every fortified wall,
16　against every Tarshish ship,
　　against all the impressive vessels.
17　Human loftiness will bow down,
　　individuals' exaltedness will fall down.
Yahweh alone will be on high on that day;
18　　idols—they will completely vanish.
19　People will go into caves in the crags,
　　into holes in the dirt
before the fearfulness of Yahweh,
　　from the dreadfulness of his majesty,

> when he arises to terrify the country.
> 20 On that day humanity will throw away
>   its silver idols and its gold idols,
> which they made for it to bow down to,
>   to the moles and bats.
> 21 to go into the clefts in the crag,
>   into the crevices in the rocks,
> before the fearfulness of Yahweh,
>   from the dreadfulness of his majesty,
>   when he arises to terrify the country.
> 22 Get yourselves away from humanity,
>   that has breath in its nostrils,
>   because what is it to count for?

It's Holy Week, and for more than twenty years a magnificent church not far from where we live put on a glorious Easter pageant in the weeks leading up to Easter, "the largest and most spectacular passion play" in the world. The church seats over 2,500 and has been filled several times on a Sunday. Its pipe organ is one of the five biggest in the world. But over the past decade it got into financial trouble and couldn't pay its bills to people such as the woman who hired out camels and other animals for its pageants. It went bankrupt and a few weeks ago finalized the sale of its premises to another church. There were no sex scandals or financial scandals, though there were problems over the "succession" from its founder.

It is hard if not impossible to get big and stay big. The bigger they are the harder they fall. Isaiah implies that a theological principle underlies this fact. When you get big, you become godlike. Your success may mean you get proud or overconfident, but Isaiah's point is that merely in your greatness, your majesty, your loftiness, your exaltation you become godlike, and it may be inappropriate for you to stay that way and obscure the truth about who is really God.

So "**Yahweh Armies** has a day against all majesty and exaltedness," the **Day of the Lord**. It's not merely a day when individuals will be judged. It's a day when all human and earthly majesty will be put down. The Old Testament often uses the imagery of a violent storm with the associated quivering of the ground to picture **Yahweh's** coming to act powerfully in the world. Isaiah pictures the tumultuous arrival of Yahweh's day as a storm that fells trees, shakes mountains and hills, demolishes walls and towers, and wrecks oceangoing ships. (There are several possible identifications of Tarshish in countries such as Lebanon, Turkey, Carthage, and Spain, but the point is they were big ships.) All those objects are strong and impressive; they would have seemed indestructible and unassailable, like the *Titanic* and the twin towers once seemed.

Before speaking of the Day that is coming, Isaiah has already identified the strengths in which Judah is trusting. The country is full of horses and chariots, the ancient equivalent to tanks and Humvees. It's also full of financial resources that can keep its army well-equipped, make it possible to fortify its cities, and enable them to last out a siege. Judah has every reason to feel safe. Interwoven with the description of its material resources is reference to its spiritual resources. There are its idols, the images of gods other than Yahweh; how foolish to be bowing down to something their own hands made! There are its means of guidance such as divination, learned from the peoples around them, to which it looks rather than to the Torah and to prophets such as Isaiah. With some poetic justice, whereas they have been bowing down to those idols, they will now find themselves bowing down in a different way and for a different reason. They will leave their idols to the moles and bats, because they will have been proved useless.

It's not surprising that Yahweh has abandoned Judah. Isaiah opens this section with that horrifying statement addressed to Yahweh, "you have abandoned *your people*." It doesn't mean they're simply doomed. Isaiah does have an ironic exhortation to them—go on then, try hiding from this storm. Hide in a cave. The second half of the line suggests how ironic the exhortation is, when it bids people hide in the ground. Caves and pits in the ground were burial places. Isaiah's words recall the reminder in Amos and in Psalm 139 that there's nowhere you can hide from Yahweh, who can reach you even in **Sheol**, the realm of death.

The chapter closes with another exhortation of a less ironic kind, challenging the hearers to dissociate themselves from the general run of humanity among whom they live, people who have the kind of attitude and follow the kind of practices the chapter has described. You could say that Isaiah is challenging people to become a faithful **remnant**. But the chapter also implicitly issues another invitation. The prophet wants Judah as a whole to heed his warning. He wants the entire community to turn from idols and from its trust in its wealth and its weaponry. He doesn't directly tell the community as a whole that it needs to repent and that Yahweh will then cancel the coming of his Day. Prophets often omit to issue a call to repentance. They speak as if catastrophe is inevitable. It's how they seek to break through to people. There's another example of Isaiah's indirect form of speech in his bidding Yahweh not to **carry** the people in their rebelliousness—that is, not to forgive them. He of course wants Yahweh to forgive them, but he knows they have to be brought to their senses in order for them to seek forgiveness, and expressing the desire that they may not be forgiven as long as they continue as they are is both a way of honoring God and another way of trying to break through to them.

Nor is it surprising that Yahweh is coming in that storm to show who is really God. The description of their trust in their resources (military, financial, and religious) points toward what Yahweh's chastisement will more literally look like. It will involve military invasion and humiliation, the capture and destruction of cities. It will involve the devastation of places of worship. It will involve the loss of wealth. It will involve the imposition of another culture's laws and policies. Subsequent chapters of Isaiah will describe how Isaiah's warning came true; indeed, we have already seen that the opening chapter has included at least one prophecy from the time of fulfillment. It wouldn't be surprising if one of the reasons why Isaiah's prophecies were preserved and ended up as Scripture is the way they were fulfilled and vindicated.

ISAIAH 3:1–4:6

On Dresses, Shawls, and Purses

3:1 Because there—
    the Lord Yahweh Armies

is removing from Jerusalem and from Judah
supply and support—
all supply of bread
and all supply of water,
2   warrior and soldier, authority and prophet,
diviner and elder,
3   centurion, important person, counselor,
the person expert in charms
and knowledgeable in chanting.
4   I will make youths their officials;
infants will rule over them.
5   The people will oppress one another,
each his neighbor.
The youth will be arrogant toward the elder,
someone belittled toward someone honorable.
6   Because a man will seize one of his brothers,
his father's household:
"You have a coat, you will be our leader,
this ruin will be under your charge."
7   On that day he will shout,
"I won't be one to bind up.
In my house there's no bread and no coat—
you won't make me leader of the people."
8   Because Jerusalem has collapsed,
Judah has fallen.
Because their tongue and their deeds were toward Yahweh,
rebelling against his glorious eyes.
9   The look on their faces testifies against them;
they declare their offence like Sodom
and don't hide it.
10   Aagh, for their lives,
because they have brought about evil for themselves.
Say of the faithful person, "It will be good,"
because they will eat the fruit of their deeds.
11   Aagh, for the faithless person, "It will be evil,"
because the reward of his hands will be done to him.
12   My people—infants are their bosses,
women rule over them.
My people—your guides make you wander;
they have swallowed up the course of your paths.

18

13 Yahweh is taking his stand to contend,
　　he is rising to decide for peoples.
14 Yahweh will come with authority
　　to his people's elders and their officials.
　"You—you have ravaged the vineyard,
　　the lowly person's plunder is in your houses.
15 What do you mean that you crush my people,
　　grind the faces of lowly ones?"
　（a declaration of the Lord Yahweh Armies).

16 Yahweh has said:
　　because Zion's daughters are lofty
　and walk outstretched with their neck,
　　flirting with their eyes,
　walking and mincing as they walk,
　　and they jingle with their feet,
17 my Lord will bare the crowns of Zion's daughters,
　　Yahweh will expose their forehead.

18 On that day my Lord will remove the splendor of the anklets,
the bands, and the necklaces, 19 the earrings, the bracelets, and
the veils, 20 the hats, the armlets, the scarves, the amulets, and
the charms, 21 the rings and the nose rings, 22 the dresses, the
capes, the shawls, the purses, 23 the gowns, the vests, the tiaras,
the veils, and the sashes.

24 It will come about [that]:
　　instead of perfume there will be a stench;
　　　instead of a wrap, a rope;
　　instead of a hairstyle, a shorn head;
　　　instead of a robe, wrapping of sack;
　　　branding instead of beauty.
25 Your men will fall by the sword,
　　your manhood by battle.
26 Her gates will lament and mourn;
　　she will be empty, she will sit on the ground.
4:1 Seven women will take hold of one man
　　on that day, saying,
　"We will eat our food,
　　we will wear our clothes,

only may your name be pronounced over us—
  take away our shame."

2 On that day, Yahweh's shoot will be
    for beauty and for honor
  and the country's fruit [will be]
    for majesty and for splendor for Israel's survivors.
3 What is left in Zion,
    what remains in Jerusalem—
  "holy" will be said of it,
    everyone who has been written down for life in
      Jerusalem.
4 When my Lord has washed away
    the filth of Zion's daughters,
  and cleanses in its midst
    the blood shed in Jerusalem,
  by a spirit of authority
    and a spirit of fire,
5 Yahweh will create over the entire site of Mount Zion
    and over its meeting place
  a cloud by day, and smoke,
    and a brightness of flaming, by night,
  because over all the splendor will be a canopy,
      6 and it will be a shelter
  for shade by day from the heat
    and for refuge and a hiding place
    from storm and from rain.

When we are going out for the evening, and if the time of year requires it, I will put a sweater on top of whatever I have been wearing all day. It's a delight to me when, in contrast, my wife disappears into the closet and reappears in her finery for us to go out, having chosen an appropriate combination of earrings and bracelets and gowns and scarves. I don't know why it should be that women bear chief responsibility for dressing up. In our local arboretum it's the male peacocks that possess exotic finery and look as if they really enjoy displaying it. I'm glad I don't have to do so, and I would be grieved if my wife couldn't do so, because I'm proud to go out with someone who can make herself look so fine.

The middle paragraph from this section of Isaiah looks as if it presupposes the same attitude and is therefore disturbing both for men and for women. So far Isaiah's polemic has mainly concerned the **Judahite** men. They're the leaders, the warriors, the elders, the people who exercise **authority** who are in a position to contend for the weak, who sign the contracts for purchasing the military hardware. The women no doubt exercise some influence over their husbands behind the scenes, but their official job is to look nice, and it's the oppression on the part of their husbands in which they collude that makes it possible for them to look nice.

So the judgment declared on them in this middle paragraph presupposes that not being directly part of the action or the decision-making doesn't exempt us from the judgment that comes on our society. In the women's case it corresponds to their position and role in the capital's life. It will include the loss of their men with the indignity that will bring in a patriarchal society, which assumes that every woman needs to take the name of a man and cannot imagine women looking after the community's affairs. The first paragraph portrays other aspects of the social disorder that will result from **Yahweh's** act of judgment. The city will be run by children. Parallel to the picture of seven women seeking the protection of one surviving man is the picture of one man trying to get another to take charge of a family's affairs on the basis of his having managed to maintain some vestige of respectable appearance. He doesn't want to accept any leadership responsibility in the chaotic situation that is presupposed.

The prophecy again issues challenges and makes promises to individuals as well as declaring the destiny of the community as a whole. Its aim is to turn the community around. But it knows that God deals with individuals, too. Sometimes people put too much stress on the individual, but it's also possible for individuals to evade responsibility or abandon hope because they think their own destiny is determined by the community. The prophecy reminds them of truths they know about God's involvement with individuals. Things will go well for the faithful person and badly for the faithless person; both will eat the fruit of their deeds. It makes clear its recognition that things don't always work out that way; it refers to the way lowly people who count as Yahweh's people are being crushed and ground down. It's nevertheless a generalization not to forget.

The last paragraph makes for a nice contrast with the paragraph about the trouble coming on the women. While Isaiah prophesies in order to get people to change, the arrangement of the book also envisages their failing to do so. What happens then? The picture of the city's restoration pairs with the earlier picture of Jerusalem drawing the whole world, but this second picture focuses on the good news for the city itself. The Bible often pictures Israel as like a tree, so Israel's judgment is like the felling of a tree. Here God promises that the felling of the tree won't be the end. God will make new growth come from the felled tree. Indeed, this new growth will be more splendid than anything one could imagine (again there's a parallel with that earlier vision of a new Jerusalem). The people there may be only survivors, only leftovers, but they have survived; it means they're people who have been written down for life. They're the nucleus of a holy people, a people whom God is marking off in connection with his purpose as the holy one. They will be a people whom God has cleansed. They will experience the kind of protection that Israel experienced on its original journey to the promised land. In due course, the fall of Jerusalem will bring the worst embodiment of Yahweh's Day so far in Israel's history, and after that event it's a message that the little beleaguered community in Judah and Jerusalem will have good reason to find encouraging.

ISAIAH 5:1–24

A Singer-Songwriter's Strange Song

1 I'm going to sing a song for my friend,
    my love song about his vineyard.
My friend had a vineyard
    on a fertile ridge.
2 He dug it and stoned it,
    and planted it with choice vine.
He built a tower in the middle of it,
    and also hewed a press in it.

He looked for it to produce grapes,
　　but it produced bad grapes.
3　So now, population of Jerusalem, people of Judah,
　　decide, will you, between me and my vineyard.
4　What more was there to do for my vineyard
　　that I did not do in it?
　Why, when I looked for it to produce grapes,
　　did it produce bad grapes?
5　So now I'm going to let you know
　　what I'm doing about my vineyard:
　remove its hedge so it will be for destroying,
　　demolish its wall so it will be for trampling,
6　　with the result that I will make an end of it.
　It will not be pruned and it will not be hoed;
　　briar and thorn will grow.
7　Because the household of Israel
　　is the vineyard of Yahweh Armies.
　The people of Judah
　　are the planting in which he delighted.
　He looked for the exercise of authority
　　but there—blood pouring out;
　　for faithfulness, but there—a cry.

8　Hey, people adding house to house,
　　people who join field to field,
　until there's no room, and you're made to live alone
　　in the midst of the country.
9　In my ears Yahweh Armies [has said],
　If many houses do not become for desolation,
　　big and good ones without inhabitant . . .
10　Because ten acres of vineyard will produce one measure,
　　and a ton of seed will produce a quart.
11　Hey, people who get up early in the morning
　　so they can chase liquor,
　　and stay up late in the evening
　　so wine can inflame them.
12　There'll be guitar and harp, tambourine and pipe,
　　wine at their parties.
　But they won't look to Yahweh's act,
　　the work of his hands they do not see.

¹³ Therefore my people are going into exile
        because of not acknowledging,
    its [people of] honor—hungry people,
        its multitude—parched with thirst.
¹⁴ Therefore Sheol has widened its throat,
        opened its mouth without limit.
Its [people of] splendor and its multitude will go down,
        its din and those who exult in it.
¹⁵ Humanity bows down, the individual falls down,
        the look of the lofty falls down.
¹⁶ Yahweh Armies is lofty in exercising authority;
        the holy God shows himself holy in faithfulness.
¹⁷ Lambs will graze as in their pasturage,
        fatlings (strangers) will feed on the ruins.
¹⁸ Hey, people who haul waywardness with cords of deceit,
        and offense like cart ropes,
¹⁹ who say, "He should hurry,
        he should speed up his work, so that we may see.
    The plan of Israel's holy one
        should draw near and come about, so we may
            acknowledge."
²⁰ Hey, people who say about evil, "Good,"
        and about good, "Evil,"
    who make darkness into light
        and light into darkness,
    who make bitter into sweet,
        and sweet into bitter.
²¹ Hey, people who are wise in their eyes,
        who are understanding in their own view.
²² Hey, warriors at drinking wine,
        people who are able at mixing a drink,
²³ who declare the faithless person to be faithful
        in return for a bribe,
    and the faithfulness of the faithful people
        they remove from them.
²⁴ Therefore:
        like the consuming of straw in a tongue of fire
            when hay sinks down in the flame,
    their root will become pure rot
        and their blossom will go up like dust,

> because they have rejected the teaching of Yahweh Armies,
>   spurned the word of Israel's holy one.

My wife and I often listen to songwriters performing their songs and note how much the singers tell us about how they came to write a particular song. Occasionally this is illuminating. I have a CD by a singer who tells us how a song arose out of the tension between her and her father over whether it was a good idea for her to spend her life driving around the country in a pickup singing for tips (from people like me). More often the explanations are frustrating. A good song stands on its own; knowing how it came to be written (the story usually involves a romantic breakup) doesn't help one appreciate it. Indeed, such appreciation likely involves listeners letting the song interact with their own experience. Information on what the song meant to the singer may lessen rather than boost the listener's appreciation.

Isaiah the songwriter cleverly introduces his song with an explanation that turns out to be devious. One can imagine him standing in the temple courtyards where he often preached and where people got used to ignoring his negative message. This time things have changed. He has written a love song for a friend who is about to get married, or who at least has his eye on a girl and hopes his family will be able to negotiate an arrangement with her family. It's a song about a vineyard, but people would have no trouble understanding that it concerns the girl he loves; the Song of Songs shows how a vineyard is a common image for a girl. Isaiah's friend has worked hard at "cultivating" his relationship with the girl in question. But then the song goes wrong; it becomes a song about unrequited love, like the songs of most singer-songwriters. His attentiveness didn't work. Isaiah asks his audience what else his friend could have done. Then it somersaults into something from a horror movie as he declares his intention to destroy the vineyard.

Isaiah has been stringing his audience along and saying the same kind of thing as usual, though winning their attention with his song may still mean they take more notice than they really wanted to. (Jesus will take up Isaiah's technique in his parables and take up the theme of the vine in a threatening way.) While a vineyard can stand for a girl, in a theological context it can also stand for Israel. Isaiah's punchline involves a double paronomasia (a play on words, but it's not playful). The Hebrew word for "the exercise of **authority**" is *mishpat*; the word for "blood pouring out" is *mispah* (actually it's a non-word—Isaiah seems to have invented it, but people would be able to guess from similar words what he meant). Similarly "**faithfulness**" is *tsedaqah*, and "a cry" (that is, a cry of pain from suffering people) is *tse'aqah*. The point about the paronomasia is that the similarity between the words belies and underlines the contrast between what God hoped for and what happened.

The rest of the section spells out what would issue from this cry of pain. Whereas every family was supposed to own a piece of land off which it could live, some people have found ways of appropriating other people's land by semi-legal means and depriving its owners of their livelihood. They indulge themselves in drinking and music. They don't believe talk about God intending to act against **Judah**. They think they have insight, but they lack it. They think they're important, but they're dispensable. Their homes will be devastated. Their crops will fail. They will lose their land. They will die and find themselves in **Sheol.**

ISAIAH 5:25–6:13

How to Frighten People into Repentance

5:25 On account of this
  Yahweh's anger flared against his people;
  he stretched out his hand against it and struck it.
 Mountains shook, and their corpses became
  like refuse in the middle of the streets.
 For all this his anger did not turn;
  his hand was still stretched out.
26 He will lift a signal to the nations from afar,
  he will whistle to one from the end of the earth,
  and there—with speed, quick, it will come.
27 There's none weary, there's none collapsing, in it;
  it doesn't slumber, it doesn't sleep.

26

The belt on its thighs doesn't come loose,
    the thong on its sandals doesn't break.
²⁸ Its arrows are sharpened,
    all its bows are drawn.
Its horses' hooves are reckoned like flint,
    its [chariot] wheels like a whirlwind.
²⁹ Its roar is like a cougar's;
    it roars like lions.
It growls and seizes prey,
and carries it off and there's no one to rescue. ³⁰   It will
    growl over it on that day,
    like the growling of the sea.
One will look to the land, and there—
    troublesome darkness;
    the light has gone dark with its thunderclouds.

^{6:1} In the year King Uzziah died, I saw my Lord sitting on a throne, high and lofty, with his train filling the palace. ² Seraphs were standing above him; each had six wings. With two it would cover its face, with two it would cover its feet, with two it would fly. ³ One would call to another, "Holy, holy, holy, Yahweh Armies, his splendor is the filling of the entire earth." ⁴ The doorposts on the sills shook at the sound of the one who called, and the house filled with smoke. ⁵ I said, "Aagh, for me, because I'm lost, because I'm someone polluted of lips, and I live in the midst of a people polluted of lips, because my eyes have seen the King, Yahweh Armies." ⁶ But one of the seraphs flew to me, in his hand a coal that he had taken with tongs from on the altar. ⁷ He made it touch my mouth, and he said, "There: this has touched your lips, and your waywardness will go away, your offense will be expiated." ⁸ Then I heard my Lord's voice saying, "Whom shall I send, and who will go out for us?" I said, "Here I am, send me." ⁹ He said, "Go, and say to this people:
    'Keep on listening, but don't understand,
      keep on looking, but don't acknowledge.'
¹⁰ Fatten this people's mind,
    make its ears heavy, smear its eyes,
  so that it doesn't see with its eyes
    and listen with its ears
  and its mind understands and it turns
    and there is healing for it."

¹¹ So I said, "For how long, my Lord?" He said,
   "Until cities have crashed into ruins
      so that there is no inhabitant,
   and houses so that there is no one,
      and the country crashes into ruins, a desolation."
¹² Yahweh will send the people away;
      vast will be the abandonment in the midst of the
         country.
¹³ When there is still a tenth in it,
      it will again be for grazing,
   like a terebinth tree or like an oak
      of which there is a stump after their felling.
   Its stump is the holy seed.

A little while ago I went to preach at a new church that is part of
the "emerging church" movement, which started in Australasia
and the UK and spread to the United States. Its background is
an awareness that the traditional churches are in deep trouble,
an awareness that was obvious earlier in the UK and Australasia than in the United States, and a disillusionment with the
churches' traditionalism and the distance that separated them
from the wider culture. The service took place in a school hall
rather than a church building and didn't have any of the set
prayers that feature in many traditional churches, though neither does it aspire to be a megachurch. The people present were
nearly all young adults. Another such church where I have
preached (it met in a theater) eventually failed when its members started becoming not only married but parents, and they
didn't quite know how to be an emerging church for people
with young families.

I don't know whether the emerging church is a new shoot
that promises new life for the church. If it is, it will be a kind of
fulfillment of the tiny promise at the end of Isaiah's vision of the
holy one, the promise expressed in those words "its stump is
the holy seed." The words are admittedly a little enigmatic, and
they come as the conclusion of an enigmatic sentence or two,
but the implication of the closing part of this section is clear
enough in the context.

Isaiah's account of his vision opens two or three chapters that
take the form of story rather than bare reports of the content

of his preaching. The book's arrangement is thus a little like the flow of a movie that begins in the middle of things then takes you back to explain the background to what you have seen so far. What we have read so far is a summary of Isaiah's message as a whole, with its warnings, its pointing out how warnings have been fulfilled, and its promises. The first paragraph above has itself noted how judgment has fallen but also how the judgment that has fallen won't be the final such judgment (if people fail to heed its message). Imaginatively it then pictures an imperial army such as **Assyria** or **Babylon**, coming from away to the north and east, frightening in its ruthless efficiency and rigor.

Isaiah's account of his vision tells how he came to be declaiming this message. His vision came in the year that King Uzziah died after his long reign, when his son Jotham or his grandson Ahaz thus became sole king after reigning alongside Uzziah. Isaiah's failure to name the new king puts him in his place and draws attention to his focus on another King. He has a vision of the Lord on his throne. The word "Lord" comes often in English translations, but it usually represents God's actual name, **Yahweh**. Here Isaiah uses the word Lord and does so three times, along with a description of him as King and as Yahweh Armies. His vision thus emphasizes who is the real Lord and King.

It wouldn't be surprising if Isaiah had his vision in the temple, but if so, it becomes a vision of the King on his throne in his palace in the heavens. Hebrew has no special word for "temple"; it uses the regular words for "house" or "palace" (so "palace" comes in the first verse) because the temple is the heavenly King's dwelling. The seraphs are creatures that combine some animal-like, some bird-like, and some humanlike features. They cover their eyes so as not to look directly at the holy God; the reference to their covering their feet likely suggests demureness (feet can be a euphemism for genitals). Their declaration of Yahweh's holiness links with the distinctive importance of this theme in Isaiah. While holiness can be attributed to other heavenly beings, the threefold declaration affirms that Yahweh's holiness is of an unequaled kind. Yahweh is holy to the power of three. The outward manifestation of that holiness is then the splendor that fills the earth as Yahweh shines out in blessing the world.

Isaiah's problem, however, is that he is an impure human being living among an impure people. They cannot join in the seraphs' praise. Perhaps his associating himself with his people's defilement simply implies a recognition that as individuals we are inevitably implicated in the wrong done by the group we belong to (family, church, city, nation). Or perhaps his vision compares with Paul's vision on the Damascus road, which revolutionizes his self-understanding; maybe up till this moment he has not realized how polluted Judah is and how polluted he is. But God cleanses his lips by a sacramental action that will enable his lips to become a means of serving Yahweh.

Whereas Yahweh specifically drafts Moses and Jeremiah, Isaiah responds to a need for volunteers. Yahweh's asking the question (not least with its "us") implies Yahweh is surrounded by his cabinet, with whom he consults when there are decisions to be taken. Isaiah is in a position to answer the question that Yahweh puts on the table for the cabinet.

His volunteering is regularly where Christian reading of this story ends, which isn't surprising in light of what follows. Yahweh is looking for someone to declare judgment on this polluted people. The judgment will take the form of telling them they're never going to understand what God is saying to them and doing with them. Indeed, the aim of Isaiah's preaching is to bring about that incomprehension so that they won't repent and find healing. Not surprisingly, Isaiah is appalled; he will perhaps be regretting the way he volunteered without knowing what the commission would be. His question "For how long?" is the question that recurs in the Psalms when someone protests about how long God intends to let some calamity continue. The answer makes things even worse until you reach that last phrase about the holy seed, which promises that the end won't be the end. A holy seed will survive, as a holy seed survives of the church in Europe and Australasia, and will survive in the United States.

On the surface the story implies that judgment is inevitable. But Yahweh's aim in telling people what he intends to do is to provoke a response. It's always the aim of a message of judgment that it should make it possible for God not to implement it, though that aim may fail, and then the judgment will indeed happen. When Jesus quotes this passage in Mark 4 to provide the rationale for his speaking in parables, the same framework applies.

ISAIAH 7:1–17

Stand Firm, Or You Won't Stand At All

[1] In the days of Ahaz son of Jotham son of Uzziah, king of Judah, Rezin the king of Syria and Pekah the son of Remaliah king of Israel went up to Jerusalem for a battle against it, but they couldn't do battle against it.

[2] So it had been reported to David's household, "Syria has leaned on Ephraim," and his heart and his people's heart shook like the trees in a forest shaking before the wind. [3] Yahweh said to Isaiah, "Go out, will you, to meet Ahaz, you and Remains-Will-Return, your son, at the end of the conduit of the Upper Pool, at the Launderer's Field road. [4] Say to him, 'Take care and be calm; don't be afraid, your heart is not to falter on account of these two stumps of smoking firewood, because of the angry burning of Rezin and Syria and the son of Remaliah. [5] Because Syria has planned evil against you [with] Ephraim and the son of Remaliah, saying [6] "We will go up against Judah and terrify it and break it open for ourselves and enthrone as king within it the son of Tabeel," [7] my Lord Yahweh has said this:

> "It won't come about,
>   it won't happen.
> [8] Because the head of Syria is Damascus,
>   and the head of Damascus is Rezin.
> Within yet sixty-five years
>   Ephraim will shatter from being a people.
> [9] The head of Ephraim is Samaria,
>   and the head of Samaria is the son of Remaliah.
> If you don't stand firm in trust,
>   you won't stand firm at all.'"'"

[10] Yahweh spoke further to Ahaz: [11] "Ask for yourself a sign from Yahweh your God. Make it deep, to Sheol, or make it lofty, up

to the heights." [12] Ahaz said, "I won't ask, I won't test Yahweh." [13] [Isaiah] said, "Will you listen, household of David? Is it too small for you, wearying human beings, that you weary my God as well? [14] Therefore my Lord—he will give you a sign. There—a girl is pregnant and is going to give birth to a son, and she will call his name God-is-with-us. [15] He will eat yogurt and honey in knowing how to reject what is evil and choose what is good. [16] Because before the boy knows how to reject what is evil and choose what is good, the land of whose two kings you're terrified will be abandoned. [17] Yahweh will bring upon you and upon your people and upon your father's household days that have not come since the day Ephraim turned away from Judah (the king of Assyria)."

I mentioned in an early volume of The Old Testament for Everyone receiving a call from a Jewish lawyer in Los Angeles who had self-published a book titled Twenty-six Reasons Why Jews Don't Believe in Jesus and wanted me to make sure that his statements about Jesus and about Christian faith were accurate. A significant part of the book concerned the way Christians use texts from the Old Testament to prove that Jesus is the Messiah but introduce a new meaning into the texts in doing so. (Ironically, the way Christians so interpret Scriptures is similar to the way other Jews in New Testament times did.) I got in trouble with a number of Christians for acknowledging that he was right. The New Testament itself doesn't address people who don't believe in Jesus in order to prove from the Prophets that he is the Messiah. It does use the Prophets to help people understand aspects of their confession that Jesus is the Messiah. The passage about a virgin conceiving and having a son who would be called Immanuel, which Matthew takes up, is a notable example.

The story about Isaiah and Ahaz starts with something like a news headline. The first sentence summarizes the story before the main part gives the details. The detailed story refers to Syria and **Ephraim**, which makes clear that the headline's reference to **Israel** means the northern kingdom, which can also be less confusingly referred to as Ephraim. Its geographical position made Ephraim more vulnerable to **Assyrian** interest in extending its control in the countries toward the Mediterranean, and

Syria and Ephraim together are intent on resisting Assyria's expansion of its empire. They want **Judah** to join them, but geography makes Judah less interested in taking on the superpower. So Syria and Ephraim are seeking to lean on Judah and are prepared to force a regime change there to put on the throne someone more amenable to their policies.

Isaiah doesn't draw attention to the horrifying implication that one part of the people of God is thus allying with a foreign nation in order to invade the other part of the people of God, but the opening reference to Ephraim as Israel (the name that theologically unites Ephraim and Judah) ironically underlines the point. The same point emerges in the description of the Judahite government as "David's household." When Ephraim made a unilateral declaration of independence from Jerusalem two centuries ago, it cut itself off from David's household, as well as from the temple that Yahweh had agreed should be built in Jerusalem. It's now not merely ignoring David but attacking his dynasty.

Isaiah's later reference to David's household, addressed to Ahaz himself, suggests that Isaiah's direct point lies elsewhere. It reminds Ahaz of his theological position. He isn't merely the king of a small Middle Eastern nation who needs to think practically and politically about policies for his people. He is the current head of David's household, the heir to God's promises to David and his successors. He has to live in the world but to do so without implying that worldly considerations are the only ones to be taken into account. It's always a tough aspect to a leader's position. Isaiah underlines the point by referring to Pekah the Ephraimite king as "the son of Remaliah" and to the man they want to put on the Judahite throne as "the son of Tabeel" (we don't know his actual name) without using their own names. They're not sons of David, like Ahaz. Each king needs to be seen as the current representative of a dynasty.

In trying to be practical, Ahaz is out checking the city's water supply. In a country such as theirs, people commonly built their cities on a hill, which was a good defensive position. Yet it meant water supply was a problem; a besieging army could sit tight and wait till the city ran out. So cities tried to safeguard and protect their water supply; Ahaz is out doing so.

It's the responsible thing to do. Isaiah doesn't say it's wrong but does warn Ahaz to avoid assuming that such action is the key to surviving the expected siege. The decisive fact is that Yahweh has made a declaration about what will happen to Syria and Ephraim, their capitals, and their kings. They're not Israel (in the theological sense), their capitals are not Jerusalem, and their kings don't belong to David's household. Ephraim is on the verge of obliteration. It fell to Assyria a decade later; the "sixty-five years" looks like an allusion to an event referred to in Ezra 4. Judah's job is to stand firm in trust in Yahweh if it wants to stand firm as a people; Isaiah uses two forms of the same verb to make the point about the connection between these two forms of standing firm.

It's in that connection that Yahweh offers Ahaz a sign. You have to admire Ahaz for the theological correctness with which he seeks to evade receiving it. Sometimes God disapproves of people who want signs, but sometimes God grants signs. Maybe there's a difference between people who want to believe but need help and people who don't want to believe and want an excuse for avoiding doing so. Ahaz comes in the latter category.

The sign involves a girl having a baby. Isaiah's words may mean "a virgin will get pregnant," but he doesn't imply that the birth itself is going to be a miracle. If she is at the moment a virgin, she will be an unmarried girl who is going to marry and conceive in the usual way. We don't know who the girl is – indeed, Isaiah doesn't need to have a particular girl in mind. The point is that by the time a few months have passed and the girl has had her baby, the crisis that preoccupies Ahaz will be over. It will have been proved that "God is with us," and she will be able to call her baby God-is-with-us, Immanuel. The comment about him eating baby food and being able to recognize food he likes and food he doesn't like then nuances the point. Hundreds of years later, Jesus came and was born of a girl who was a virgin when she conceived and whose baby turned out to be "God is with us" in a more personal sense, and Matthew can utilize the words in Isaiah to help his Christian readers understand something of the wonder of that event.

The sign will do Ahaz no good because of the attitude he brings to it. The Assyrians who will devastate Syria and Ephraim will also invade Judah. It's one implication of the name of the son Isaiah takes with him when he confronts Ahaz. The name could be a promise that "[only] the **remains** [of Assyria] will return [home]." But it could be a warning that "[only] the remains [of Judah] will survive." It could also imply that "[at least] some remains [of Judah] will survive." It could be a call to people to separate themselves from the stance of the people as whole: "the remains must return [to Yahweh]." You have to work out what it signifies in light of who you are.

ISAIAH 7:18–9:1a

Where to Look for Guidance?

7:18 On that day Yahweh will whistle to the fly that is at the end of the streams of Egypt and to the bee that is in the country of Assyria. 19 They will come and settle, all of them, in the steep washes and the craggy clefts and all the thorn-bushes and all the watering holes. 20 On that day my Lord will shave with a razor hired beyond the Euphrates River (with the king of Assyria) the head and the hair on the feet, and it will also sweep away the beard. 21 On that day someone will keep alive a heifer from the cattle and two [goats] from the flock, 22 but from the abundance of the milk they produce he will eat yogurt, because everyone who is left within the country will eat yogurt and honey. 23 On that day every place where there used to be a thousand vines worth a thousand sheqels of silver will be for briar and for thorn. 24 With arrows and a bow a person will come there, because the entire country will be briar and thorn. 25 But all the hills that are hoed with a hoe—the fear of briar and thorn won't come there; it will be for the roaming of oxen and the trampling of sheep.

8:1 Yahweh said to me, "Get yourself a big panel and write on it in ordinary letters, 'For Plunder-hurries-loot-rushes.'" 2 I invoked as trustworthy witnesses for me Uriah the priest and Zechariah ben Jeberechiah. 3 I had sex with the prophetess and she got pregnant and gave birth to a son. Yahweh said to me, "Call him Plunder-hurries-loot-rushes, 4 because before the

boy knows how to call 'father' and 'mother,' someone will carry
off Damascus's wealth and Samaria's plunder before the king of
Assyria."
⁵   Yahweh again spoke to me further:
⁶ Because this people has rejected
        the waters of Shiloah, which go gently,
        and rejoices at Rezin and the son of Remaliah,
⁷ Therefore, now: my Lord is bringing up against them
        the waters of the Euphrates, powerful, vast
        (the king of Assyria and all his splendor).
    It will rise up over all its channels
        and go over its banks.
⁸ It will sweep through Judah, flood as it passes over;
        it will reach as far as its neck.
    Its wings spread out will be
        the filling of the breadth of your country.

    God is with us:
⁹   do evil, peoples, and shatter.
    Give ear, all you distant parts of the earth;
        equip yourselves and shatter,
    Equip yourselves and shatter;
¹⁰   make a plan, but it will be frustrated.
    Speak a word, but it won't stand,
        because God is with us.

¹¹ Because Yahweh said this to me as he took hold of my hand
so that he might train me out from the way of this people:
¹² "You shall not say 'conspiracy'
        about everything that this people calls 'conspiracy.'
    What they are in awe of, you shall not be in awe of,
        and not dread.
¹³ Yahweh Armies—regard him as holy;
        he is to be the object of your awe, your dread.
¹⁴ He is to be a holy place, but a stone to trip over,
        a crag to stumble over,
    for the two houses of Israel—
        a trap and a snare for Jerusalem's inhabitants.
¹⁵ Many people will stumble on them,
        they will fall and break, be snared and caught."

¹⁶ Bind up the testimony, seal the teaching among my disciples. ¹⁷ I will wait for Yahweh, who is hiding his face from Jacob's household, and I will be expectant of him. ¹⁸ Here am I and the children Yahweh has given me as signs and portents in Israel from Yahweh Armies who dwells on Mount Zion. ¹⁹ So when they say to you, "Inquire of the mediums and the experts who chirp and whisper. Is a people not to inquire of its gods, of the dead on behalf of the living, ²⁰ for teaching and testimony?"— they will indeed speak in accordance with this word, for which there will be no dawn. ²¹ [The people] will pass through [the country] wretched and hungry. When it is hungry it will rage and belittle its king and its gods. It will turn upward ²² and look to the earth, but there: trouble and darkness, oppressive gloom, driven murkiness, ^{9:1} because there will be no dawn for [the country] that experiences oppression.

In Mexico, and in Mexican communities in places such as Los Angeles, there's a lively movement of prayer to Santa Muerte, Saint Death. You pray to her for protection from the dangers of the night, in the conviction that she can protect you from attack, accident, and violent death. She can also bring trouble to someone who has attacked you unjustly. Prayer to Santa Muerte goes back to the religious life of people in the area before the gospel came to the Americas. Nowadays most people who pray to Santa Muerte would also view themselves as Christian, but their observance is forbidden by the church and they pray to her in secret while also maintaining their membership in the church.

The situation was similar in Israel. While the story of **Yahweh's** involvement in Israel's life and the related teaching about how to reach out to Yahweh, incorporated in the Torah, were supposed to shape Israel's faith and life, in practice traditional religion remained alive underground and may have affected people's lives more than the facts and instructions in the Torah. This reality is at the background of Isaiah's depiction of people's faith when he speaks of them inquiring of ghosts and experts who chirp and whisper. People assumed that the dead had access to information inaccessible to the living, and they would seek to make contact with dead people in **Sheol**, especially their relatives, to get guidance for the future or advice about coping with illnesses and other crises. The dead people aren't gods in our sense, but Hebrew can use its word for gods to cover any beings other than live human beings.

Isaiah knows that the real God has spoken through him and that the people are taking a terrible risk in looking to such beings for "teaching and testimony." It is he they should be looking to. At the end of the section he again speaks of the frightening consequences of ignoring Yahweh and thinking that these other resources are trustworthy. People are seeking to avoid trouble and darkness but will be walking into them, even creating them. Maybe the most solemn thing Isaiah says to them is that he has given up on them, now that God has hidden his face from them. When God's face shines on you, you experience blessings. When God's face turns away, blessing departs.

The people are not listening. He fears they never will. But he knows his warnings will come true. So he has his message written down and sealed so that when it comes true, there will be no doubt that he gave it. Then people will have to acknowledge that he was right. But in a strange way that acknowledgment will open up the possibility of facing the future with Yahweh. In the context of Isaiah's ministry as he preaches in the temple courts, the warnings and the declaration about writing down his message are designed to jolt people to their senses, like the account of his commission to make them blind and deaf. In the context of the writing down of this story they're designed to show why disaster came.

The opening verses offer four pictures of how the calamity will come about. They include hints that it will involve devastation but not simply terminate the people's life. When it happens, such hints could give people the courage to go on. One can see the pictures becoming reality and one can imagine these dynamics operating when the **Assyrians** devastate **Judah** in the time of Hezekiah and again when the **Babylonians** destroy Jerusalem itself. (Lamentations describes how things were for people then.)

The second paragraph reminds people of the promise that Yahweh urges people to accept, as Syria and **Ephraim** are putting pressure on Judah. Isaiah has another son (presumably "the prophetess" is his wife, but she has a prophetic ministry of her own, like Huldah in Jeremiah's day) and gives him another significant name. Writing the promise down in a way that no one can escape both puts Isaiah's prophetic authenticity on the line and gives people no excuse for saying they didn't know about the promise. Their unwillingness to trust it is the background to the saying about the waters of Shiloah (Siloam). The water supply Ahaz was inspecting in the previous chapter comprises a stream emerging from a spring. It provides an image for the unspectacular way Yahweh provides for Jerusalem. If they don't trust that provision, it will be the Assyrian flood that overtakes them. The positive challenge is backed up by the further promise framed by the double declaration "God is with us." That fact means that if peoples like Syria and Ephraim (or Assyria) threaten Judah, Judah need not be anxious.

Knowing you have such a message to deliver doesn't necessarily make it easy to distance yourself from the way everyone else thinks. The conspiracy Isaiah describes might be a plot to replace Ahaz, the inside version of the plan by Syria and Ephraim, or it might be a plot to silence Isaiah and his supporters. It's easy to be in awe of the wrong people; the person to be in awe of is God. It would also be easy for people who half believed Isaiah's message to rejoice in the prospect of Ephraim getting its comeuppance. Isaiah reminds such people that Yahweh is potentially a threat to both halves of Israel, to Judah as well as Ephraim.

ISAIAH 9:1b–10:4

A Sign of Hope

9:1b As the earlier time has humiliated
      the country of Zebulun and the country of Naphtali,
  the later one has honored the Way of the Sea,
      the other side of the Jordan, Galilee of the nations.
2 The people walking in darkness
      has seen great light.
  Those living in deathly gloom—
      light has shone on them.
3 You have made the nation many,
      you have given it great joy.

They have rejoiced before you like the rejoicing at harvest,
    like people who celebrate at the dividing of plunder.
4 Because the yoke that burdened it,
    the rod on its shoulder,
the boss's club over it,
    you have shattered as on the day at Midian.
5 Because every boot of someone trampling with a roar,
    and the coat rolled in blood,
have been for burning,
    consumed by fire.
6 Because a child has been born to us,
    a son has been given to us,
    and government has come onto his shoulder.
People have called him
    "An-extraordinary-counselor-is-the-warrior-God,
the-everlasting-Father-is-an-official-for-well-being."
7 Of the growing of government and of well-being
    there will be no end, on David's throne and on his reign,
to establish it and support it,
    with authority and faithfulness,
from now and forever;
    the passion of Yahweh Armies will do this.

8 My Lord has sent out a word against Jacob,
    and it has fallen on Israel.
9 But the people, the entirety of it, acknowledge it
    (Ephraim and the inhabitants of Samaria)
    with loftiness and big-headedness:
10 "Bricks have fallen, but we will build with stone;
    sycamore-figs have been cut down,
    but we will put cedars in their place."
11 But Yahweh has lifted high
    the adversaries of Rezin over it,
and spurred on its enemies,
12   Syria from the east, the Philistines from the west,
    and they have devoured Israel with open mouth.
For all this, his anger did not turn;
    his hand was still stretched out.

13 The people did not turn to the one who hit it;
    it has not inquired of Yahweh Armies.

14 So Yahweh cut off from Israel head and tail,
   palm branch and reed, in one day.
15 The elder and the important person, he is the head,
   and the prophet who teaches falsehood, he is the tail.
16 The guides of this people became ones who make them
      wander;
   the ones who were guided were people who were
      confounded.
17 Therefore my Lord does not rejoice over its picked troops
   and does not show compassion for its widows and orphans,
   because the entirety of it is impious and does evil,
      and every mouth speaks mindlessness.
   For all this, his anger did not turn;
      his hand was still stretched out.

18 Because faithlessness burned like fire,
      which consumes briar and thorn.
   It set light to the thickets of the forest,
      and they swirled as a column of smoke.
19 By the fury of Yahweh Armies
      the country was scorched.
   The people became like a fire consuming;
      one person did not spare his neighbor.
20 He carved to the right but was hungry,
      and ate to the left but was not full;
      one person eats the flesh of his offspring.
21 Manasseh, Ephraim, Ephraim Manasseh;
      altogether against Judah.
   For all this, his anger did not turn;
      his hand was still stretched out.

10:1 Hey, you who inscribe wicked statutes,
      who write oppressive decrees,
2   to subvert the case of poor people
      and steal the rights of the lowly among my people,
   so that widows become their spoil
      and orphans their plunder.
3   What will you do on the day when you get attention,
      when disaster comes from afar
   (to whom will you flee for help,
      and where will you abandon your splendor?),

41

4 except cower beneath a captive,
    fall beneath the slain?
For all this, his anger did not turn;
    his hand was still stretched out.

My wife's son-in-law returned yesterday from one of his recurrent trips to meet with Darfuri refugees in Chad to encourage them, show some interest on the part of people from the United States, and look for ways of advocating for them. The focus of activity on this occasion was the hope of sending a soccer team from Darfur to the upcoming Viva World Cup, a competition for peoples such as the Iraqi Kurds who cannot take part in the regular World Cup. They took with them two soccer coaches and organized a competition for players from the different camps to identify a squad to take part in the competition if the diplomatic and practical hurdles can be overcome (and they can get the proper footware; the Darfuri usually play barefoot). It may seem an inconsequential, frivolous project; yet play can be important aid to healing, and the creation of the team and the prospect of their being able to join in the tournament is a monumental sign of hope for a people who have no hope.

For **Judahites**, when people have experienced darkness, defeat, and oppression, the birth of a new son in the royal household is a sign of hope. This section's opening paragraph mostly speaks of **Yahweh's** act of restoration as if it's past, but the restoration had not happened in Isaiah's day, so it likely speaks by faith of what Isaiah knows God is going to do. He can speak as if the events have happened because they have already begun; it's a common feature of the way Scripture works. The event that has actually happened is the birth of a son to the king, perhaps the birth of Hezekiah to Ahaz. People would look back to his birth as a significant moment, given his greatness as a reformer and as one who saw Yahweh marvelously preserve Jerusalem from falling to **Assyria**.

So he has that complicated name, "An-extraordinary-counselor-is-the-warrior-God, the-everlasting-Father-is-an-officer-for-well-being." Like earlier names in Isaiah (God-is-with-us, **Remains**-Will-Return, Plunder-hurries-loot-rushes), the name is a sentence. None of these names are the person's everyday name—as when the New Testament says that Jesus will be called Immanuel, "God with us," without meaning this expression is Jesus' name. Rather, the person somehow stands for whatever the "name" says. God gives him as a sign of the truth of the expression attached to him. The names don't mean that the person *is* God with us, or *is* the remains, or *is* the plunder, and likewise this new name doesn't mean the child *is* what the name says. Rather he is a sign and guarantee of it. It's as if he goes around bearing a billboard with that message and with the reminder that God commissioned the billboard.

The name makes some declarations about God. The warrior God is an extraordinary counselor or planner. That is, Yahweh is expert at determining what the future should bring and seeing that it does so; and Yahweh is capable of making plans that bring about events that one would never have guessed. Further, the everlasting Father is an officer who brings well-being. Isaiah 1 bemoaned how the children have disdained their father, and they have paid for it, but their father isn't finished with them. The Hebrew word for an officer often denotes an army officer, which links with the description of Yahweh as the warrior God. In this context *shalom* will then include the idea of peace, but the word commonly has the broader meaning of **well-being**—life as a whole going well. This prospect is what the child's name promises Judah.

The child's birth is a sign that God will restore his people. As David exercised government with faithfulness, so will this child (unlike his father). Remarkably, Isaiah starts from the restoration of **Ephraim**: the far northern clans of Zebulun and Naphtali, the Mediterranean region, the northeastern areas across the Jordan, and Galilee, to which the Assyrians transported other peoples. The birth of a new son to David's household underwrites the future of Israel as a whole. In his mind's eye Isaiah can see light dawning over the whole land, light that contrasts with the darkness of which chapter 8 spoke. He can see the Assyrian yoke broken, its army turning tail, as chapters 36–37 will describe. Judges 6–8 recounts the deliverance from Midian. Neatly, Jesus started his preaching in the north, so Matthew 4 can look at his ministry in light of Isaiah's vision. Jesus hasn't brought about the fulfillment of the entire vision, not any more than Hezekiah did, but he was another sign and guarantee that God will bring about its fulfillment, and a more compelling one. He wasn't merely wearing a billboard; he embodied its message.

Meanwhile, the book reverts to the critique and warning that characterized earlier chapters. They addressed their "Hey" to people who were using their power and resources to act oppressively, and they spoke of God's anger not having turned away and his hand being still stretched out. That analysis, confrontation, and warning recurs, completing a frame around the account of Isaiah's commission and ministry. People have experienced reversals but have determined to take control of the situation and have declined to recognize a need to turn to Yahweh. Yahweh has put down their misleading leaders but also holds the ordinary and vulnerable people responsible for following them. The nation has seen a total disintegration of its community ethos and its people's mutual commitment—within the northern kingdom, and that of the northern kingdom against Judah. It's still not over. They still need to turn.

ISAIAH 10:5–32

On Mixed Motives

5   Hey, Assyria, my angry club—
        and the mace in their hand is my wrath.
6   Against an impious nation I send it;
        I commission it against a people toward which I am wrathful,
    to take plunder and seize spoil,
        and make it into something trampled like mud in the streets.
7   But it doesn't think this way;
        its mind doesn't reckon this way.
    Because in its mind is to destroy,
        to cut off nations not a few.
8   Because it says,
        "Are my officers not kings, altogether?
9   Isn't Calno like Carchemish, or Hamath like Arpad—
        or Samaria like Damascus?

44

10 As my hand reached the nonentity kingdoms
    (and their images were more than [those of] Samaria
       and Jerusalem)—
11 as I did to Samaria and its nonentities,
    shall I not do the same to Jerusalem and its images?"
12 But when my Lord finishes all his action
    against Mount Zion and against Jerusalem:
  "I will attend to the fruit of the king of Assyria's
     big-headedness
  and to the lofty splendor of his look."
13 Because he said, "By the might of my hand I have acted,
    by my wisdom, because I have understanding.
  I have removed the borders of peoples,
    I have plundered their treasures,
    as a mighty one I have subdued inhabitants.
14 My hand reached, as [into] a nest,
    for the wealth of peoples.
  Like one gathering abandoned eggs,
    I myself gathered the entire earth.
  There was not one flapping a wing,
    or opening its mouth and chirping."
15 Does the ax glorify itself over the person who chops with it,
    or the saw magnify itself over the person who wields it,
  as if the club wields the person who lifts it up,
    as if the mace raised the one who is not made of wood?
16 Therefore the Lord Yahweh Armies will send off
    a wasting disease against his well-fed ones.
  Beneath its [people of] honor it will burn,
    with a burning like the burning of fire.
17 The light of Israel will become fire,
    its holy one a flame.
  It will burn and consume its thorn
    and its thistle, in one day.
18 The splendor of its forest and its farmland
    it will finish off, body and soul.
  It will be like the wasting away of a sick person;
19   the remains of the trees in its forest will be so few
    that a boy could write them down.

20 On that day the remains of Israel
    and the survivors of the household of Jacob

will not again lean on the one that hit them.
They will lean on Yahweh,
Israel's holy one, in truth.
21 The remains will turn, the remains of Jacob,
to God, the warrior God.
22 Though your people, Israel,
should be like the sand of the sea,
it will be remains of it that will turn;
a finishing is determined, overwhelming faithfulness.
23 Because a finish, a thing determined—
the Lord Yahweh Armies is doing it,
in the midst of the entire country.

24 Therefore the Lord Yahweh Armies has said this:
"Don't be afraid, my people
who dwell on Zion, of Assyria,
which hits you with a club
and lifts its mace against you in the manner of the
Egyptians.
25 Because in a very little while more,
my wrath will finish,
and my anger will be toward their destruction."
26 Yahweh Armies is lifting up a whip against it
like the hitting of Midian at the Oreb Crag,
like his mace over the sea,
and he will raise it in the manner of Egypt.
27 On that day its burden will move away from your shoulder,
and his yoke from upon your neck;
the yoke will be destroyed in the face of your stoutness.

28 He has gone against Aiat, he has passed by Migron,
at Mikmas he stationed his equipment.
29 They crossed at the pass;
"Geba will be lodging for us."
Ramah trembles,
Gibeah of Saul has fled.
30 Yell aloud, Bat-gallim, pay heed, Laishah,
answer, Anatot!
31 Madmenah ran away,
the inhabitants of Gebim sought refuge.
32 Yet this day at Nob, standing,
he will wave his hand.

at the mount of Ms. Zion,
    the hill of Jerusalem.

Next week my wife and are to speak at a retreat for students aimed at helping people maintain a connection with God while they're studying theology. I'm looking forward to this event because we have the experience of going through seminary and watching generations of students do so, so we have experiences to share, lessons we have learned, and reflections to offer. I'm pretty confident that students will appreciate at least some things we say, and I won't object if they say so afterward. Of course I may be totally wrong, but whether I am or not, the problem is that my keenness to be useful to students and my keenness to serve God is mixed up with my enjoyment of performing in a way that people will appreciate. As a pastor I'm always faced by the question of whether I'm doing my work for God's sake or for people's sake or for my sake—or, rather, if these three motivations are always mixed up.

Maybe they were mixed up for Isaiah. Certainly they were mixed up for the **Assyrians**, if not at the level of conscious motivation. The Assyrians were serving **Yahweh** but didn't realize it. They were rampaging around the Middle East carving out an empire, and their rampaging in **Ephraim** and **Judah** was the means of God acting there. They were the club or mace that God wielded in expressing anger at the people's wrongdoing. The Bible often sees the superpowers as means whereby God's purpose is fulfilled, for good or ill. But in neither connection are they trying to serve God. Their motivation isn't mixed. They just want to serve their own interests (but this doesn't stop God using them). They operate with the self-confidence that's natural to a superpower. They know their resources are bigger than anyone else's; they can beat anyone. They have a proven strategic track record.

The trouble is that they're thus more impressed with themselves than they are with the God whom they're unconsciously serving. And the basis upon which God evaluates them isn't whether God finds them strangely useful. It's the nature of that motivation. God doesn't see anything unjust in utilizing people's wrong instincts yet still evaluating them on the basis of those instincts. The Assyrians will be judged in the same way as their victims are judged. They get cut no slack because God uses them. They will find the God who is the light of Israel setting them alight.

The message concerns Assyria but it's designed for Judah to hear. We get no indication that a prophet such as Isaiah went off to address the Assyrian king. It's usually the case that when prophets speak as if they're addressing other nations, it's Israel that they're directly addressing. Their job is to enable the people of God to understand what God is doing in the world and to live their lives in light of that understanding. The point is more explicit when Isaiah goes on to tell people not to be afraid of Assyria. You could say it's a strange exhortation. Judah has every reason to be afraid of Assyria in the short term. The final paragraph gives a vivid imaginary description of the frightening advance on Jerusalem by the Assyrian army. But Judah continues to be "my people." Assyria's destructiveness won't be the end of the story. The pattern in the putting down of Egypt at the Reed Sea at the exodus and of Midian in Gideon's day (see Judges 6–8) will be repeated.

Thus when Isaiah goes on to speak of the people who form the leftovers in Judah when the superpower is finished with them, and of how they will behave in the future, he is again addressing Judah, and his words are again not mere predictions but challenges and promises designed to influence Judah in the present. The section keeps moving between declarations about Assyria's and Judah's future and warnings to Judah, and this reflects the way it sets different challenges and scenarios before Judah, designed to provoke a response. Judah has an unfortunate penchant for relying on people who will then turn on them, people such as the Assyrians themselves. Eventually they will see sense and realize whom they should rely on. A people will survive who are mere leftovers, a tiny people that Yahweh allows to survive to avoid wiping out the whole people when Yahweh's wrath overwhelms Yahweh's instinct to be faithful and not act in judgment. They will be a **remnant**, in the traditional translation. But that tiny people will turn to Yahweh and become faithful leftovers, a faithful remnant.

ISAIAH 10:33–12:6

A Day When There Will Be a Song to Sing

10:33 There is the Lord Yahweh Armies,
lopping off boughs with a crash.
The loftiest in height are being felled,
the tall ones fall down.
34 The thickets in the forest will be struck down with an ax,
and Lebanon will fall by the Mighty One.
11:1 But a shoot will come out from Jesse's stump,
a branch will sprout from his roots.
2 Yahweh's breath will rest on him,
a wise and understanding breath,
a breath of counsel and strength,
a breath of acknowledgment and awe for Yahweh;
3 his delight will be awe for Yahweh.
He will not exercise authority by the seeing of his eyes,
or reprove by the hearing of his ears.
4 He will exercise authority with faithfulness for the poor,
and reprove with uprightness for the lowly people in the
country.
He will hit the country with the club in his mouth,
with the breath from his lips.
5 Faithfulness will be the belt around his thighs,
truthfulness the belt around his waist.
6 Wolf will sojourn with lamb,
leopard will lie down with goat,
calf, lion, and yearling together,
with a little boy leading them.
7 Cow and bear will graze,
their young will lie down together.
Cougar, like ox,
will eat straw.
8 A baby will play over the cobra's burrow;
an infant will hold its hand over the viper's hole.
9 People will not do evil, they will not destroy,
in all my holy mountain.
Because the country will be full of the acknowledgment of
Yahweh
as the waters cover the sea.

49

¹⁰ On that day, Jesse's root which will be standing
     as a signal for peoples –
nations will inquire of him,
     and his abode will be [a place of] splendor.

¹¹ On that day my Lord will again apply his hand
     to get the remains of his people that remain,
from Assyria, from Egypt, from Pathros,
     from Sudan, from Elam, from Shinar,
     from Hamat, and from the coasts of the [Mediterranean]
      Sea.
¹² He will lift up a signal to the nations,
     and gather the men of Israel who were thrown out,
and the women of Judah who were scattered he will collect,
     from the four corners of the earth.
¹³ Ephraim's jealousy will go away,
     and harassers within Judah will be cut off.
Ephraim won't be jealous of Judah,
     and Judah won't harass Ephraim.
¹⁴ They will fly against the back of the Philistines to the west;
     together they will plunder the easterners.
Edom and Moab will be [subject to] the extending of their
     hand;
     and the Ammonites will be their obedient people.
¹⁵ Yahweh will dry up the tongue of the Egyptian sea,
     and will wave his hand over the Euphrates
     with the heat of his breath.
He will hammer it into seven washes,
     and let people make their way in sandals.
¹⁶ There will be a highway for the remains of his people,
     which remain from Assyria,
as there was for Israel,
     on the day it came up from the country of Egypt.

¹²:¹ You will say on that day:
     I will confess you Yahweh,
because whereas you were angry with me,
     your anger turned and you comforted me.
² There is God, my deliverance,
     I will trust and not be fearful,
because Yah, Yahweh,
     is my strength and might.

³ You will draw water with joy,
      from the fountains of deliverance.
⁴ You will say on that day:
      Confess Yahweh, proclaim his name.
   Make his deeds known among the peoples,
      make mention that his name is on high.
⁵ Make music for Yahweh, because he has acted in majesty;
      this is to be acknowledged in the entire earth.
⁶ Yell and resound, inhabitants of Zion,
      because great in your midst is Israel's holy one.

Our city's annual Black History Parade this year had the theme "Looking back and remembering: we've come a mighty long way." The words reminded me of the hymn, "We've Come This Far by Faith." But in my head I can hear some African American people rightly adding, "But we have a long way to go yet before we have a full place in our society. There are too many African Americans in prison and not enough in college. Our teenagers still get slain by police or vigilantes." The dean of one of the schools in my seminary has been stopped by the police for driving while black. Do you stress the positive or the negative? There are people who see the glass as half full and others who see it as half empty. Both play an important role in the community.

This section of Isaiah presupposes versions of that tension. Isaiah sees the **Assyrian** forest being felled. He sees it only in vision; it won't happen for another century. Maybe he was disappointed not to see it fulfilled in his lifetime. But he has the vision, and hope depends on a vision. Likewise he can see the felling of Jesse's tree—that is, the fall of David's dynasty. This fall he can also see only in a vision, but he can also look beyond it and see a new shoot growing from the felled tree. Earlier he applied the imagery of felled tree and new shoot to the destiny of the people as a whole; here it applies to David's household. The new shoot will lack the weaknesses that the Davidic kings have usually shown; he will realize the Davidic ideal in showing both compassion for the weak and toughness toward the oppressor. The context thus suggests that the picture of killers in the animal world being turned into pets is another image for the same deliverance.

51

There's more that **Yahweh** intends to achieve through this new shoot. His significance will extend beyond Israel to the entire world. The sequence here implies the idea going back to God's promise to Abraham, that what God does in Israel will be so impressive that the world will flock to Jerusalem to seek blessing and guidance from Yahweh. Here the draw is the achievement of the Davidic shoot in bringing about a transformation of **Judahite** society.

The middle paragraph also talks in terms of a signal summoning the nations but does so in connection with another aspect of Israel's own need. There's need for social renewal; there's also need to bring back to the country **Ephraimites** and Judahites who have been transported all over the known world. The Ephraimite transportation happened in Isaiah's day, but the Judahite transportation happened over a century later, suggesting that this prophecy comes from a later prophet than Isaiah himself, like the prophecies in subsequent parts of this book. (In the event, a return of the people scattered all over the world never happens, partly because they like life where they are, then in due course their being spread over the world becomes an alternative means of God's reaching out with his revelation to the whole world.)

The vision goes beyond the mere return of people to the land. It envisages a healing of the longstanding tension within Israel between Ephraim and Judah, a tension going back to the split within the nation two centuries before Isaiah's day that will reappear after the **exile** in the story told in Ezra and Nehemiah. Both periods also saw recurrent tension between Judah and its neighbors in Philistia, Edom, Moab, and Ammon; the story in Ezra and Nehemiah makes especially clear little Judah's vulnerability to these people after the exile.

The final paragraph gives Judah a song to sing "on that day," a song rather like the thanksgivings or testimonies that appear in the Psalms, for singing when God has done something amazing for people. This "psalm" also assumes that God's acts for his people are not significant just for them. Their praise deserves to be heard among other nations so that they're drawn to acknowledge Yahweh.

The song brings the first major section of Isaiah to a close. You could say that the whole story is contained in these twelve chapters. There has been confrontation, warning, and promise, and the community is invited to live within this story, facing the challenges of the present but also (when the warnings have been fulfilled) living by the promises for the future. Providing the people with a song that they will be able to sing one day is another way of inviting them to live in hope. If they yield to the song, they're virtually praising God for fulfilling his promises before the fulfillment happens. Wherever they are, they're invited to see that they have come this far by faith and can continue in hope, not because their faith or hope is big but because the God they trust and hope in is big. It fits that the last clause in Isaiah 1–12 is a declaration about "Israel's holy one."

It's hard to acknowledge after 2,700 years that Isaiah's vision has been fulfilled only in little ways (the glass is only half full), though Jesus' coming does constitute God's "Yes" to his promises. It thus makes it the more possible to keep believing in them and to keep singing the song in anticipation.

ISAIAH 13:1–14:2

The Downfall of the Superpower

13:1 A prophecy about Babylon, which Isaiah ben Amoz saw.

2 On a bare mountain lift up a signal,
      raise your voice to them.
   Wave your hand,
      so that they will come through the leaders' gates.
3 I myself have commanded the people I have sanctified,
      I have called my warriors on behalf of my wrath,
      the people who exult in my majesty.
4 The sound of uproar on the mountains,
      the semblance of a great company,
   the sound of the din of kingdoms, nations assembling—
      Yahweh Armies is mustering an army for war.
5 They are coming from a distant country,
      from the end of the heavens,

Yahweh and the instruments of his wrath,
   to devastate the entire earth.
6   Howl, because Yahweh's day is near;
      like destruction from the Destroyer it comes.
7   Therefore all hands go limp,
      every human heart melts.
8   They are terrified, spasms and throes seize them,
      they thrash about like a birthing woman.
   One person looks aghast at his neighbor;
      their faces are flaming [red] faces.

9   There, Yahweh's day is coming, ruthless,
      with fury and angry blazing,
   to turn the earth into a desolation,
      so that it can destroy its offenders from it.
10   Because the stars in the heavens, and their constellations,
      will not flash their light,
   the sun will have gone dark when it comes out,
      the moon will not shine its light.
11   I will attend to its evil upon the world,
      and to their waywardness upon the faithless.
   I will put an end to the majesty of the arrogant,
      and bring down the dignity of the violent.
12   I will make people scarcer than pure gold,
      human beings than Ophir gold.
13   Therefore I will make the heavens quake,
      and the earth will shake out of its place,
   at the fury of Yahweh Armies,
      on the day of his angry blazing.
14   Like a hunted gazelle,
      like sheep with no one gathering them,
   each person will turn to his people,
      each will flee to his country.
15   Everyone who is found will be run through,
      everyone who is swept up will fall by the sword.
16   Their little ones will be smashed before their eyes,
      their homes will be plundered, their wives bedded.

17   There am I, stirring up the Medes against them,
      who don't count silver, and gold—they don't want it.

54

¹⁸ Their bows will smash the young,
>   they won't have compassion on the fruit of the womb,
>   their eye won't spare children.
¹⁹ So Babylon, the most splendid of kingdoms,
>   the majestic splendor of the Kaldeans,
>   will become like God's overturning of Sodom and
>   Gomorrah.
²⁰ It will not be inhabited ever,
>   it will not be dwelt in to all generations.
> Arab will not camp there,
>   shepherds will not pasture there.
²¹ Wild creatures will lie down there;
>   their houses will be full of owls.
> Ostriches will dwell there,
>   wild goats will leap about there.
²² Hyenas will live in its strongholds,
>   dragons in its luxurious palaces.
> Its time is near coming,
>   its days will not drag on.

^{14:1} Because Yahweh will have compassion on Jacob
>   and will again choose Israel.
> He will settle them on their land and the alien will join
>   them
>   and attach themselves to the household of Jacob.
² Peoples will take them
>   and bring them to their place.
> The household of Israel will possess them
>   on Yahweh's land as male and female servants.
> They will be captors to their captors
>   and will rule over their bosses.

Last Sunday's newspaper included three reviews of books on "the state of the union," one by a Brit, two by Americans, all written by people who love the United States, but all concerned about its decline as the world's one superpower. It's often said that the United States has endless capacity to reinvent itself, and (the books and the reviewers argue) it needs to draw on that capacity not merely for its own sake but for the world's sake, because while the country may be in a dysfunctional state, the current world order is in a more parlous one. "Given what else is out there, the world still needs America," one of the writers affirmed. Someone has to be dominant in the world, and the United States being masters of the world is better than any plausible alternative.

I'm not sure what I think of that argument; I do think that both Testaments emphasize the down side to the idea that someone has to dominate the world, and they make clear that sooner or later the superpower does fall. **Babylon** is a great example—as is the tellingly-entitled Tower of Babel.

This chapter is the first of eleven chapters concerning the nations around **Judah**. Most of these peoples would presumably never know about the prophecies. They were meant for the Judahites to hear, to enable the people of God to look at their world in the right way. The particular significance of each prophecy would vary according to the significance of that nation for Judah's life. Babylon was important to Judah in two ways, in different contexts. In Isaiah's day, Babylon (modern Iraq) was a relatively unimportant nation far away to the east, but a nation with ambitions. It saw itself as making a challenge to **Assyrian** domination of its world, and it was interested in making allies with other nations to that end; we will come back to that dynamic in Isaiah 39.

But Babylon's ambitions in Isaiah's day wouldn't make it important enough to take it as seriously as happens in the first two chapters of these prophecies about foreign nations. Its prominence here reflects the fact that it did realize its ambitions. A century after Isaiah's day, it took Assyria's place as the one superpower, and Judah became one of its underlings. When Judah rebelled against being in that position, the Babylonians came, destroyed Jerusalem, and took many of its people off in **exile** to Babylon. It's this fact that lies behind Babylon's prominence in these prophecies about the nations. Whatever the origin of individual prophecies in the book, it wasn't Isaiah who organized it but people who saw the ongoing importance of his prophecies, and their work reflects the situation when Babylon is the superpower and the Judahites are in exile.

After the opening line of the section, in the first two paragraphs there's no mention of Babylon at all. In part that functions to arouse suspense. You can imagine people listening to the prophecy and wondering who on earth it's about. They could think that the army is the Babylonian army, and they could then wonder who are its victims. Only in the third paragraph do they discover that the army is the Medes, from further east (modern Iran) and that the Babylonians or **Kaldeans** are the victims.

The way the prophecy works also reflects how Babylon's fall to the Medes is just one embodiment of a pattern—Assyria yields to Babylon, Babylon to the Medes and Persians, the Medes and Persians to the Greeks, the Greeks to the Romans. The pattern doesn't hold independently of God's activity. God is involved. Without realizing it, the Medes are an army dedicated to God's service. Their rise indeed brings one embodiment of the **Day of the Lord**. The event has such world-shaking significance, it's as if the whole cosmos goes dark. Isaiah pictures God sending his staff to raise an army with the gusto to join in this project that God has commissioned it for, to effect the downfall of people with whom God is wrathful, with repercussions for the whole world that it controls. The event's connotations are frightening even for people who will benefit from it. The picture of calamity for one people melds into a picture of calamity for the world as a whole. It cannot simply point at the superpower and exult in its downfall but must see the superpower's waywardness as an enhanced form of its own waywardness. Any downfall it experiences presages the world's downfall.

The picture is expressed hyperbolically. When the Medes and Persians conquered Babylon, they didn't destroy it or smash its children (this element in the prophecy is the basis for the hyperbolic prayer in Psalm 137). But they did bring it to an end. The last two verses make explicit the significance of this action for people in Judah two hundred years after Isaiah's day. It will mean the reestablishing of the Judahite community, foreigners coming to join it, and their former masters becoming their servants.

ISAIAH 14:3-27

So You Have Fallen from the Heavens!

³ On the day Yahweh gives you rest from your suffering, from your turmoil, and from the hard service that was imposed on you, ⁴ you will take up this poem about the king of Babylon:

Ah, the boss has stopped,
   the storm has stopped!
5   Yahweh has broken the mace of the faithless,
      the rulers' club,
6   that hit peoples with fury,
      a hitting without breaking off,
   that subdued nations in anger,
      a persecution without holding back.
7   The entire earth is at rest, it's still;
      people have broken out in resounding.
8   The juniper trees have rejoiced over you, too,
      the cedars of Lebanon:
   "Now you have lain down,
      no one will come up who will cut us down."
9   Sheol below has been astir regarding you,
      to meet your coming,
   rousing the ghosts regarding you,
      all earth's big guys,
   raising from their thrones
      all the nations' kings.
10   All of them respond and say to you,
      "You too have been made weak as we are,
      you have become like us!"
11   Your majesty has been brought down to Sheol,
      the sound of your harps.
   Beneath you worm is spread out,
      maggot is your covering.

12   Ah, you have fallen from the heavens,
      bright one, son of dawn!
   You have been felled to the earth,
      enfeebler of nations!
13   You're the one who said within yourself,
      "I will go up to the heavens.
   Above the highest stars
      I will raise my throne.
   I will sit on the mount of assembly,
      on the extremities of Zaphon.
14   I will go up on cloud tops,
      I will be like the One on High."
15   Yet you are brought down to Sheol,
      to the extremities of the Pit.

58

¹⁶ The people who see you stare at you,
    they wonder about you.
"Is this the man who shook the earth,
    who disturbed kingdoms,
¹⁷ Who made the world an absolute wilderness
    and destroyed its cities?
Its prisoners he did not release to [go] home,
    ¹⁸ all the nations' kings."
All of them lay down in honor,
    each in his "house."
¹⁹ But you have been thrown out away from your tomb,
    like abominable carrion,
clothed in the slain,
    pierced by the sword,
people who go down to the stones of the Pit
    like a trampled corpse.
²⁰ You won't be one with them in burial,
    because you destroyed your country,
you slaughtered your people;
    the offspring of evildoers will not be named forever.
²¹ Prepare a place of slaughter for his children
    because of the waywardness of their ancestors.
They are not to arise and possess the earth,
    so that cities cover the world's surface.

²² I will arise against them
    (a declaration of Yahweh Armies)
and cut off for Babylon name and remains,
    offspring and descendants (Yahweh's declaration).
²³ I will make it into the possession of the owl,
    pools of water.
I will sweep it with a destructive sweeper
    (a declaration of Yahweh Armies).

²⁴ Yahweh Armies has sworn:

Yes, as I envisaged, so it is happening;
    as I planned, it comes about:
²⁵ to break Assyria in my country—
    I will crush him on my mountains.

His yoke will depart from upon them,
>   his burden will depart from upon his shoulder.
²⁶ This is the plan that has been made for the entire earth,
>   this is the hand that is stretched out over all the nations.
²⁷ Because Yahweh Armies has made a plan,
>   and who can frustrate it?
His hand is stretched out,
>   and who can turn it back?

Last night we watched a documentary about a young man on death row who was about to be executed. Ten years ago as a teenager he and a friend had murdered a woman, her son, and her son's friend, all for the sake of stealing their fancy car. They were drunk and on drugs. The murderer's own father was in his second life term for killing people. There seemed to be no mother around. When his penniless brother called their grandfather to ask what was going on, the grandfather refused to pay for the call. Words such as dysfunctional are insufficient to describe the family's life. It reminded me of comments in the Gospels about Satan entering Judas and Jesus addressing Peter as Satan, as a way of explaining how people can do or say horrific things. So how did Satan become able and inclined to act that way?

John Milton's poem *Paradise Lost* took Isaiah 14 to provide the answer. It describes how Satan could deceive Eve because "his pride / had cast him out from heaven, with all his host / of rebel angels, by whose aid aspiring / to set himself in glory above his peers, / he trusted to have equaled the Most High, / if he opposed; and with ambitious aim / against the throne and monarchy of God / raised impious war in heaven and battle proud / with vain attempt. Him the Almighty Power / hurled headlong flaming from the ethereal sky / with hideous ruin and combustion down / to bottomless perdition, there to dwell / in adamantine chains and penal fire, / who durst defy the Omnipotent to Arms."

Isaiah is indeed talking about someone trying to usurp God's position of authority in the world, but he isn't describing a supernatural being but talking about the **Babylonian** king as the head of the superpower. Our word "superpower" gives the game away. The claim to be a superpower is a claim to have usurped God's authority. The prophecy sees the desire to control the entire world as a desire to have a godlike position over it.

Isaiah makes the point by taking up a theme people would have known (Ezekiel 28 does the same). For much of the year, Venus gets very bright just before dawn so that it can be called the son of dawn, the morning star. But for much of the year, in the morning Venus is eclipsed by the sun's own brightness. Middle Eastern religions saw the planets and stars as representing the gods and representing things going on between the gods, and a Canaanite story saw these events in the sky as reflecting a failed attempt by Venus to become top god, to become president of the assembly of the gods.

The prophecy is using that story to describe the king of Babylon attempting to achieve a godlike position over the world, trying to become top dog or top god. It may refer to someone such as Nebuchadnezzar or Nabonidus, but it names no single king and it is inherently transferable to any ruler who makes the attempt it refers to. In Isaiah's own day, it would refer to an **Assyrian** king such as Sennacherib, whose overreaching and downfall is the subject of Isaiah 37–38. (Assyria indeed gets a mention later in this section.) Either way, in Isaiah (and Ezekiel) it's a prophecy about events in this world.

It's a prophecy with a promise. When the **Judahites** look at the Assyrian or Babylonian king, they see someone who looks all-powerful, more powerful than God. In the vision God gives Isaiah, the king has been cast down from the godlike position over the world that he sought. He has gone from the height of heaven to the depth of **Sheol**. His predecessors as kings stand up to welcome him. But he doesn't get the splendid burial that other kings got. His corpse is more like that of an ordinary person killed in battle, lying on the battlefield in a heap of corpses, a long way from the mausoleum he expected to occupy.

God hasn't yet given Judah rest from its suffering, turmoil, and servitude to the superpower. But in his vision Isaiah has seen the superpower's downfall, and his people are invited to live in the certainty that rest will come. They will be able to take up his poem; it will be reality, not just hope. And it happened. Assyria fell. Babylon fell. It's not only one king who falls. Whole dynasties do so. The dictator's sons don't get a chance to take over from their father; they're put down too.

In these promises there's also comfort for the Assyrians and Babylonians themselves. It's not only other peoples that suffer at the hand of a superpower's king. His own people suffer.

ISAIAH 14:28–16:14

Compassion and Openness to Learning

14:28   In the year King Ahaz died, this prophecy came:

29   Don't rejoice, all you Philistines,
        because the club of the one who hit you has broken.
     Because from the snake's root a viper will come out,
        its fruit a flying seraph.
30   The firstborn of poor people will pasture,
        the needy will lie down in safety.
     But I will kill your root with hunger,
        I will slay the remains of you.
31   Howl, gate; cry out, city;
        melt, all you Philistines.
     Because a cloud is coming from the north;
        there's no one going astray in its appointed ranks.
32   What will one answer the nation's aides?—
        that Yahweh has established Zion,
        and on it the lowly of his people will rely.

15:1 A prophecy about Moab.

     Yes, by night Ar has been destroyed,
        Moab has been devastated.
     Yes, by night Qir has been destroyed,
        Moab has been devastated.
2   Dibon has gone up to the house,
        to the high places, to weep.
     Over Nebo and over Medeba
        Moab howls.
     On every head in it there is shornness,
        every beard is cut off,
3   in its streets they wear sackcloth.
     On its roofs, in its squares,

62

everyone in it howls, falling down with weeping.
4   Heshbon and Elealah cry out,
their voice makes itself heard in Jahaz.
Therefore the armed men of Moab shout,
its spirit trembles within it.
5   My heart cries out for Moab—
its fugitives as far as So'ar,
as far as Eglat-shelishiyah.
Yes, the ascent of Luhit—
with weeping they climb it.
Yes, the road to Horonaim—
they raise a shattering cry.
6   Yes, the waters of Nimrim
become a great desolation.
Yes, the grass is dry, the vegetation is finished,
greenery has ceased.
7   Therefore the abundance they've made and what they have
in their charge—
they carry them across the Willows Wash.
8   Yes, the cry has surrounded Moab's border,
as far as Eglaim its howl,
and in Beer-elim its howl.
9   Yes, the waters of Dimon are full of blood,
yet I will put more on Dimon—
a lion for the survivors of Moab,
for the remains of the land.

16:1 Send a ram belonging to the country's ruler,
from Sela in the wilderness to the mountain of Ms. Zion.
2   Like a bird flitting, a nest thrown out,
are the Moabite women at the fords of the Arnon.
3   "Bring us counsel, make a decision,
make your shadow like night at midday.
Shelter the banished, don't betray the fugitive;
4 the people banished from Moab should sojourn with you.
Be a shelter for them
from the face of the destroyer."
When the oppressor is no more, when destruction finishes,
when the devastator has come to an end from the country,
5   a throne will be established with commitment,
there will sit on it in truthfulness

in David's tent one who exercises authority,
    inquiring after judgment, and quick in faithfulness.

6   We have heard of Moab's majesty,
    very majestic,
its majesty, its loftiness, and its arrogance—
    its empty talk is not like that.
7   Therefore Moab should howl,
    everyone in it should howl for Moab,
for the blocks of raisins from Qir-hareset you should moan,
    utterly stricken
8   Because the terraces of Heshbon languish,
    the vines of Sibmah.
The nations' lords have struck down their clusters
    that had reached as far as Jazer,
that wandered into the wilderness;
    when their shoots spread, they crossed to the sea.
9   Therefore I weep with Jazer's weeping
    for Sibnah's vines.
I drench you with my tears,
    Heshbon and Elealeh.
Because over your summer fruit and over your harvest
    the cheering has died.
10   Rejoicing and gladness are gathered up from the farmland,
    in the vineyards no one resounds, no one shouts.
Wine in the presses—the treader doesn't tread;
    I have made the cheering stop.
11   Therefore my heart moans for Moab like a guitar,
    my spirit for Qir-heres.
12   When Moab appears, when it wearies itself,
    at the high place,
when it comes to its sanctuary to pray,
    it will not avail.

13 This is the word that Yahweh spoke for Moab previously.
14 But now Yahweh has spoken: "In three years in accordance
with the years of an employee, Moab's splendor with all its great
multitude will be humbled. The remains will be a small thing,
tiny, not much."

I have mentioned that my wife's daughter and son-in-law give their lives to seeking to make known the plight and needs of the hundreds of thousands of Darfuri refugees who fled from genocide in Sudan ten years ago and have been living since then in camps in Chad. My wife gets discouraged because it seems impossible to get the world to take their plight seriously and do something about it. It's as if Satan or God has blocked the world's ears to their cry. One reason why Satan or God has been able to do so is what is often termed the world's compassion fatigue. There's a limit to the energy available in the world to care about the needs of desperate peoples, and the Darfuri are the victims of this dynamic.

Maybe Isaiah helps Judah in this connection in his prophecy about Moab, just east of Judah, across the Dead Sea. The Old Testament expresses two attitudes to Moab. It tells scandalous stories about Moab, for instance casting aspersions on its origins (Genesis 19). These stories reflect the tensions between neighbors who were often fighting each other; in Isaiah's day, Moab joined the peoples rebelling against **Assyria**. But the Old Testament also tells a story about a Moabite woman called Ruth who came to believe in **Yahweh** and commit herself to a **Judahite** family, and in particular to her widowed mother-in-law, and about the way the Judahites of Bethlehem welcomed her into their community so that she became David's great-grandmother.

Isaiah begins his Moab chapters with a vision of Moab's destruction, or rather of its situation after its destruction. Like the prophecy about **Babylon**, it likely describes something that has happened in the prophet's imagination, not yet in actuality. One of its functions is to get Judah to understand Moab's potential destiny and be forewarned about the danger of allying with Moab. The closing verses of the section declare that the vision is about to find fulfillment.

The first paragraph about Moab describes cities scattered through Moab coping with the consequences of invasion, the grief that consumes people, and the places toward which people from those cities fled for refuge, carrying their possessions like those Darfuri refugees fleeing genocide in Sudan. Their cry makes itself heard throughout the country—Isaiah uses the word for the Israelites' cry in Egypt. His own feelings are suggested by the way he himself cries out for Moab; it's the same word. Yet he also tells us that Yahweh isn't yet finished with bringing calamity on Moab.

The middle paragraph about Moab begins with either Isaiah or Yahweh urging Moab to send a present from its king to Jerusalem. Apparently the leadership has taken refuge at Sela in Edom, which later became the Nabataean city of Petra, while Moabite women whose men have lost their lives cross the Arnon (the Israel-Moab boundary) looking for refuge. Perhaps it's these women in their female wisdom who utter the plea to Judah to offer Moab protection. They declare that turning to Jerusalem and to the Davidic king isn't merely a temporary expedient to get them through a crisis. Somehow their experience has made them willing to look to the Davidic king for the truthful, committed, faithful exercise of **authority**. So it is in the prophet's vision. The place where Yahweh dwells is the only place for a nation in despair to turn—and even Moab can turn there.

The last paragraph takes us back to the disaster; the section isn't arranged chronologically. Moab's impressiveness, its proper national pride, and its self-confidence have been extinguished. Its impressive vineyards that seemed to reach across the world, and the rest of its farmland, have been devastated. In response to his vision, once again the prophet mourns for Moab. The Moabites may turn to their gods, but it will get them nowhere. There's no suggestion that calamity comes on Moab as an act of judgment, still less judgment for Moab's enmity to Judah. Many events in history don't have that kind of significance. They are just things that happen. They do open up possibilities. As Jesus puts it in Luke 13, the collapse of a tower in Siloam didn't mean the victims were worse sinners than others. The question the story raises is what other people will learn from the event. Here, the question is whether Judah will learn from it. For Moab, the question would be whether it draws them to turn to Yahweh, preferably before disaster comes.

The opening paragraph in this section suggests that **Philistia** was tempted to rebel against Assyria, like Moab. An

Assyrian king has died, and the Philistines think it might be a good moment for people like Philistia and Judah to assert their independence. Don't be so silly, Isaiah says. The next king will be even worse. Once again the audience of Isaiah's prophecy includes Judah itself; its point is to get Judah to live by trust in Yahweh, not by political calculation. People who do so will find pasture and will live in safety. If Philistia does rebel, it will pay a price. But the prophecy is sparing in the way it specifies who can be the beneficiaries of its invitations. It's open to the Philistines to count themselves among the people who find pasture and safety, who find refuge in **Zion** and its God. Such is the message to the envoys from Philistia. As with Moab, it's open to Philistia to turn to Yahweh.

ISAIAH 17:1–18:7

Who Would Want to Be a Superpower?

17:1 A prophecy about Damascus.

> There is Damascus, removed from [being] a city;
>   it will become a fallen ruin.
> 2 The cities of Aroer will be abandoned,
>   they will be for flocks,
>   and they will lie down with no one disturbing.
> 3 Fortress will cease from Ephraim,
>   kingship from Damascus.
>   The remains of Syria
>   will become like the Israelites' splendor
>   (a declaration of Yahweh Armies).
> 4 On that day Jacob's splendor will become poor,
>   the fat of his body will become thin.
> 5 It will be like the gathering of the standing harvest,
>   when someone's arm harvests the ears,
>   like the gleaning of ears in the Vale of Repha'im.
> 6 There will remain gleanings in it,
>   like the beating of an olive tree:
>   two, three, berries on the top (the height);
>   four, five, on a fruitful bough
>   (a declaration of Yahweh, the God of Israel).

7   On that day a person will turn to his maker,
    and his eyes will look to Israel's holy one.
8   He won't turn to the altars that are the work of his hands,
    he won't look to what his fingers made,
    both the columns and the incense stands.

9   On that day his strong cities will be
    like the abandoned piece of woodland and height
  that people abandoned before the Israelites,
    and it will be a desolation.
10 Yes, you have put out of mind the God who delivers you;
    your strong crag you have not kept in mind.
  Therefore you may plant the plants of the Lovely One
    and sow the cutting of an alien [god].
11 On the day you plant, you may get them to grow,
    and in the morning you sow, get it to blossom;
  the harvest flees
    on the day of sickness and mortal pain.

12 Aah, the uproar of many peoples,
    that roar like the seas' roar,
  the din of nations,
    that make a din like the din of mighty waters!
13 Nations make a din like the din of many waters,
    but he bellows at it and it flees far away,
  driven like the chaff on the mountains before the wind,
    like tumbleweed before the storm.
14 Toward evening time there—terror;
    before morning, it is no more.
  This is the share of the people who despoil us,
    the lot of the people who plunder us.

18:1 Hey, country of the buzzing of wings,
    that is beyond the rivers of Sudan,
2   which sends envoys by sea
    in papyrus boats on the water's surface.
  Go, swift aides,
    to a nation towering and smooth,
  to a people feared far and near,
    a nation characterized by gibberish and aggressiveness,
    whose country streams divide.

3 All you inhabitants of the world,
      people who dwell in the earth!
   At the raising of a signal on the mountains, you should look,
      and at the sounding of the horn, you should listen.
4 Because Yahweh has said this to me:
      "I will be quiet and I will look to my place,
   like glowing heat in the sunshine,
      like a dew cloud in the heat of harvest."
5 Because before harvest, when the blossom is done
      and the flower becomes a ripening grape,
   he will cut the shoots with pruning knives,
      and the tendrils he has removed he will have taken away.
6 They will be abandoned, all of them,
      to the birds of prey of the mountains
      and the animals of the earth.
   The birds of prey will summer on them
      and all earth's animals will winter on them.
7 At that time
      tribute will be brought to Yahweh Armies,
   (a people towering and smooth,
      a people feared far and near,
   a nation characterized by gibberish and aggressiveness,
      whose country streams divide)
   to the place of the name of Yahweh Armies,
      Mount Zion.

Two days ago the news reported that for every soldier who dies on the battlefield in Afghanistan, twenty-five veterans commit suicide at home. It's such an unbelievable statistic I have just checked it again. Yesterday the news reported that the Taliban had undertaken a concerted offensive in Kabul that suggests an increasing sophistication and discipline and has made a former White House Afghanistan director express concern at the implied intelligence failure. Today's news includes suggestions about a similarity between the position of the United States today and that of Britain in 1945 when it could no longer afford to run an empire and had lost the willpower to do so. It's hard being an imperial power, even a soft one.

The center of this section has something to say about an imperial power, but the outside two paragraphs concern

69

further individual peoples. It begins with Damascus, the capital of Syria; Isaiah 7 already critiqued the alliance of **Ephraim** with Syria designed to resist **Assyrian** ambitions in their area. This new prophecy restates its declarations about calamity coming on Syria and again associates Ephraim with its fate. For Syria and Ephraim alike, there will be only **remnants** of their present splendor. They'll be like an emaciated person or the leftovers of a harvest—just a few olives on a branch too high to reach. Yet that word "remnant" continues to be capable of having its meaning turned upside down. If there are only remnants left, at least there are remnants. The first "on that day" prophecy envisages them seeing the error of their ways and finding their way back to **Yahweh**. Even for Ephraim, the end need not be the end. Indeed, the prophecy doesn't make explicit that it's talking about Ephraim. If the entire prophecy is "about Damascus," the possibility of turning to Yahweh is open to Syria too.

The last paragraph takes us in the opposite direction, turning away from the north to the south from Judah. It talks about Sudan because a Sudanese dynasty ruled Egypt in Isaiah's day, and Egypt directly impacts Judah as the big power to the south. From their insect-ridden land, the land of the Nile with its delta, the Sudanese send their envoys to Jerusalem by sea, along the Mediterranean coast. Isaiah bids the envoys go home to their tall, smooth-skinned people, widely respected in the world of the day.

The rationale for his brisk response is the same as applies to similar overtures from Ephraim and Syria. **Judah** isn't in the business of playing politics. Isaiah presents his message as one for the whole world to recognize. Decisions in politics are not made by people like Syria, Ephraim, Judah, Egypt, Sudan, or Assyria itself. They're made by Yahweh. At the moment Yahweh is just sitting there watching. There are moments when he is active and moments when he bides his time. Our human attempts to control our destiny sometimes simply fail, because they don't fit into the intentions he is pursuing and the timeframe he is working with. Yahweh is like a farmer sitting waiting in the heat of summer for the right moment to harvest the crops. But before the grape harvest there's further tough pruning and discarding to be done. Yes, there's a divine purpose at work at a quite different level from the one at which the politicians are operating.

Again the implication isn't simply that there's never to be a relationship between Yahweh and a far-off nation such as Sudan. A time will arrive when they will come to Jerusalem not just on a political mission. These tall, smooth-skinned, frightening, aggressive people with their strange language will come back to bring Yahweh an offering, to recognize the significance of **Zion** in a new way.

The paragraphs about Syria-Ephraim and Sudan-Egypt form the frame around this section. At the center stand two shorter paragraphs that don't name their addressees but imply their identity clearly. The first begins by talking about an abandoned land; it uses a word that came in the warning to Judah in Isaiah 6 and comes nowhere else in the Bible. It addresses "you," and "you" is feminine singular, speaking the way one speaks to Jerusalem. If Judahites and Jerusalemites were comforted by declarations about trouble coming on people such as Syria-Ephraim and Sudan-Egypt, they had better shape up. The lovely one and the stranger are the alien gods that people in Judah also prayed to. People think their harvest will then flourish, but actually it will be a disaster.

The paragraph about "the nations" has the potential for being good news, though only if its challenge is also accepted. "The nations" often means the empire as a whole—in Isaiah's day, Assyria. The pressure of peoples such as Syria-Ephraim and Sudan-Egypt correctly presupposed that Assyria is a great threat to their area. Isaiah declares that people need not fear the roar of the Assyrian beast. When Yahweh bellows, it will run away. In the evening it may terrify you; by morning, it can be gone. The story in Isaiah 37–38 will put flesh on the bones of this declaration. Once again Isaiah challenges people to trust that Yahweh is capable of having things in hand. It would also be a means of witnessing to Yahweh's sovereignty in the world and of embodying what it means to follow Yahweh.

ISAIAH 19:1–25

Egypt My People

¹ A prophecy about Egypt.
  There is Yahweh, riding on a swift cloud,
      coming to Egypt.

71

Egypt's nonentities will tremble before him,
    and Egypt's heart will melt within it.
2 I will stir up Egyptians against Egyptians,
    and one will fight against his brother,
one against his neighbor, city against city,
    kingdom against kingdom.
3 Egypt's spirit will drain away within it,
    and I will confound its plan.
They will inquire of the nonentities and the ghosts,
    of the mediums and experts.
4 But I will put Egypt
    into the hand of a hard master.
A powerful king will rule over them
    (a declaration of the Lord Yahweh Armies).
5 Water will dry up from the sea,
    the river will wither and parch.
6 Rivers will stink as they get low,
    the channels of Egypt will dry up.
Reed and rush will wither,
7   the plants by the Nile, by the mouth of the Nile.
Everything sown at the Nile will wither,
    blow away, be no more.
8 The fishermen will lament and mourn,
    all those who throw a hook into the Nile.
The people who spread a net
    on the water's surface will have languished.
9 The workers with combed flax will be shamed,
    and the weavers of linen.
10 Its textile workers will become crushed,
    all the wage-earners troubled in spirit.
11 The officials at So'an are simply dense,
    Pharaoh's wise counselors—stupid counsel.
How can you say to Pharaoh,
    "I am a son of wise people,
a son of the kings of Qedem?"—
12   where on earth are your wise people?
May they please tell you, may they acknowledge
    what Yahweh Armies has planned against Egypt.
13 The officials at So'an have become fools,
    the officials at Noph have deceived themselves.

They have made Egypt wander—
  they, the cornerstone of its clans.
14 Yahweh has mixed within it
  a spirit of distortion.
They will make Egypt wander in all it does,
  like the wandering of a drunk in his vomit.
15 Nothing will be done by Egypt
  that head or tail can do, palm branch or reed.

16 On that day, the Egyptians will be like women, and will be trembling and fearful before the shaking of the hand of Yahweh Armies, which he is shaking against them. 17 The land of Judah will be a terror to the Egyptians. Everyone to whom someone makes mention of it will be fearful because of the plan of Yahweh Armies, which he is formulating against them. 18 On that day, there will be five cities in the country of Egypt speaking the tongue of Canaan and taking oaths to Yahweh Armies. "Sun City," one will be called. 19 On that day there will be an altar for Yahweh in the heart of the country of Egypt and a column for Yahweh at its border. 20 It will be a sign and testimony for Yahweh Armies in the country of Egypt; when they cry out to Yahweh before oppressors, he will send them a deliverer and contender to rescue them. 21 Yahweh will make himself known to the Egyptians, and the Egyptians will acknowledge Yahweh on that day. They will serve with sacrifice and offering, and make promises to Yahweh and fulfill them. 22 Yahweh will strike Egypt, striking and healing. They will turn to Yahweh and he will let himself be entreated by them and will heal them. 23 On that day there will be a highway from Egypt to Assyria. Assyria will come to Egypt and Egypt to Assyria. Egypt will serve with Assyria. 24 On that day Israel will be the third for Egypt and Assyria, a blessing in the midst of the earth, 25 because Yahweh Armies has blessed it, saying "Blessed be my people Egypt, my handiwork Assyria, and my own possession Israel."

Yesterday I had dinner with two people home from working in the Middle East, one in a Christian university to the north of Israel, the other in a seminary to the south. In both countries the Christian community is a minority in a tough context where increasing numbers of Christians leave for places such as the United States. Yet the presence of many fewer expatriate Christian workers than were there in the past has some positive implications. The churches have more capacity for accepting responsibility for their mission than might once have seemed the case. In both countries the Christian community has known ups and downs, but it has a history that goes back to the earliest decades of the church.

You could see the existence of the church in countries either side of Israel as a fulfillment of the promises at the end of Isaiah 19. The chapter as a whole provides the most spectacular example of the way these prophecies about other nations combine warnings of calamity with declarations of the positive concern God has for them. We have to keep reminding ourselves that whether or not these nations knew of the prophecies about them, the prophecies were given to Israel—hence their being in Israel's Scriptures. They are there to help the people of God think about the world and about God's involvement in the lives of nations.

So the first paragraph's warnings about disaster coming to Egypt are there to warn **Judah** about treating Egypt as a resource, an ally in Middle Eastern politics, as it was inclined to do (Isaiah 30–31 will make that point more explicit). When **Yahweh** acts, Egypt's nonentities (its tin-pot gods) will be helpless, its people will panic and turn on each other, and a foreign power will conquer it. While Yahweh might issue such threats against any people, and there's no necessity to look for a link with a specific context, the **Assyrian** king Sargon did conquer Egypt in Isaiah's day. Two threats look more customized for Egypt. One is the failure of its great natural resource, the Nile, with consequences running through the nation's entire life. The other is the failure of the intellectual resources upon which it based its political policies. The government thought it had the best research program in the world, and Israelites were familiar with the intellectual achievements of Egyptian scholarship. But the best planning in the world gets you nowhere if Yahweh has a plan in a different direction.

So on that day there will be disaster for Egypt; but also on that day things will be spectacularly different. Cities in Egypt will be speaking Hebrew and taking oaths in Yahweh's name, one of them being historically a city dedicated to the sun god. There will be an altar for worship of Yahweh at the heart of the country and a border sign announcing that it belongs to Yahweh. Egypt will have the same experience that Israel itself had in Egypt, of crying out and being delivered. The Egyptians will know Yahweh, worship Yahweh, and make and keep commitments to Yahweh. They will know chastisement but they will also know healing. It's hard to see it as pure coincidence that there later developed a flourishing Jewish community in Egypt, that the translation of the Scriptures into Greek for the sake of Gentiles as well as Jews happened there, and that Egypt became one of the most important early centers of Christian faith.

And there will be that freeway between the great imperial center north of Israel and the great imperial center to the south. Yahweh's intention to make Abraham's people a blessing to the world will be fulfilled. While Israel is Yahweh's own possession, Egypt will be "my people" and Assyria "my handiwork"—terms elsewhere that apply distinctively to Israel. Judah's thinking about nations such as Egypt and Assyria has to include both their vulnerability to Yahweh (so don't rely on them or fear them) and their destiny as Yahweh's people and Yahweh's handiwork.

ISAIAH 20:1–21:17

Prophet as Crazy Man

20:1 In the year the commander-in-chief came to Ashdod when Sargon, the king of Assyria, sent him, and made war on Ashdod and took it—² at that time Yahweh spoke by the hand of Isaiah ben Amoz. "Go, loose the sackcloth from on your thighs and take the sandal from on your feet." He did so, going stripped and barefoot. ³ Yahweh said, "As my servant Isaiah has gone stripped and barefoot three years as a sign and portent for Egypt and Sudan, ⁴ so the king of Assyria will drive off the captives of Egypt and the exiles of Sudan, young and old, stripped and barefoot, bare of buttock, Egypt's nakedness. ⁵ People will be shattered and shamed because of Sudan their trust and Egypt their splendor. ⁶ The one who lives on this foreign shore will say on that day, 'There, such is the state of the

one we trusted, where we fled for help, for rescue from the king
of Assyria. How can we ourselves escape?'"

21:1 The prophecy about the Sea Wilderness.

Like storms in the Negev passing through,
    from the wilderness it comes, from a fearful country.
2 A hard vision has been told me:
    "The betrayer is betraying, the destroyer is destroying!
Go up, Elam, lay siege, Media—
    I have put an end to all its groaning."
3 Therefore my thighs are full of convulsing,
    pains have seized me, like the pains of someone giving
       birth.
I'm too struck down to listen, I'm too terrified to look;
4   my mind wanders, shuddering has overwhelmed me.
The evening that I loved,
    he has turned to horror for me.
5 Setting the table, spreading the rug, eating, drinking . . .
    "Get up, officers, oil the shield!"
6 Because Yahweh my Lord has said to me,
    "Go, set a watch, so he may tell what he sees.
7 He will see a rider, a pair of horsemen,
    a donkey chariot, a camel chariot.
He is to pay attention, with attention,
    great attention."
8 The lookout called:
    "On the watch I have been standing, my Lord,
    continually by day,
and on my watch I have been taking my position
    every night.
9 And there, a chariot of men is coming,
    a pair of horsemen."
He testified, "Babylon has fallen, fallen,
    all its gods' images.
He had smashed to the ground 10 my crushed one,
    my son on the threshing floor."
What I heard from Yahweh Armies,
    Israel's God, I have told you.

11 A prophecy about Dumah.

Someone is calling to me from Se'ir:
  "Watchman, what is there of the night,
  what is there of the night?"
12 The watchman said,
  "Morning came, and night, too;
  if you inquire, inquire; come back again."

13 A prophecy in the steppe.

In the forest, in the steppe, you lodge,
  caravans of Dedanites.
14 Meet the thirsty one, bring water,
  you who inhabit the country of Tema,
  present the fugitive with his food.
15 Because they have fled before swords,
  before the drawn sword,
before the bent bow,
  before the weight of war.
16 Because my Lord has said this to me:
  Yet a year according to the years of an employee,
  all the splendor of Qedar will finish.
17 The remains of the number of the bows,
  the warriors of the Qedarites, will be few,
  because Yahweh, Israel's God, has spoken.

The installing of a professor in his or her "chair" is an occasion for making fun of the person as well as for making seriously congratulatory speeches. I was not surprised that when I was installed one of the people who had been asked to speak made fun of my clothes. Indeed, the seminary president makes fun of them on various occasions. I like T-shirts and bright colors. On the other hand, I don't much care for my clerical collar and hardly ever wear it. While I can provide you with a theological rationale for the abolition of the collar, the truth is that I don't care for going around as a marked man in that way, even though I also know that people can sometimes find it helpful that someone is identifiable as a priest and can feel free to approach the person as a priest.

What would I have felt if I had been asked to do what Isaiah did? Prophets were often called to embody in their lives and actions some aspect of what God intended to do. Embodying it was more than merely an illustration. Because a prophet like Isaiah is God's representative, it suggests he is putting into effect what he says. He was already embodying his message in his person when he went around in "sackcloth." Sackcloth isn't uncomfortable clothing but the kind you would normally wear only at home. Wearing it in public was a sign that something was wrong, that you were too poor or too preoccupied to dress properly. Maybe it was common wear for prophets, or maybe Isaiah was symbolizing his mourning for the moral and spiritual state of the people or for the fate that threatened them. Either way, by wearing sackcloth, Isaiah was already saying something. When he took off the sackcloth, this need not mean he was naked—quite likely he still had on something like underwear, which would still mean he was cold in a Jerusalem winter. The point was to embody the fate coming on the victims of **Assyria**.

The story has the same background as the previous chapter. Ashdod on the Mediterranean coast led a rebellion against Sargon and tried to involve Egypt and its Sudanese dynasty, but Sargon came and destroyed Ashdod. Be careful, then, Isaiah says to **Judah**. Don't get sucked in. Look at me if you want to see where it will lead. Don't trust in these people.

When people heard the reference to the Sea Wilderness that opens the next prophecy, they might have been puzzled. What immediately follows might have made them wonder if it referred to Judah's southern wilderness, but the prophecy turns out to be another announcement of the fall of **Babylon**. So "Sea Wilderness" perhaps refers to Mesopotamia, across the desert from Judah, and the area near the Persian Gulf. A frightening message comes to the prophet, one referring to action by Elam and Media, far away to the east of **Babylon**. It's action that will be good news for Judah, the fall of the betrayer and destroyer, the power that will later bring Judah trouble and groaning, smashing and crushing.

Dumah is an oasis in the desert west of Babylon. The message about it pictures its people there hearing with the approach of morning that an immediate threat of attack is over, yet warned that one deliverance of that kind doesn't mean the end of the story. Dedan and Temah are also desert oases, south of Dumah. In the vision there has been a battle and the inhabitants of these oases are bidden to show compassion to people who have escaped with their lives. These fugitives are the remains of the people of Qedar, who live in that desert area. These three prophecies have little directly to do with Judah; they remind Judah that Yahweh is Lord of their histories too and that his activity lies behind the events in their history.

ISAIAH 22:1–25

Meanwhile, Back in Jerusalem

1 A prophecy about Vision Valley.

   What are you doing here, then,
      that you have gone up, all of you, onto the roofs,
2 you, full of noise, tumultuous city,
      exultant town?
   Your slain were not slain by the sword,
      they were not dead in battle.
3 All your leaders fled together,
      without the bow they were captured.
   All those of you who were found were captured together,
      they ran far away.
4 Therefore I have said, "Look away from me,
      I will express bitterness in weeping.
   Don't try to comfort me
      over the destruction of the daughter of my people."
5 Because the Lord Yahweh Armies had a day of tumult,
      trampling, and confusion,
   in Vision Valley someone tearing down the wall,
      and a cry for help to the mountain.
6 Elam carried the quiver,
      with chariotry of men, horsemen;
      and Qir bared the shield.
7 Your choicest vales became
      full of chariotry and horsemen.
   They took their stand at the gate
8   and it exposed Judah's covering.

You had looked on that day
    to the armory in the Forest House.
9   The breaches in David's city—
    you had considered them, that there were many.
You had collected the water of the Lower Pool
10   and counted the houses in Jerusalem.
You had torn down the houses to strengthen the wall
11   and made a basin between the two walls
    for the water from the old pool.
But you did not look to the one who made it,
    you did not consider the one who formed it long before.

12   The Lord Yahweh Armies
        summoned on that day,
    to weeping and lamenting,
        shaving the head and putting on sackcloth.
13   But there—rejoicing and celebration,
        slaughtering of cattle and killing of sheep,
    eating of meat and drinking of wine:
        "Eat and drink, because tomorrow we will die!"
14   Yahweh Armies revealed himself in my ears:
        "If this waywardness of yours is expiated before you die . . ."
    the Lord Yahweh Armies has said.

15 The Lord Yahweh Armies said this: "Come, go to this administrator, to Shebna, who is over the house. 16 'What are you doing here, and whom do you have here, that you have hewn a tomb for yourself here, one who has hewn his tomb on high, who has chiseled a dwelling for himself in the crag? 17 There: Yahweh is going to hurl you far, warrior, he is going to grasp you firmly. 18 He is going to roll you up tightly, rolling you up like a ball, to a country broad on both sides. There you will die; there will be your splendid chariots, a humiliation to your master's house. 19 I will thrust you out from your position; you will be ousted from your office. 20 On that day I will summon my servant Eliaqim son of Hilqiah. 21 I will put your uniform on him and fasten him with your belt, and put your authority in his hand. He will be a father to the inhabitants of Jerusalem and the household of Judah. 22 I will put the key of David's household on his shoulder; he will open and no one will shut, he will shut and no one will open. 23 I will fix him as a peg in a reliable

place; he will be an honorable throne for his father's household.
[24] All the honor of his father's household will hang on him, off-spring and shoots, all the little things, from the bowls to all the jars." [25] On that day (a declaration of Yahweh Armies) the peg fixed in a reliable place will depart. It will be hacked off and it will fall, and the load that is on it will be cut down (because Yahweh has spoken).

I have just come off the phone from a conversation with a former student in England who was in tears about failing a degree program. She doesn't claim that her exam performance was brilliant; she sees herself as a poor examinee. But she doesn't think her work deserved to fail. The failure comes at the end of two or three years in which she has always thought that her mentor, the examiner, treated her in a mean way. On her account, he has been known to read her work and then incorporate her ideas in his own work without attributing them. She thinks part of the problem may be that he is prejudiced against her for her Christian faith. She is more sure that he is prejudiced against her because she is a woman; there are other women who have received similar treatment from him. I have only her side of the story, but I do know that such things happen and that power corrupts.

Such corruption has overcome Shebna, who is something like the White House chief of staff. Isaiah 36–37 will tell us more of him (if it's the same Shebna) and of the responsibility he had; this chapter's preoccupation is what he has done with his power. It involves not his relationships with people but his using his position to glorify himself. Having a splendid tomb will perpetuate his memory, but even now it will draw attention to his importance." "That Shebna must be very important, look at the tomb that awaits him!" God takes extraordinarily seriously his pretensions to high honor. Perhaps the warning about dying in exile is a metaphor and the warning about losing his position is the more literal picture of what will happen.

The earlier part of the chapter (like the previous chapter) starts in a way that will have puzzled its hearers and made them think. As they wondered what "Vision Valley" was, the immediately following lines might not help them. The prophecy addresses people who are celebrating something; they are having parties on the flat roofs of their houses. They have had a narrow escape, something like the relief of a siege. But should they really be partying when many of their leaders have been killed—not heroically in battle but having turned tail and run? In light of the suffering of the city, tenderly described as "the daughter of my people," lamenting would be more appropriate than partying.

It's actually the **Day of the Lord** that has come upon this people in Vision Valley. It has involved the breaching of the city's walls and a cry to the sanctuary at the city's height. Eventually the prophecy makes explicit that it's referring to Judah and to David's city. Vision Valley is a term for the slope outside the city. The mountain toward which the cry goes up is Mount **Zion** where the temple sits. Troops from Elam and Qir will have been an element in the **Assyrian** army that attacked Jerusalem in 701, when the city almost fell; Isaiah 36–37 again gives a fuller account. As the crisis approached, the city had looked hard at its defenses (the Forest House in Jerusalem had cedar columns, making it look a little like a forest), at its water supply. But people hadn't turned to **Yahweh**, who lay behind the Assyrian invasion. They had missed the point.

Jerusalem's miraculous escape was now a moment when Yahweh gave the city another chance to turn to weeping and lamenting. Instead they're giving themselves to those parties. The proverbial saying "Eat and drink, because tomorrow we will die" occurs in many cultures. Here it's not the people's words but Isaiah's typically ironic comment. "Go on, enjoy yourselves, because your refusal to learn from the way Yahweh acts toward you means your troubles are by no means over." His explicit word from Yahweh underscores the point. There's no way their waywardness can be expiated if they won't turn to Yahweh. As usual, the critique, the irony, and the warning are all designed to drive the people into changing, but by the time the book comes together the warning has been fulfilled and they function to urge future generations to learn the lesson from these events.

The prophet's ministry to **Judah** reflects the fact that they're special in Yahweh's sight. The location of this chapter about Jerusalem among the chapters about all the other nations reflects the fact that they behave no better than other people, and experience Yahweh relating to them in the same way as other people. As the other nations hear Yahweh's invitations and promises in these chapters, so Judah hears Yahweh's critique and warning. Sometimes the people of God behave more like the world than the world does.

ISAIAH 23:1–18

What to Do with a Whore's Fee

1   A prophecy about Tyre.
Howl, Tarshish ships,
because it has been destroyed from [there being] a
house.
After they came from the country of Cyprus,
it was revealed to them.
2   Be still, inhabitants of the coast,
merchants of Sidon.
Seafarers filled you,
3   by many waters the seed of Shihor.
The harvest of the Nile was its revenue,
and it became the marketplace of the nations.
4   Be shamed, Sidon, because the sea has said,
"The stronghold of the sea!"
"I have not labored, I have not given birth,
I have not brought up young men or raised girls."
5   When the news [came] to Egypt, they were in anguish,
when the news [came] about Tyre.
6   Pass over to Tarshish;
howl, you inhabitants of the coast.
7   Is this your exultant one,
whose antiquity is from ancient days,
whose feet carried it
to a nation far away?
8   Who planned this for Tyre,
the bestower of crowns,
whose merchants were leaders,
its traders the most honored in the earth?
9   Yahweh Armies planned it,
to defile all its splendid majesty,

83

to humiliate all the most honored in the earth.
¹⁰ Pass through your country like the Nile,
    Ms. Tarshish; there is a harbor no more.
¹¹ Someone stretched out his arm over the sea,
    shook kingdoms.
It was Yahweh gave a command regarding Canaan,
    to destroy its fortresses.
¹² He said, "You will no more exult,
    oppressed maiden, Ms. Sidon.
Get up, cross over to Cyprus;
    even there will be no rest for you."
¹³ There, the country of the Kaldeans—
    this is the people that exists no longer.
Assyria founded it for ships;
    they set up its watchtowers.
They stripped its fortresses,
    they made it into a ruin.

¹⁴ Howl, ships of Tarshish,
    because your stronghold has been destroyed.
¹⁵ On that day, Tyre will be forgotten for seventy years,
    like the days of one king.
At the end of seventy years
    it will be for Tyre like the song about the whore:
¹⁶ "Take the guitar, go about the city,
    forgotten whore.
Be nice, play, sing many a song,
    so that you may be remembered."
¹⁷ Because at the end of seventy years
    Yahweh will attend to Tyre.
It will return to its charge and its whoring
    with all the world's kingdoms on the earth's surface.
¹⁸ But its profit and its charge will be holy to Yahweh;
    it won't be treasured, it won't be stored,
because its profit will be
    for the people who live before Yahweh,
    for eating until they are full and for fine clothes.

Education and health have been realms where Christians get involved both to benefit people in other cultures and to draw people to Christ. I recently heard about an Indian with the same vision for his software company. He runs a commercial enterprise but runs it as a kingdom business. A big business has to focus on maximizing shareholder wealth; any business needs to be making a profit in order to function. In this man's business, the main purpose is "to provide human, technological, and financial resources to grow God's kingdom in India and worldwide." He recognizes the built-in conflict between kingdom interests and business interests in our imperfect world. It's hard for a business to survive without serving unethical market demands. He implies that he just has to live with that fact.

Isaiah's prophecy about Tyre recognizes that conflict by comparing Tyre's trading business with the sex trade. Who would have thought God would declare that a prostitute's fees would go to the maintenance of the temple, even as a metaphor? Yet God does so. In a strange way God honors, while also judging, the trading activity of Tyre.

Tyre, south of modern Beirut, was one of the premier trading cities of the Middle Eastern and Mediterranean world, superbly located on the eastern Mediterranean coast, north of Egypt, west of **Assyria**, south of Turkey and east of **Greece**, Rome, and Spain. It had a magnificent natural harbor from which ships could thus ply in three directions, and it was engaged in bringing grain from Egypt from the Nile Delta; Shihor is one of the branches of the Nile. It's "the stronghold of the sea."

The trouble is that any sort of greatness makes a people rival God in its own eyes or in other people's. Thus Tyre is bound to be put down. The theme recurs from Isaiah 2, which also refers to Tarshish ships. Here, that term refers to Tartessus in Spain, with which Tyre had a trading relationship. The vision pictures events from the perspective of the ships from Tarshish, which are appalled to discover as they come from Cyprus (the big island 150 miles from Tyre) that the port they were bound for has been destroyed. The vision imagines the response of other cities on the coast of Lebanon, which Isaiah refers to as Canaan, such as Sidon, a sister city twenty miles north of Tyre. They are evidently affected by the disaster and share the shame. They might as well seek refuge in Cyprus, even in Tarshish itself. Tyre's southern trading partner, Egypt, is likewise appalled.

Even the sea joins in the grief, being so familiar with Tyre and its ships. It's like a woman who has lost her children.

Who brought about this disaster? It is **Yahweh**, the one who makes things happen in the world. Yahweh's power isn't confined to Israel. As usual, the prophecy doesn't assume the disaster it announces is bound to happen; it urges Tyre to note the fate of **Babylon** and learn the lesson. Once again the prophecy's point as a message addressed to Judah may be to warn Judah about either its inclination to have too high an estimate of its own importance or about its inclination to resist Assyrian authority. While Tyre did pay a price for its resistance, it was not destroyed, at least until the time of Alexander the Great, though that event would be irrelevant to people in Isaiah's day. Literal fulfillment was evidently not necessary in order for the message to make its point.

Isaiah's reference to prostitution suggests an evaluation of the city's focus on trade. By implication, economics is designed to be an activity within a community, within something like a family. I have more grain than I need, you have more olives, so we trade some. Nobody is concerned to make a profit. Instead, trade becomes a means of me increasing my resources, having a bigger share to enjoy for myself. Making money by means of trade is like prostitution. Tyre's destruction would therefore mean the whore unable to continue to ply her trade. But for Tyre as for the other nations there is hope, in its case the hope of being free to resume its trade. And for Tyre as for other peoples, its destiny is to acknowledge Yahweh, acknowledge Israel as Yahweh's people, and acknowledge Jerusalem as the place where Yahweh dwells. Its trade will enable it to make substantial subventions of the service of Yahweh for which Israel is especially responsible. It won't simply put its profits into the bank. Even the profits of its unholy trade will become holy.

ISAIAH 24:1–23

The Broken World Covenant

1   There: Yahweh is laying waste to the earth and making it
        desolate,
     twisting its surface and scattering its inhabitants.

2 It will be: as people, so priest;
        as servant, so his master;
   as female servant, so her mistress;
        as buyer, so seller;
   as creditor, so borrower;
        as lender, so the one to whom he lends.
3 The earth will be totally laid waste,
        it will be totally plundered,
        because it is Yahweh who has spoken this word.
4 The earth dries up, withers;
        the world languishes, withers;
        the height languishes with the earth.
5 The earth was profane under its inhabitants,
        because they transgressed the teachings.
   They violated the statute,
        broke the age-old covenant.
6 Therefore a curse has consumed the earth;
        the people who live in it have paid the penalty.
   Therefore earth's inhabitants have burned up;
        few people remain.
7 The wine has failed, the vine has languished,
        all the people who were joyful in heart groan.
8 The rejoicing of tambourines has stopped,
        the noise of the exultant has ceased,
        the rejoicing of the harp has stopped.
9 They do not drink wine with a song,
        liquor tastes bitter to the drinker.
10 The empty town has broken up,
        every house is shut up against entering.
11 There is a cry over wine in the streets,
        all celebration has reached evening,
        earth's rejoicing has gone into exile.
12 Desolation remains in the city;
        the gate is battered, a ruin.
13 Because thus it will be in the midst of the earth,
        among the peoples,
   like the beating of an olive tree,
        like gleanings when the harvest finishes.

14 Those people lift their voice, resound,
        because of Yahweh's majesty they have shouted from the west.

¹⁵ Therefore honor Yahweh in the east,
    in shores across the sea,
    [honor] the name of Yahweh, Israel's God.
¹⁶ From the end of the earth we have heard music,
    "Glory belongs to the Faithful One."
But I said, I waste away,
    I waste away! Oh, me!
Traitors have betrayed,
    traitors have betrayed—betrayal.
¹⁷ Terror and pit and trap
    for you who inhabit the earth!
¹⁸ The one who flees at the sound of terror
    will fall into the pit.
The one who climbs out of the pit
    will be caught in the trap.
Because sluices have opened on high,
    and earth's foundations have shaken.
¹⁹ The earth has quite broken up;
    earth has quite split up;
    earth has quite tottered down.
²⁰ The earth has quite reeled like a drunk,
    swayed about like a lodge.
Its rebellion weighs heavy upon it;
    it will fall, and not rise again.

²¹ On that day Yahweh will attend
    to the army of the height, in the height,
    and to the kings of the earth, on the earth.
²² They will be gathered as a gathering,
    a captive in a pit.
They will be imprisoned in a prison,
    and after many days will receive attention.
²³ The moon will feel shamed,
    the sun will feel disgrace.
Because Yahweh Armies will have begun to reign
    on Mount Zion and in Jerusalem,
    and his splendor [will be] before his elders.

The media have been showing scary pictures of places affected
by the hundred tornadoes that have struck the central plains

in the United States. The one that most horrified me pictured a man standing in the midst of his father's house in Oklahoma. It was simply a mess of broken timber. His mother had miraculously survived, as she had survived the much more devastating tornado that hit her town in 1947, because she had heeded warnings on the radio. The event recalled the severe tornadoes last year when (for instance) the college town of Tuscaloosa in Alabama was "in some places torn to the slab." As rescuers worked away the evening after the tornadoes, "cries could be heard into the night" from people buried in the debris.

Such experiences and images enable us to picture the scene Isaiah 24 portrays. Whereas Isaiah 1–12 focused on events in Judah and Isaiah 13–23 broadened the horizon to speak of the nations around Judah that affected its life, Isaiah 24–27 broadens the horizon still further, making hardly any references to particular peoples. The nightmare picture concerns the earth, the world. Once again the prophet sees a devastating event happening before his eyes. It affects all sorts of people; status or wealth doesn't save you.

Why does **Yahweh** intend to bring this calamity? The prophecy presupposes that the world knows teachings, statutes, the terms of a covenant. These are expressions usually applied to Israel, but the Bible assumes that the world as a whole knows the basic facts about God and about God's expectations of humanity. It doesn't need a special revelation to be told that murder, adultery, and theft are wrong; God made us with that awareness. If we've lost that awareness, it's because we have turned our backs on it. Genesis 9 uses the expression "age-old covenant" or "eternal covenant" to refer to God's covenant with Noah and with all humanity after him, and that reference makes sense here. The Noah covenant involved nothing you could precisely call conditions, but it presupposed some expectations about matters such as shedding blood. Notwithstanding God's covenant commitment, a humanity that behaved as if God and God's expectations didn't exist could hardly expect to get away with this lifestyle forever. In the vision, then, God's curse has consumed the earth again (as in Genesis).

The prophet hears voices that respond with satisfaction to this scene of devastation. The voices are anonymous; the point is the proclamation, not the proclaimers. Yahweh's majesty is honored by the devastation of the world that has ignored his teaching, his statutes, his covenant. But the prophet finds it impossible to join in the rejoicing. The vision was too horrifying for it to generate a sense of satisfaction. Yes, the world is characterized by unfaithfulness between peoples, but that fact doesn't make him able to look forward to the destruction for which it's destined, which he goes on to describe with some further concrete images.

It's not only earth that is the object of God's judgment. In passing, the first paragraph spoke of "the height" languishing, as well as the earth, and the last paragraph takes up that note. It's not only the earth that is the scene of rebellion against God; the heavens are also. The morally appalling nature of life on earth doesn't derive from mere human rebellion but from heavenly rebellion. The Bible never tells us how this rebellion happened; it does assume it to be a reality. It's more interested in how the rebellion will be stopped. Yahweh intends to terminate it. The reference to sun and moon being shamed links with the way people turn these into deities that rule the earth: the reference isn't to the sun and moon as parts of God's creation with a proper role to fulfill but to the sun and moon as objects of inappropriate trust and reverence.

One significance of the chapter as a whole for the people with whom the vision is shared comes in the last line. Even if we hesitate to rejoice in the idea of judgment, like the prophet, we can rejoice in the fact that it will mean Yahweh has begun to reign. The book of Isaiah is realistic about the fact that Yahweh's reign is often not a reality on earth or in the heavens. Jesus will make the same assumption as he declares that the reign of God is now coming. Naturally, Jerusalem is the place where Yahweh will locate his throne over the world, and the elders will be there, as they were at Sinai and as they are in John's vision in Revelation. There is a sense in which God reigns now, but much of what happens in the world does not reflect his will. From time to time he asserts that will.

ISAIAH 25:1–26:6

Grief Brought to an End

25:1 Yahweh, you are my God, I will exalt you,
　　　I will confess your name,
　　because you have done something extraordinary,
　　　plans from a distant time, truthfulness, truth.
2　Because you have made out of a city a heap,
　　　a fortified town into a ruin.
　　The citadel of foreigners is no longer a city;
　　　it won't be built up ever.
3　Therefore a strong people will honor you,
　　　a town of violent nations will revere you.
4　Because you have been a refuge for the poor person,
　　　a refuge for the needy person in his trouble,
　　a shelter from rain,
　　　a shade from heat,
　　when the spirit of the violent was like winter rain,
5　　the din of aliens like heat in the desert.
　　You subdue the heat with a cloud shade;
　　　the music of the violent fades away.
6　And Yahweh Armies will make
　　　for all peoples on this mountain
　　a party with rich foods, a party with aged wines,
　　　juicy rich foods, refined aged wines.
7　He will destroy on this mountain the layer of wrapping,
　　　the wrapping over all the peoples,
　　the covering that is spread out over all the nations;
8　　he will have destroyed death forever.
　　My Lord Yahweh will wipe the tears
　　　from on all faces.
　　The disgrace of his people
　　　he will take away from all the earth;
　　　because Yahweh is the one who has spoken.

9　On that day one will say:
　　There, this is our God,
　　　we waited for him and he delivered us.
　　This is Yahweh, we waited for him;
　　　let's celebrate and rejoice in his deliverance.

^{10} Because Yahweh's hand will rest
  on this mountain.
Moab will be trodden down in its place
  like the treading of straw at Madmenah.
^{11} It will spread out its hands in its midst
  as a swimmer spreads his hands to swim.
[Yahweh] will bring down its majesty
  with the spoils of its hands.
^{12} The towering fortification of its walls
  he will have laid low, brought down,
  knocked down to the earth, right to the dirt.

$^{26:1}$ On that day this song will be sung in the country of Judah:
  We have a strong city;
  he makes walls and rampart into deliverance.
^{2} Open the gates so that the faithful nation may come in,
  one that keeps truthfulness.
^{3} A mind that is sustained, you keep in well-being,
  in well-being because it is filled with trust in you.
^{4} Trust in Yahweh forever, because in Yah—
  Yahweh is a lasting crag.
^{5} Because he has laid low the people who live in the height;
  the towering town he brings down.
He brings it down right to the earth,
  knocks it down right to the dirt.
^{6} The foot treads it down, the feet of the lowly person,
  the soles of the poor.

In a movie called *Grace Is Gone*, Grace is a sergeant in the army on active service. Her husband, Stan, looks after a supply store back home. One morning the feared and terrifying visit comes from army representatives with the task of telling Stan that Grace has been killed in action. Without explaining why he is doing so, he takes his two daughters on a car ride that turns into a spontaneous trip to the eight-year-old's favorite place, a Florida amusement park. On the way, they stop at his mother's house, where his brother is staying. Stan's twelve-year-old is old enough to realize there's something mysterious about the strange journey and her father's uncharacteristic behavior. It's only at the end of the entire trip that Stan can face telling his daughters the news. Doing so of course involves facing it himself.

How we long for the day when God will destroy "the face of wrapping," the shroud that people put over their faces as a sign of mourning, when God has destroyed dying forever and wiped away the tears of people like Stan and his daughters. Israel was only too familiar with invasion and defeat, with the experience of losing people in war. One of the most horrifying of its stories concerns an event a century after Isaiah's day, when the **Babylonians** capture the last king of Jerusalem, Zedekiah, and blind him; but first, they kill his sons before his eyes, so that the sight of their death is the last thing he ever sees. The prophecy knows that other peoples go through the same pain. People in the United States and Europe know at the time I write that Iraqis and Afghanis and members of the Taliban go through the same pain as they do. The prophecy promises that God won't merely destroy the wrapping over Israelite faces but "the wrapping over all the peoples, the covering that is spread out over all the nations." He will wipe the tears from all faces.

Chapters 24–27 continue to maintain the dynamic of chapters 13–23 as they interweave warnings about judgment on the world with promises of restoration for the world, as chapters 13–23 interwove warnings about disaster for individual nations with invitations to those nations to seek **Yahweh**. At the same time, the section begins from the fact that ending grief will issue from God's taking action to put down the oppressors who generate war and cause the grief. It presupposes God's fulfilling the promise to destroy the great imperial capital. It will be this act that shows Yahweh to be a refuge for the needy and a shade from the heat. The middle paragraph also affirms that individual nations choose their destiny. Maybe the reason for singling out Moab for mention is the temptation offered by the place name Madmenah. There are places with a name of this kind in **Judah** and in Moab, but it's also the Hebrew word for a cesspit. It thus gives the prophet the chance to indulge in a wondrously scatological image for Moab's fate. Any people will be wise to substitute its name for Moab and to make sure it qualifies as a people that is looking to Yahweh rather than one that ends up with the fate described here.

The positive aspect to God's promise is the vision of the party to end all parties on Mount **Zion**. That element is one feature suggesting that this vision restates the earlier one of nations flocking to Jerusalem, in Isaiah 2. It also implies the reversing of Israel's humiliation. People who have seen Israel defeated and **exiled** will see Israel honored as the banquet happens on Mount Zion.

It's not surprising that the visions in chapters 24–27 interweave promises with acts of praise; this section begins and ends that way. The third paragraph notes that it's the faithful nation that can come into the strong city that Yahweh makes a safe place for people. That qualification points once more to the way a nation has to make its decision to be a people that turns to Yahweh if it's to avoid Moab's fate. Israel itself has to make sure it's a people of that kind.

Where does one look for the fulfillment of these great promises? We still live in a world characterized by oppression, arrogance, hatred, conflict, death, and mourning. Thus the last chapters of the Bible (Rev. 19–22) take up these words from Isaiah in promising a day when God will finally judge the imperial powers, wipe away tears, and invite people to his banquet. Yet Israel also knew times when it saw some fulfillment of the vision, as God put down **Assyria** or **Babylon**, delivered Jerusalem, and comforted his people, while Revelation assumes that Jesus brings some anticipation of the vision's fulfillment, as well as confirming that its final fulfillment will arrive.

ISAIAH 26:7–27:13

Wishing and Hoping and Thinking and Praying, Planning, and Dreaming (1)

26:7 The path is clear for the faithful person;
  you level a clear track for someone who is faithful.
8 Yes, on the path determined by your decisions,
    Yahweh, we have waited for you.
  The longing of our entire being
    has been for your name and your renown.
9 With my entire being I have longed for you by night;
    yes, my spirit within me seeks urgently for you.
  Because when your decisions are in the earth,
    the inhabitants of the world learn faithfulness.

10 If the faithless person is shown favor,
   he doesn't learn faithfulness.
  In a country characterized by uprightness he does wrong,
   and doesn't regard Yahweh's majesty.
11 Yahweh, they don't see your hand raised;
   they should see and be shamed.
  Your passion for the people,
   yes, your fire for your adversaries should consume them.
12 Yahweh, may you institute well-being for us,
   because you accomplished for us all the things we have
    done.
13 Yahweh our God, lords apart from you have controlled us,
   but of you alone we will make mention—of your name.
14 Dead people don't live,
   ghosts don't rise.
  Therefore you attended to them and destroyed them
   and put an end to any mention of them.
15 You added to the nation, Yahweh;
   when you added to the nation you were honored,
   you extended all the country's borders.
16 Yahweh, during trouble they attended to you,
   a whispered prayer during your correction of them.

17 Like a pregnant woman who draws near to giving birth,
   who writhes, cries out in her pain,
  so have we become because of you, Yahweh.
18 We were pregnant, we writhed,
   it is as if we gave birth to wind.
  We don't achieve deliverance in the earth;
   the inhabitants of the world don't fall.

19 Your dead will live, my corpse will rise;
   wake up and resound, you who dwell in the dirt!
  Because your dew is the dew of the lights,
   and you make the country of ghosts fall.
20 Go, my people, enter your rooms,
   and lock your door after you.
  Hide for a little moment,
   until wrath passes.
21 Because there—
   Yahweh is going to come out from his place

95

to attend to the waywardness of the earth's inhabitants
    upon them.
The earth will uncover its shed blood
    and will no more cover its slain.
27:1 On that day Yahweh will attend with his sword,
    hard and great and strong,
upon Leviathan the fleeing serpent,
    upon Leviathan the twisting serpent,
    and will slay the dragon that is in the sea.

2   On that day,
        a delightful vineyard, sing of it!
3   I Yahweh am going to watch over it;
        every moment I will water it.
    Lest someone attend to it,
        night and day I will watch over it.
4   I have no fury;
        if anyone produces for me briar and thorn,
    in battle I will march against it
        and set fire to them altogether.
5   Or he can take hold of my refuge,
        he can make peace with me,
        peace he can make with me.
6   Coming days:
        Jacob will root, Israel will bud and blossom,
        and the world's surface will be full of produce.

7   Did he hit it like the hitting of the one who hit it,
        was it slain like the slaying of the ones slain by him?
8   By driving away, by sending off, you contend with it;
        he removed it by a hard blast on a day of east wind.
9   Therefore by this Jacob's waywardness will be expiated;
        this is the entire fruit of the removing of its offense.
    Through his making all the altar stones
        like shattered blocks of limestone,
        sacred columns and incense altars won't stand.
10   Because the fortified city is desolate,
        the habitation rejected and abandoned like the
            wilderness.
    There a calf grazes,
        there it lies down and consumes its boughs.

¹¹ When its branches wither, they break;
>>women come, set light to them.
>Because it is not a people of understanding;
>>therefore its maker will not have compassion on it,
>>its former will not be gracious to it.

¹² On that day
>>Yahweh will thresh from the Euphrates channel
>>to the Wash of Egypt,
>and you will be gleaned
>>one by one, Israelites.
¹³ On that day
>>there will be a sound on a great horn.
>The people who are perishing
>>will come from the country of Assyria,
>>and the ones who are scattered in the country of Egypt.
>They will bow down to Yahweh
>>on the holy mountain, in Jerusalem.

On Thursday I took part in interviewing a prospective new faculty member and on Friday my wife and I took part in a student retreat, and I now see a feature these events had in common. The interviewee referred to forwarding God's kingdom, and it reminded me that the Bible never talks about our having that responsibility. One reason we take it on is that we can't see God doing so. The theme of the retreat was maintaining connection with God, and one presupposition is that it's our responsibility to do so. One reason people think they have to do so is that God doesn't seem to. God has withdrawn.

That awareness underlies this section. Maybe it's appropriate that as a whole it's jumbled and unclear. Its starting point is clear enough, making the kind of statement of faith that Israel was committed to. The prayer that follows expresses the awareness that life isn't working out the way the statement of faith says. Thus the prayer is like a psalm. Like much of Isaiah 24–27, it presupposes a time in Israel's life in or after the **exile** where people have been waiting for God to act but can't see God's activity either in restoring them or in putting down the superpower. They have sat waiting for **Yahweh** to make the kind of **decisions** that are needed in the world and to implement them, but God isn't doing so. Previous sections have described the nations as due to be objects of Yahweh's grace, in that they will have opportunity to recognize Yahweh, but at the moment Yahweh is letting them carry on in their faithlessness and disregard for Yahweh. What good is that kind of mercy?

The converse need is that Yahweh should do something about instituting Israel's **well-being**, about which the chapter's opening made a statement of confidence. They can look back on their story as a people and see Yahweh's past activity, when Yahweh delivered them from overlords who ruled over them (who are now dead and won't come back to life) and extended Israel's own territory. When trouble came, they looked to Yahweh, and Yahweh responded. Yet Yahweh is no longer operating that way, and they cannot bring about their deliverance.

The third paragraph constitutes Yahweh's and the prophet's response. Sometimes the prophet speaks for Yahweh (so Yahweh speaks directly as "I"), sometimes the prophet reports what Yahweh has to say (referring to Yahweh as "he"). Whereas those other overlords are dead and gone, Yahweh intends to bring Israel back to life as a people, and they can start believing and behaving as a people Yahweh is bringing back to life. The picture of a people brought back to life from the death of exile parallels Ezekiel's vision of the valley full of bones. Way back, Isaiah 5 sang a frightening song about God's vineyard; Isaiah 27 has a more encouraging one. No one is going to spoil or attack the vineyard now; its potential spoilers will have a chance to make Yahweh their refuge instead. Yahweh now feels no wrath toward it. While Israel has been devastated by Yahweh and taken off into exile, it has not been annihilated, as its overlords have been or will have been. By its chastisement, its faithlessness has been dealt with. Its false forms of worship have been destroyed. Its scattered people will be brought home.

Associated with its renewal and gathering is the postponed judgment on Israel's present overlords, the occupants of the fortified city (unnamed, so it can apply to the capital of any oppressor) and on the supernatural power of evil (in a context such as this, Leviathan is an Old Testament equivalent of Satan). So like the Israelites in Egypt when Yahweh acts against the Egyptian firstborn, they need to take shelter until the moment of wrath is passed, lest they get affected by the fallout.

The people's prayer assumes that you can have absolute boldness in telling God what is wrong with a situation and what he should do about it (at worst, God will answer back and explain why he isn't doing as you suggest). It also assumes that Israel is in no position to do what needs doing; it's just a little people under the control of a big power. Unlike us, it cannot kid itself about its capacity to further God's kingdom. All it can do is cast itself on God. But helplessness is a wonderful aid to prayer and may even drive God to respond to prayer. As with the promises in the previous section, one can see moments in Israel's experience when God did what the answer promises, moments such as the deliverance from the **Babylonians** and the much later deliverance from the **Seleucids**. Thus the section encourages subsequent readers to pray the way it does.

ISAIAH 28:1–29

God's Strange Work

1 Hey, the majestic crown of Ephraim's drunks,
    whose glorious beauty is a fading flower,
  which is on the head of a fertile valley—
    people struck down by wine.
2 There, my Lord has someone strong and powerful,
    like a hail storm, a destructive hurricane.
  Like a storm of water, forceful, rushing,
    he has brought it down to the earth with power.
3 The majestic crown of Ephraim's drunks
    will be trampled underfoot.
4 The fading flower, the glorious beauty,
    which is on the head of a fertile valley,
  will be like a fig before harvest,
    which someone sees,
  and the one who sees it—
    while it's still in his palm, he eats it.
5 On that day
    Yahweh Armies will become

99

a beautiful crown and a glorious diadem
    for the remains of his people,
6 an authoritative spirit
    for the one who presides over the exercise of authority,
    and the strength of the people who turn back the battle
      at the gate.

7 But these also wander because of wine,
    stagger because of liquor:
priest and prophet wander because of liquor,
    they're confused because of wine,
    they stagger because of liquor.
They wander about in seeing,
    they go astray in giving judgment.
8 Because all the tables are full of vomit, filth—
    there is no place.
9 "To whom does he teach knowledge,
    to whom does he explain a message?
People weaned from milk,
    moving on from the breast?
10 Because command upon command,
    command upon command,
rule upon rule, rule upon rule,
    a little here, a little there.
11 Because with mockings of lip and with an alien tongue
    does he speak to this people,
12 the one who said to them,
    'This is the resting place, rest,
    for the weary person, yes this is the place of repose.'"
They were not willing to listen,
13   and to them Yahweh's word
will be command upon command,
    command upon command,
rule upon rule, rule upon rule,
    a little here, a little there,
so that they may go, but fall back,
    and be broken and snared and captured.

14 Therefore listen to Yahweh's word,
    you scorners,

who rule this people,
    which is in Jerusalem.
15 Because you have said,
    "We have sealed a covenant with death,
    with Sheol we have made a pact.
The sweeping flood, when it passes,
    won't come to us,
because we have made a lie our refuge,
    we have hidden in falsehood."
16 Therefore my Lord Yahweh has said this:
    "Here am I founding in Zion a stone,
    a testing stone, a valuable corner stone,
a well-founded foundation;
    the one who stands firm in faith will not be hasty.
17 I will make authority the measuring line,
    faithfulness the weight.
Hail will sweep away the lying refuge;
    water will flood the hiding place.
18 Your covenant with death will be covered over,
    your pact with Sheol won't stand.
The sweeping flood, when it passes—
    you will be for trampling it.
19 The times when it passes, it will get you,
    because it will pass morning by morning,
    by day and by night."
It will be simply a horror,
    understanding the message.
20 Because the bed will be too short for stretching out,
    the blanket too narrow for gathering around oneself.
21 Because Yahweh will arise as on Mount Perizim,
    he will be astir as in the Vale of Gibeon,
to do his work—strange is his work,
    to perform his service—foreign is his service.
22 So now, don't be scornful,
    or your chains will strengthen.
Because I have heard of a finish, a thing determined,
    by the Lord Yahweh Armies,
    against the entire country.

23 Give ear, listen to my voice,
    attend, listen to what I say.

101

²⁴ Is it every day that the plowman plows to sow,
    breaks up and harrows his ground?
²⁵ When he has leveled its surface,
    does he not scatter caraway and sprinkle cumin,
  set wheat (millet), barley in its place,
    and spelt in its border?
²⁶ He disciplines it with judgment;
    his God teaches him.
²⁷ Because caraway isn't threshed with a sled,
    and the wheel of a cart isn't rolled over cumin.
  Because caraway is beaten with a rod,
    and cumin with a club.
²⁸ Cereal is crushed,
    yet the thresher doesn't thresh forever.
  The wheel of his cart may rumble,
    but he doesn't crush it with his horses.
²⁹ This too comes from Yahweh Armies;
    he formulates extraordinary plans,
    he shows great skill.

The other Sunday we were singing the hymn "Great Is Thy Faithfulness," and I was reflecting wryly that it's a shame nobody realizes where its basic ideas come from, as is the case with the related chorus "The steadfast love of the Lord never ceases." They come from Lamentations, which follows the book of Jeremiah, and the context adds depth to that declaration of faith, because Lamentations is a series of poems expressing people's feelings and prayers after Jerusalem was destroyed, as Isaiah warns that it will be if people are not careful. It's quite something that the declaration comes in that context. But the same prayer poem also declares the related conviction that God doesn't act in a destructive way willingly—it doesn't come from God's heart.

Isaiah makes the same point when he describes the coming destruction of the city as something that is God's "strange" work. It's "foreign" to **Yahweh** to act in this way. Sometimes people can get the impression that Yahweh is basically a God of wrath who likes acting in judgment, or at least that love and wrath are equally balanced within Yahweh. Like other parts of the Old Testament, Isaiah knows that on the contrary, Yahweh's basic inclination is to be gracious and merciful. Yahweh is capable of making himself act in judgment, but it's his "strange" work; it's a bit alien to him. Maybe it links with that fact that Isaiah strangely describes Yahweh's action as a piece of service, like the work of a servant. Who is the master if Yahweh is the servant? I guess Yahweh is serving himself and serving what is right, but it's not the kind of action a person would freely choose.

But **Judah** needs to recognize that Yahweh is prepared to make himself do it. After the widening of the horizon in chapters 24–27 to consider the destiny of the world as a whole, chapters 28–33 focus down on Judah again. Their drift thus returns to that of chapters 1–12, but some of their allusions show that the situation has moved on and the setting is now the reign of Ahaz's son Hezekiah. Yet initially this focus isn't explicit because he begins by talking about the **Ephraimites** and about the judgment coming on them at the hand of **Assyria**, with them too busy drinking to think about it. He speaks in disrespectful and flippant fashion, and one can imagine some of the Judahites sniggering and others appalled at what is going to happen. For the latter the closing words of the first paragraph offer the consoling reassurance that even for Ephraim devastation won't be the last word. The **remnant** of Ephraim that survives will come to recognize where their real splendor lies and will have the leadership and strength that they currently lack.

But the talk about Ephraim is mostly lead-in to a declaration to Judah: "but you lot are no better!" As usual there were other prophets than Isaiah as well as priests who were giving Judah a very different message and were dismissive of the naïve simplicity of Isaiah's message just to do what Yahweh said and trust him to make everything work out.

In the third paragraph he points out the implication of their attitude. He of course doesn't mean they think they have made an agreement with death whereby death is going to let them off (as we might think with our means for prolonging life; it's said that Californians like to feel that death is voluntary). They think they have made some politically wise plans that will protect them from being overwhelmed by the Assyrians. But they're deceiving themselves. That simple message that they dismiss, the message about standing firm in faith which is unchanged since he gave it to Hezekiah's father, is the key to security. Alongside that is the expectation that **authority** will be exercised with **faithfulness** in the city. Trust in Yahweh and the faithful exercise of authority are the key to survival and flourishing. The Judahite leadership is interested in neither. But it will find that actually its attitude will lead to Judah being overwhelmed. Its policy will offer it scant protection, like a bed that is too short or a blanket that is too skimpy. Yahweh will act as he did in David's day (see 2 Samuel 5). But the strange thing will be that he will now be acting against Jerusalem, not for it. So the people had better listen to his simple advice if they want to avoid his warning coming true.

But the book of Isaiah doesn't like to end a chapter on a totally bleak note, and the parable about the farmer offers a modest hint that a determination to finish Judah off cannot be the end of the story. A farmer knows that there's a time for sowing and a time for planting, that threshing doesn't go on forever, that crushing is subject to limitations. He knows, because God teaches him. So God is wise enough to apply the same principles to the way he goes about "farming" and making plans for the achievement of his purpose in the world by means of his people.

ISAIAH 29:1–24

Worship That Issues from Human Instinct

1 Hey, God's Hearth, God's Hearth,
     town where David camped!
  Add year to year;
     the festivals may come around.
2 But I will oppress God's Hearth,
     and there will be sorrow and sighing.
  It will be to me God's real hearth;
3   I will camp against you with a real encircling.
  I will lay siege against you with a rampart,
     set up siege works against you.
4 When you're lower than the ground you will speak,
     your words will be lower than the dirt.

104

Your voice will be like a ghost from the earth,
    your words will chirp from the dirt.
5 But like fine dust will be the multitude of your adversaries,
    like passing chaff the multitude of the violent.
In an instant, suddenly,
6   by Yahweh Armies you will be attended,
with thunder, shaking, and a loud voice,
    storm and hurricane and a flame of consuming fire.
7 It will be like a dream, a vision in the night—
    the multitude of all the nations,
which are making war against God's Hearth,
    and all its besiegers and its stronghold and its oppressors.
8 Like someone hungry who dreams
    and there—he is eating,
    but he wakes up and his mouth is empty,
or like someone thirsty who dreams
    and there—he is drinking,
but he wakes up and there—
    he is faint and his throat is craving.
So will the multitude of nations be
    that are making war against Mount Zion.

9 Wait about and be stupefied,
    blind yourselves and be blind!
They are drunk but not from wine,
    they totter but not from liquor.
10 Because Yahweh has poured over you
    a spirit of coma.
He has closed your eyes, the prophets,
    and covered your heads, the seers.
11 The vision of everything has become for you
    like the words of a sealed scroll,
which they give to someone who knows how to read,
    saying "Read this out, will you,"
but he says, "I can't,
    because it's sealed."
12 So the scroll is given to someone who doesn't know how to
    read,
    saying "Read this out, will you,"
    but he says, "I don't know how to read."

¹³ My Lord has said,
  "Because this people has drawn near with its mouth,
    and with its lips has honored me,
  but has kept its mind far from me,
    and their awe for me has been a learned human
      command:
¹⁴ therefore here I am,
    once more doing something extraordinary with this
      people,
    acting in an extraordinary way, something extraordinary.
  The wisdom of its wise will perish,
    the understanding of its people of understanding will
      disappear."
¹⁵ Hey, you who go deeper than Yahweh
    to hide a plan,
  whose act is in the dark and who say,
    "Who sees us, who knows about us?"
¹⁶ Your overturning [of things]!—should the potter be reck-
      oned as like the clay,
    or should the thing made say of its maker,
    "He didn't make me"?
  Or should the pot say of its potter,
    "He didn't understand"?

¹⁷ In yet a little while, won't Lebanon turn into farmland,
    and the farmland be reckoned as forest?
¹⁸ On that day,
    deaf people will listen to the words of a scroll,
  and out of murk and darkness
    the eyes of blind people will see.
¹⁹ The lowly will regain joy in Yahweh,
    and the neediest of people will rejoice in Israel's holy one.
²⁰ Because the violent will not exist,
    the arrogant person will be finished,
    and all the people who are keen about wickedness will be
      cut off,
²¹ the people who turn someone into an offender by means of
      the statement they make,
    who trap the judge at the gate,
    and who turn aside the faithful person by means of
      empty words.

> [22] Therefore, Yahweh has said this to Jacob's household,
>> the one who redeemed Abraham:
> "Jacob won't now be shamed;
>> his face won't now be pale.
> [23] Because when he (his descendants) sees the work of my
>> hands in his midst,
>> he will sanctify my name."
> People will sanctify Jacob's holy one
>> and stand in awe of Israel's God.
> [24] The people who wander in spirit will acknowledge
>> understanding,
>> and the people who complain will accept learning.

The most disappointing and frustrating church service I have attended in California took place one Mother's Day, when I played hooky from our church because I wanted to avoid a service preoccupied by the topic of mothers and went to another church where it was even more preoccupied by mothers. It seemed to have nothing much to do with worship of God and listening to God. It just reflected our culture. I had the same thought this morning as I took part in worship in seminary chapel. In its own way it also reflected our culture and the life and practice of the church in our time. Then I thought again about the regular worship of my own Episcopal congregation, dominated by set prayers (and I love it that way), which thus contrasts with anything clearly present in Scripture. It's tradition.

The third paragraph in this section suggests that Isaiah sees something similar in **Judah**. His people have drawn near to **Yahweh** with their mouth, have honored Yahweh with their lips, but have kept their mind far away from Yahweh. Their awe for God (their worship of God, some translations say, quite appropriately) is something they have learned from human teaching, human tradition, human culture. But it looks as if the problem Isaiah sees isn't merely that their worship followed humanly devised forms. It's that their minds are miles away from Yahweh. Many translations speak of their heart being far away from Yahweh, but to us that suggests a problem about their feelings. When the Bible speaks of the heart it's usually speaking about what we would call the mind—about our thinking, our attitudes, our way of making decisions (to refer to emotions, the Bible more often uses words referring to the guts or the soul). From his first chapter, Isaiah has been concerned about the way Israel could be enthusiastic in its worship, but there's a disjunction between this enthusiasm and the life it lives outside the temple. When Britain was engaged in the slave trade, the slavers were in church on Sunday. During the big financial scandals in the United States early in the present century, the swindlers were in church on Sunday.

The slavers and swindlers in church were clever people, and the people in the temple for the great festivals were clever too. Yet in another sense they're totally stupid—or as Isaiah puts it in the second paragraph, they're like people who are blind or drunk. They have no clue what is happening. Tell them where their policies will lead, and they have no idea what you're talking about. They think they can hide their plans—once more Isaiah speaks not in terms of what they would admit but of the implications of their attitude. They behave as if they're the potter instead of the clay that the potter shapes. Their incomprehension is actually God's will. It's an aspect of God's judgment on them. They decline to understand, so God makes it impossible for them to understand. Of course, telling them so reflects the assumption that it might still be possible to shake them to their senses. It's never over until it's over.

The problem God has in relating to them is that there's a compelling case for casting them off because of their wrongdoing but also a compelling case for staying with them because of the commitment he has already made. God has various ways of squaring this circle. The one Isaiah speaks of in the first paragraph involves making use of the instinct of Israel's enemies to attack Jerusalem and letting them very nearly take it, then turning around at the last minute and crushing the attackers instead. In addressing Jerusalem, God gives it a new name, "Altar Hearth." In ordinary usage the term refers to the hearth around the temple altar where animals were burned in sacrifice. Jerusalem as a whole had a position of this kind around the temple. Isaiah's point is that fire is now going to consume the altar and the hearth itself. It's a metaphor for destruction by enemies. But miraculously, the destruction will be called off at the last minute. Judah will be delivered and its attackers unbelievably disappointed. Isaiah 36–37 relates how this came about.

Like other sections in this part of Isaiah, the chapter cannot end before giving people something more encouraging to think about. The cedar forests of Lebanon will become farmland; the farmland of Carmel will become forest—in the context, the term suggests a forest of fruit trees. The leaders who are morally deaf and blind at the moment will see and hear and ordinary people will have reason to rejoice in Yahweh, because the factors that cause oppression for them will be resolved. The community's relationship to God will be sorted out—which means not so much feelings (our preoccupation) as living the right way.

ISAIAH 30:1–17

God Is Our Refuge and Strength, Really?

¹ Hey, rebellious sons (Yahweh's declaration),
      in making a plan but not from me,
   in pouring a drink offering but not from my spirit,
      so as to heap offence on offence:
² you who set off to go down to Egypt,
      but have not asked what I say,
   in protecting yourselves by Pharaoh's protection
      and in relying on Egypt's shade.
³ Pharaoh's protection will become shame for you,
      and reliance on Egypt's shade disgrace.
⁴ Because his officials have been at So‘an,
      his aides reach Hanes:
⁵ everyone will have come to shame
      because of a people that is no use to them,
   no help and no use,
      but shame and yes, disgrace.

⁶ The prophecy about the beasts of the Negev.

   In a country of trouble and distress,
      lion and cougar, viper and flying serpent,

they carry their wealth on the back of donkeys,
    their treasures on the hump of camels,
to a people that is no use,
7   Egypt whose help is a breath, empty.
Therefore I call this
    "They-are-Rahab-sitting."
8 Now, go, write it on a tablet with them,
    inscribe it on a scroll,
so that it may be for future days,
    a witness forever.
9 Because it is a rebellious people,
    deceitful children,
children who didn't wish to listen
    to Yahweh's teaching,
10 people who have said to seers,
    "Don't see"
and to visionaries,
    "Don't give us visions of uprightness.
Speak nice things to us,
    give us visions that are deceptions.
11 Get out of the way, turn from the path,
    terminate Israel's holy one from before us."
12 Therefore Israel's holy one has said this:
"Because you have rejected this word,
    and trusted in oppression and crookedness,
    and relied on it,
13 therefore this waywardness will be for you
    like a breach falling,
swelling out in a high wall,
    whose breaking comes suddenly, in an instant.
14 Its breaking is like the breaking of a potters' jug,
    smashed—he doesn't spare [it].
Through its smashing there cannot be found a fragment
    for picking up fire from a hearth
    or for skimming water from a pool."

15 Because my Lord Yahweh, Israel's holy one, has said this.
"By turning and resting you will find deliverance;
    in quiet and trust will be your strength,"
    but you were unwilling.

¹⁶ You said, "No, we will flee on a horse"—
    therefore you will flee.
  "We will ride on a swift one"—
    therefore your pursuers will be swift.
¹⁷ One thousand before the blast of one,
    before the blast of five you will flee,
  until you're left like a beacon on the top of a mountain,
    like a banner on a hill.

I have just read a message from an Indian Christian couple who expect tomorrow to go to another village for a day of teaching for which they expect Christians to gather from many villages in the area. They're thirsty to hear the Word of God. My friends love to go to teach there, but it's an area with much tension where there have been killings and abductions by Maoists. The number reached a peak last year, but the number of incidents in the first third of this year suggests it may top last year's figure. So they wrote asking for us to pray for them in light of Paul's words in 2 Corinthians, where he expresses the conviction that God would deliver him and his associates as God had done in the past "because you're helping by praying for us."

Isaiah would approve of their message. In speaking of protection and shade and reliance, he uses the kind of terms that Psalm 91 uses in speaking of God looking after people. The scandal of what he sees in Judah is that people are applying these words to the king of Egypt. They have turned back on the very basics of their relationship with God. It would be bad if they looked to anyone for refuge, but there's an extra level of irony in their looking to Egypt—have they forgotten their own story?

The reference to Egypt makes more explicit that the context of these chapters is Hezekiah's reign rather than that of Ahaz. In Ahaz's day the threat was **Ephraim** and Syria, the potential protection **Assyria**. By Hezekiah's day, the Assyrians have dealt with Ephraim and Syria as Isaiah said would happen, and Assyria has become the threat to **Judah** as he also said. So Judah assumes it had better make some plans to protect itself. It's surely the responsible thing to do. The drink offering will be part of the religious ceremony involved in making a covenant with Egypt. But Isaiah has referred many times to **Yahweh's** being the great planner in Judah's world. Making plans without consulting Yahweh is surely stupid, offensive, and irresponsible.

So'an and Hanes are Egyptian cities to which Judahite envoys have journeyed in this connection; the second paragraph begins with an imaginative description of their journey through the desert with the sweeteners they need. Isaiah has a nice way of ridiculing them. Rahab isn't the Rahab in Joshua (whose name is spelled differently in Hebrew) but another term for the dynamic embodiment of wild power that Isaiah earlier referred to as Leviathan. It's a poetic term for Egypt in Psalm 87. Judah hopes that Egypt will assert some feral and fierce power on Judah's behalf; Isaiah declares that Judah is in for disappointment. Rahab is just going to sit there sleepy and unroused.

Indeed, the situation is going to get catastrophically worse rather than better. Isaiah offers two frightening images. It will be like the collapse of a high wall. Or it will be like someone smashing a pot because they're annoyed, smashing it so violently that there's nothing left. People want to be told things they will like. Paradoxically, they don't want to be told to do nothing. They want to be in control of their destiny. But the only security lies in surrendering such control to Yahweh—or rather in recognizing that the control lies with Yahweh, so they might as well face facts.

ISAIAH 30:18-33

Wishing and Hoping and Thinking and Praying, Planning, and Dreaming (2)

¹⁸ Therefore Yahweh waits to be gracious to you;
    but therefore he will arise to show compassion to you.
Because Yahweh is a God with authority—
    the blessings of all who wait for him!
¹⁹ Because, people in Zion, which dwells in Jerusalem,
    you really will not weep.
He really will be gracious to you at the sound of your cry;
    as he hears it, he will have answered.

²⁰ My Lord will give you trouble bread
    and affliction water.
But your teacher will no more turn aside;
    your eyes will be seeing your teacher.
²¹ Your ears will listen to a word from behind you,
    saying, "This is the way, walk in it,"
when you turn to the right
    and when you turn to the left.
²² You will defile the plating of your silver images
    and the sheath of your gold idol.
You will scatter them like something sick;
    "Get out," you will say to it.
²³ And he will give the rain for your seed
    with which you sow your ground,
and the bread that is the produce of your ground,
    and it will be rich and fat.
Your cattle will graze on that day
    in a broad pasture.
²⁴ The oxen and donkeys that serve the ground
    will eat seasoned fodder
    that has been winnowed with shovel and fork.
²⁵ There will be, on every high mountain
    and on every lofty hill,
streams running with water,
    on the day of great slaughter,
    when towers fall.
²⁶ The moon's light will be like the sun's light,
    and the sun's light will be sevenfold,
    like the light of seven days,
on the day when Yahweh bandages his people's wound
    and heals the wound from his blow.

²⁷ There, Yahweh's name is coming from afar,
    his anger is burning, his load is a weight.
His lips are full of wrath,
    his tongue is like a devouring fire.
²⁸ His breath is like a rushing wash
    that comes half way to the neck,
to shake the nations in a deceptive shaker,
    with a halter that makes them wander
    on the peoples' jaws.

²⁹ The song will be for you,
  like the night when a festival gets itself sanctified.
The rejoicing of heart
    [will be as] when someone goes with a pipe
    to come on Yahweh's mountain, to Israel's crag.
³⁰ Yahweh will make the majesty of his voice heard,
    and show the descent of his arm,
  in angry wrath and devouring fiery flame,
    cloudburst, storm, and hailstone.
³¹ Because at Yahweh's voice
    Assyria that beats with a club will be shattered.
³² Every passing of the appointed mace,
    which Yahweh causes to descend on him,
  will be with tambourines and guitars,
    and with battles involving shaking [his arm], which he
      wages against them.
³³ Because Tophet is prepared of old;
    it too is prepared for the King.
He has made its fire pit deep and wide,
    fire and wood a-plenty,
Yahweh's breath
    like a wash of sulfur burning in it.

When I was about eight, we went for a family holiday to stay with some friends. One morning as breakfast was about to begin I went back to our bedroom to get a sweater or something (it was an English summer) and had to climb into a wardrobe to reach it. Unbeknown to me, the top part of the wardrobe wasn't fastened to the bottom part. As I climbed inside, I caused the top half to fall off its base, door downwards, with me inside. It was too heavy for me to lift so as to crawl out, but I could just lift it an inch or two off the ground to call for help. They heard me downstairs, but they decided not to respond because I had apparently done something else stupid more than once and they thought it would be good for me to wait. I waited, and they waited, for what seemed to me a very long time.

God waits to be gracious to Israel. In a sense God doesn't have to wait. God isn't constrained by time lines in the way human beings are. Yet God waits. Sometimes parents know they should make their children wait even though they could do what the children want right now. Sometimes God submits himself to human constraints and waits rather than zap people with a miracle, which would be too easy. If God shows grace to Israel instantly every time it gets itself into a mess, God encourages Israel and us to think that our actions don't matter and have no consequences. God is one who has compassion—it's the Hebrew word for the womb, so it points to the motherly feelings of one who won't forever sit there eating her breakfast while her child cries out. God is one who has **authority**, the power to take action to rescue us. So it's worth waiting for him. But we may have to wait. The church in the West is at a point in its history when it needs to start waiting (and wishing and hoping and thinking and praying) for God to return to it and restore it rather than accepting things as they are or thinking that it can and should fix things.

There are some striking features about the normality that will then return. One is that it doesn't mean an end to all problems. There will still be situations in which the people need to cry out to God. The difference will be that they will indeed cry out and God will immediately respond, rather than making them wait. Like other parts of Old and New Testaments, Isaiah doesn't assume that being God's people means a trouble-free life. Rather it means that in trouble you have someone to turn to, someone who responds.

There's an irony about the lines that follow, when the prophecy describes how things will be when God stops waiting and starts guiding his people, because it's not as if God has been failing to guide them over the centuries. They have always had God's guidance. Like us, their problem was not that they didn't know what to do but that they didn't want to do it. So there's also a kind of wistfulness about the promise: if only they would listen to the voice that seeks to guide them. (Whereas Christian talk of guidance or leading often refers to knowing whether to go to this church or that, take this job or that, date this person or that, talk about guidance or leading in the Bible characteristically refers to worshiping God in a way that fits who God is and living with other people in a way that fits who God is.)

The account of Israel's restoration also assumes that there is still a **Day of the Lord** to come. The backcloth to Israel's restoration is a day of slaughter, when towers fall. Israel will always have to recall that it can be the victim of the Day of the Lord, not its beneficiary. That is so when Isaiah's opening chapters speak of towers falling; they're towers in places like Jerusalem. But when Israel is living by the guidance of that voice and is nevertheless subordinate to superpowers with lofty towers, it can know that God puts down superpowers.

In the first paragraph the restoring of Israel's blessing lies in the foreground, the day of wrath in the background. In the second paragraph the ratio reverses. The nations (the plural term often refers to the superpower of the day) will think they have a plan to take over the world but will discover they're deceived. They will expect to be singing, but **Judah** will be the one singing as it gathers to pray for God to act and deliver and/or to praise God for doing so. Tophet is a place in one of the canyons just outside Jerusalem where children were sacrificed to "the King"—in this context, the title of a traditional god of the country. This disgusting place would be an appropriate destiny for the **Assyrian** king after he fails to conquer Jerusalem.

ISAIAH 31:1–32:20

I See Hawks in L.A.

$^{31:1}$ Hey, people who go down to Egypt for help,
    and lean on horses,
who have trusted in chariotry because it's big,
    and in horsemen because they're very strong,
and not turned to Israel's holy one,
    not inquired of Yahweh.
^{2} But he too is wise, and he has brought evil,
    and not made his words turn away.
He will arise against the household of evildoers,
    and against the help of people who do wickedness.
^{3} Egypt is human not God,
    their horses are flesh not spirit.
When Yahweh stretches out his hand,
    helper will collapse,
the one who is helped will fall,
    all of them will come to an end together.

⁴ Because Yahweh has said this to me:
"As a lion murmurs,
   or a cougar over its prey,
(when a whole group of shepherds
   is summoned against it—
at their voice it isn't shattered,
   at their uproar it doesn't succumb),
so Yahweh Armies will come down,
   to take up arms on Mount Zion and on its hill.
⁵ Like birds flying,
   so Yahweh Armies will shield Jerusalem,
shielding and saving,
   passing over and rescuing.
⁶ Turn to the one you have deeply departed from,
   Israelites.
⁷ Because on that day they will reject, each one
   his silver nonentities and his gold nonentities,
   which your hands made for you, an offense.
⁸ Assyria will fall by a sword not human;
   a sword that does not belong to a human being will
      devour it.
It will flee for its life before the sword,
   and its young men will be for conscript labor.
⁹ Its crag will pass away because of the terror,
   its officers will be shattered because of the ensign"
(a declaration of Yahweh, whose fire is in Zion,
   whose furnace is in Jerusalem).

^{32:1} There, a king will reign to promote faithfulness;
   as for officials, they will govern to promote the exercise
      of authority.
² Each will be a true hiding place from wind,
   a place of concealment from rain,
like channels of water in the desert,
   like the shade of a heavy crag, in a weary country.
³ The eyes of people who see will not be blind,
   the ears of people who listen will give heed.
⁴ The mind of the quick will understand knowledge,
   the tongue of the hesitant will be quick
      to speak dazzling words.

⁵ No more will a mindless person be called a leader,
    or a villain called a savior.
⁶ Because a mindless person speaks mindlessness,
    and his mind effects wickedness,
acting impiously,
    and speaking of wandering from Yahweh,
leaving the hungry person empty,
    and letting the drink of the thirsty fail.
⁷ The villain: his tools are evil,
    he is one who plans schemes,
to destroy the lowly by falsehoods,
    and the needy person by the way he speaks in exercising
      authority.
⁸ But a leader will plan acts of leadership,
    and that man will stand through acts of leadership.

⁹ Carefree women, arise, listen to my voice!
    secure daughters, give ear to what I say!
¹⁰ In [a few] days over a year
    you secure ones will shake,
because the harvest will be finished,
    the ingathering won't come.
¹¹ Tremble, you carefree; shake, you who are secure,
    strip, be bare, a skirt around your waist,
¹² lamenting upon the breasts for the lovely fields,
    for the fruitful vine,
¹³ for my people's soil,
    which will produce thorn and briar,
yes, for all the joyful households,
    the exultant town.
¹⁴ Because the fortress will have been abandoned,
    the uproar of the city will have been forsaken.
Citadel and tower will have become
    empty spaces forever,
the enjoyment of donkeys,
    pasture for flocks.

¹⁵ Until the spirit empties itself on us from on high,
    and wilderness becomes farmland,
    and farmland counts as forest.

¹⁶ Authority will dwell in the wilderness,
    faithfulness will live in the farmland.
¹⁷ The effect of faithfulness will be well-being,
    the service of faithfulness will be quiet
    and security forever.
¹⁸ My people will live in an abode characterized by well-being,
    in secure dwellings, in carefree places of rest.
¹⁹ Though it hails when the forest falls,
    and the city utterly collapses:
²⁰ the blessings you will have, sowing by all waters,
    letting the feet of cattle and donkeys roam free!

One of my favorite bands is called *I See Hawks in L.A.*, which is also the title of one of their early songs. In the song the hawks hover over the city as if they sense it's about to be destroyed and there will be plenty of provender for them to enjoy. "What if this place got buried alive?" What if "the big one" that Californians speak of happens? "Let the snakes take over again." It's an image from a disaster movie.

Isaiah sees hawks hovering over Jerusalem. They too sense that the city is about to be destroyed. They too look forward to the provender they will then enjoy. They're not the kind of birds that let their prey be taken by any other creature. They're like lions. Yet suddenly the picture turns upside down, as happened in chapter 29. It transpires that being in the oversight of hawks or in the lion's maw is a safe place—no one else (specifically, the Assyrians) can get you.

How stupid is **Judah** not to treat **Yahweh** as its protector, then! Instead it trusts the Egyptians, even though they're human not God, their horses flesh not spirit. Humanity and the animal world are characterized by flesh. Isaiah doesn't use the word for flesh to denote the lower or sinful nature. Flesh is our created being in its relative weakness, fragility, and vulnerability. How stupid is Judah, then, to be relying on human, creaturely resources for its protection! With some sarcasm Isaiah points out that whereas Egypt has a reputation for philosophical acumen as well as military ability, Yahweh has a touch of wisdom, too, and has also shown himself capable of making plans and implementing them (for instance, in the recent frightening fall of **Ephraim** to **Assyria**). So how stupid Judah is in not turning to Yahweh. It needs to do so.

As I write, there is a widespread disillusionment with governments around much of the world, in the United States, in Europe, in Africa, and in the Middle East. The reasons and factors in different countries vary; the disillusionment is common. It wouldn't be surprising if people in Judah had similar feelings about their government, but the paragraph about a coming king and his government promises them that things will not always be as they are. Typically, it assumes that the priority for a government is the exercise of **authority** in accordance with **faithfulness** so that it acts as a secure hiding place for the vulnerable. That is where real leadership lies. In true Isaianic fashion, the prophet includes the promise that people who won't look or listen for truth at the moment will now do so.

The paragraph addressing the women constitutes another repetition of the sequence whereby warning leads into promise. Formally, Isaiah addresses the leading women of Judah. Usually it's the men he confronts, but here it's their wives and daughters, who will have some influence over husbands and sons and some responsibility for conserving the household resources in a crisis. Isaiah isn't critiquing them but giving them something to think and worry about. At the moment they're secure and can be carefree, but in just over a year things will look very different. The scene is the harvest celebration, one September–October. The prophecy says, "Make the most of it; this time next year there won't be a harvest." It would be appropriate for them to start mourning now for the catastrophe that is coming. The reference to the city's devastation shows that the prophecy isn't speaking of a natural disaster that ruins the harvest but of invasion and defeat that devastates the entire land, as happens when an army rampages over it and appropriates everything within sight. Of course the warning doesn't affect the women alone. Formally they're the people who are bidden to listen, but no doubt the prophecy is just as much intended for their husbands and fathers and sons.

Once again you might have thought that the vision was so terminal that it must presage an actual End, but again warning yields to promise by way of the unexpected "until" that would have seemed excluded by the preceding "forever." The country is restored. Again it will be characterized by faithfulness in the exercise of authority, and again some of Isaiah's characteristic notes appear—there will be security and quiet, and women and man can be truly carefree.

The section began with that reminder that human resources are flesh not spirit. Spirit in its dynamism and power is what distinguishes God from humanity. The section closes with the vision of God's spirit or wind sweeping over the earth, emptying itself out there so as to bring about a transformation of nature and a transformation of the human community.

ISAIAH 33:1–24

The Outrageous Hope into Which the City of God Is Invited

1   Hey, destroyer who has not been destroyed,
    betrayer who has not been betrayed!
  When you finish destroying you will be destroyed,
    when you stop betraying, they will betray you.
2   Yahweh, be gracious to us,
    we have looked for you.
  Be people's arm every morning,
    yes, our deliverance in time of trouble.
3   Before the sound of uproar peoples fled,
    before your rising nations scattered.
4   Your spoil was gathered like the gathering of locusts;
    like the rushing of grasshoppers someone rushes on it.
5   Yahweh is lofty, because he dwells on high;
    he filled Zion with authority and faithfulness.
6   He will become the steadfastness of your times;
    wisdom and knowledge are the wealth that brings
      deliverance,
    awe for Yahweh—that is its treasure.

7   There—the people in God's Hearth have cried out aloud in
    the streets,
    the aides of Salem weep bitterly.
8   Highways have become desolate,
    the traveler on the road has ceased.

He has broken the covenant, rejected the cities,
    not taken account of anyone.
9 The country has withered, wasted away;
    Lebanon is shamed, it has shriveled.
Sharon has become like the steppe,
    Bashan and Carmel are shaking off [their growth].
10 "Now I will arise," Yahweh says,
    "now I will exalt myself, now I will raise myself high.
11 You will conceive hay, give birth to straw;
    your breath is a fire that consumes you.
12 Peoples will be burnings of lime,
    thorns cut off that are set on fire.
13 Listen, you far off, to what I have done;
    acknowledge, you that are near, my might."

14 Offenders in Zion are afraid,
    trembling seizes the impious.
Who of us can dwell with the consuming fire,
    who of us can dwell with the everlasting blaze?
15 One who walks in faithfulness,
    who speaks uprightly,
who rejects profit from extortion,
    who waves his hands rather than grasping a bribe,
who stops his ear rather than listening to [talk of] bloodshed,
    who closes his eyes rather than look at evil—
16 that person can dwell on the heights,
    with cliff fortresses as his high tower.
His food will be given,
    his water reliable.

17 Your eyes will see the King in his glory,
    they will look at the country stretching afar.
18 Your mind will murmur about the dread—
    where's the person counting, where's the person
        weighing?
Where's the person counting the towers?—
19   you won't see the arrogant people,
the people too way-out of speech to hear,
    so stammering of tongue that there's no understanding.
20 Look at Zion, our festival town;
    your eyes will see Jerusalem,

122

a carefree abode,
  a tent that will not move about,
whose pegs one will never pull up,
  none of whose ropes will break.
21 Rather, there the majestic one, Yahweh, will be for us
  a place of rivers, streams, broad on both sides.
No rowing vessel can go in it,
  no majestic ship can pass through it.
22 Because Yahweh is the one exercising authority for us,
  Yahweh is our lawgiver,
Yahweh is our King,
  he is the one who will deliver us.
23 Your ropes are loose,
  they cannot hold secure the base of their mast,
  they cannot spread a sail.
Then abundance of plunder is divided,
  lame people take spoil.
24 No inhabitant will say, "I'm sick";
  the people that lives in it—
  its waywardness is carried.

This past Sunday we prayed for the peace of the world, for a spirit of respect and forbearance to grow among its peoples, for people in positions of public trust to serve justice and promote the dignity and freedom of every person, for the world to be freed from poverty, famine, and disaster, and for the poor, the persecuted, the sick, and all who suffer, for refugees, prisoners, and all who are in danger, that they may be relieved and protected. We pray prayers along those lines every week, and the more we pray them, the more outrageous they seem, and perhaps the more depressing.

It would be tempting to give up were it not for promises such as Isaiah's that God is committed to those ends. Whereas much in previous chapters of Isaiah starts from the concrete situation of the **Judahites** threatened by **Assyria** and inclined to try to solve their problems by seeking help from Egypt, this chapter contains no such concrete references. It could reflect many historical situations, all variants on the same sort of experience such as the opening line announces. Israel is the victim of a destroyer: Assyria was one, **Babylon** another, **Persia** another,

Seleucid Greece another. Sometimes these superpowers acted in beneficent ways and life would be tolerable, though people would still long to determine their own affairs. Sometimes the superpower would be more directly oppressive. Indeed, referring to the superpower as a destroyer need not imply that Judah was its victim. Sometimes a prophet such as Isaiah is putting the superpower on notice because of the wrong it's doing to other people.

The chapter's lack of concrete references makes its promises significant for any of the historical contexts just noted. It also makes clearer that God's fulfilling a vision is never a random event. It means God's ultimate purpose is receiving one of its periodic partial fulfillments. When God delivered the Israelites from Egypt, or brought them back to Judah after the **exile**, or freed them from the Seleucids in the 160s, or sent Jesus to declare that God's reign was here—all these events formed a partial fulfillment of God's ultimate vision. This chapter offers an expression of that final vision by taking up motifs and phrases from previous chapters in Isaiah and using them to draw a new picture of that final fulfillment. It's a montage of images, jumping from one image to another.

It begins from a bold declaration to the superpower that it will fall, though the immediate audience for the declaration will be Judah itself, to whom it comes as a promise. Its context in their life is indicated by the appeal for God to show grace to them. Like many Old Testament prayers, the prophecy goes on to describe how God has acted in the past, putting a superpower down, appropriating its plunder, and acting with **authority** and faithfulness toward **Zion**. Such recollections function as reminders to God to act that way again and to the people concerning God's capacity to do so.

The middle paragraph focuses on the present, which forms a contrast with what God has done in the past. The people of Jerusalem (God's Hearth, Salem) grieve over the state of things in the country, given the way the destroyer has acted, ignoring his commitments to the people and despoiling the country as superpowers do. The prayer, the recollection, and the protest drive **Yahweh** into a response, a promise to act that takes the form of a warning to the superpower that Yahweh will frustrate its expectations.

It's pretty scary for the people of God itself when Yahweh takes action. The third paragraph recognizes that they may be caught by the heat when God acts in wrath. Oppression by outside powers can drag a people down to the level of their oppressors (one expression of which is the way the oppressed can behave like their oppressors when they get into power themselves). The prophecy reminds them of some basic expectations God has of them. If Yahweh is coming, they need to look at their own lives.

The section closes with a majestic portrayal of the promising side to this coming. At present people can look back on the past only wistfully. When God acts, they will be able to look back with a different kind of disbelief. Do you remember the dread we felt? Do you remember when the imperial tax collectors were going around counting everything? Do you remember how they spoke an odd language and made us feel stupid because we couldn't understand it? Now we can encourage each other to look at Zion where we celebrate the festivals, which have even more meaning than before, and where we know we are safe forever. We are never going into exile again. It's as if Yahweh is a quiet stretch of water, broad but not accessible to dangerous warships. We will be the ones profiting from the resources of the empire now, instead of being raided by it. There'll be no more sickness and no more unforgiven sin that would take us into exile. (One reason the remembering will be important is that it may hold people back from adopting their oppressors' style.)

We can pray with confidence for the ultimate fulfillment of God's purpose for the world.

ISAIAH 34:1–35:10

Putting Down Edom, Giving the Mute Their Voice

34:1 Come near to listen, nations;
    pay attention, peoples.

The earth and what fills it should listen,
    the world and all who come out from it.
2 Because Yahweh has anger for all the nations,
    wrath for all their army.
He has devoted them, given them to slaughter,
3   and their slain will be thrown out.
Their corpses—their stench will go up,
    and the mountains will dissolve with their blood.
4 All the army of the heavens will rot
    and the heavens will roll up like a scroll.
All their army will fall
    as the foliage of the vine falls
and as that of the fig tree falls,
5   because my sword will have drunk its fill in the heavens.

There, on Edom it descends,
    and on a people I have devoted, in exercising authority.
6 Yahweh's sword is full of blood,
    soaked in fat,
in the blood of lambs and goats,
    in fat from the kidneys of rams.
Because Yahweh has a sacrifice in Bosrah,
    a great slaughter in the country of Edom.
7 Wild oxen will fall with them,
    bullocks with mighty steers.
Their country will be full of blood,
    their dirt be soaked in fat.
8 Because it is Yahweh's day of redress,
    a year of recompense for Zion's cause.
9 Its washes will turn to pitch,
    its dirt to sulfur.
Its country will become burning pitch;
10   day and night it won't go out.
Its smoke will go up forever;
    from generation to generation it will lie waste.
For ever and forever
    there will be no one passing through it.
11 Hawk and hedgehog will possess it,
    owl and raven will dwell in it.
He will stretch out over it the measuring line of emptiness,
    and the weights of the void 12 over its nobles.

126

People will call it "There's no kingship there";
    all its officials will be nothing.
13 Thorns will grow up in its citadels,
    briar and thistle in its stronghold.
It will become the abode of jackals,
    the dwelling of ostriches.
14 Wildcats will meet hyenas,
    a wild goat will call to its neighbor.
Indeed, the night creature has rested there,
    has found herself a place of repose.
15 There the snake has nested and laid eggs,
    sat and hatched in its shade.
Indeed, there vultures have gathered,
    each with her mate.
16 Inquire from Yahweh's scroll, and read out:
    "Not one of these will be missing,
    none will look for its mate,
because with my mouth" he commanded,
    with his spirit he assembled them.
17 He is the one who made the share fall to them,
    his hand divided it up for them with the line.
They will possess it for all time,
    to all generations they will dwell there.

35:1 The wilderness and the dry land will rejoice,
    the steppe will celebrate and bloom like a crocus.
2 It will bloom abundantly and celebrate,
    indeed with celebration and resounding.
Lebanon's splendor will be given it,
    Carmel and Sharon's glory.
Those people will see Yahweh's splendor,
    our God's glory.
3 Strengthen weak hands,
    firm up collapsing knees.
4 Say to the hesitant of mind,
    "Be strong, don't be afraid, there is your God.
Redress will come, God's recompense,
    he will come and deliver you."
5 Then the eyes of the blind will open,
    the ears of the deaf will unfasten.

⁶ Then the handicapped person will jump like a deer,
        the mute's tongue will resound.
    Because waters will burst out in the wilderness,
        washes in the steppe.
⁷ The burning sand will become a pool,
        the thirsty ground fountains of water.
    In the abode of jackals, its resting place,
        the dwelling will be reed and rush.
⁸ There will be a highway there, a way,
        and the holy way it will be called;
        an unclean person won't pass along it.
    It will be for them—the one who walks the way;
        stupid people won't wander there.
⁹ There will be no lion there;
        violent beast won't go up on it.
    It won't be found there;
        the restored people will go.
¹⁰ The people redeemed by Yahweh will return,
        will come to Zion with resounding,
        with eternal gladness on their head.
    Joy and gladness will overtake them;
        sorrow and sighing will flee.

As a result of multiple sclerosis, my first wife, Ann, indeed had collapsing knees, as well as weak hands. When we were relocating to the United States, as we arrived at Heathrow, I was helping her transfer into her wheelchair by using a technique her nurses had taught me, bracing her knees against mine, but in swiveling from the car seat to the ground on the way to the wheelchair our knees lost contact, her knees folded, and I dropped her. In subsequent years she became mute, too. It wasn't that she knew what to say but had lost the ability to use her voice; the disease's effect on her mental workings meant she could no longer think out what she wanted to say. Maybe being unable to speak was tougher than being unable to walk.

My heart therefore thrills at the image of the handicapped person jumping like a deer. It would be a sight to behold! What a further image, that a mute person's tongue can resound! The promises' logic is that seeing God's great act of restoration will be so astonishing, it will compel such responses from limbs and mouths that lack the ability to move. The sight is a shock that electrifies them back to life, an extreme version of the way the whisper of a loved one may be able to arouse a response from someone in a coma. Perhaps it will be hearing God's voice calling or singing or whispering that will bring to birth the new life the vision portrays.

The prophecy doesn't directly portray Yahweh's act of restoration. It portrays its reverberations in nature. It's like a poem in the way it teases the reader. Who are the "those people" to whom it points as the beneficiaries of God's act? Only in the last verses are they identified. Even there, it first rules out some people—the unclean (for instance, people stained by the worship of other gods) and the stupid (people who haven't recognized that submission to **Yahweh** is the first principle of wisdom). As in English, in Hebrew the word "violent" usually applies to human beings not animals, so the lions and violent beasts may stand for another group of people who are excluded from the picture. The beneficiaries are the people redeemed and **restored** by Yahweh and brought back to **Zion** from the **exile** of which Isaiah warns.

The other animal reference, to jackals, draws attention to the way these two chapters form a diptych, a balancing pair. Like Jesus and Paul, the prophecy assumes that redress on the wayward and restoration for the committed go together, as two sides of a coin. It's as if God can't just focus on the nice idea of restoring his people but also has to face the less pleasant task of bringing punishment to the rebellious. The collocation also recognizes how the restoration of God's people commonly requires the putting down of their oppressors as its precondition. When **Judah** is in exile, being brought back to Zion will require putting down the power of the superpower that took them there. The first paragraph, then, speaks of judgment on the superpower.

The superpower isn't named, which makes it noteworthy that Edom comes into focus in the middle paragraph. For much of Old Testament times Edom did nothing more worthy of special judgment than other peoples such Moab or Ammon. But Edom later took over large amounts of Judahite territory, as far as Hebron. This might be a reason for speaking of the need for Yahweh to "take recompense for Zion's cause." Further, Edom later became the Jews' code term for Rome (like Babylon in the New Testament). Maybe in the Old Testament it's already a symbol for a power asserting itself against Yahweh and his people. Originally Edom (=Esau) was the brother of Israel (=Jacob), which could encourage this antithesis. Jacob stands for the chosen, Edom for the not-chosen. Ironically, Edom was never destroyed in the way the prophecy warns; indeed, the Idumeans (the term for the people who later lived in the area) were converted to Judaism. Perhaps you could call it a neat kind of destruction.

ISAIAH 36:1–37:20

A Politician's One Fatal Mistake

36:1 In King Hezekiah's fourth year, Sennacherib king of Assyria came up against all the fortified cities of Judah and took them. 2 The king of Assyria sent the Rabshaqeh from Lachish to Jerusalem to King Hezekiah with a heavy force, and he took a stand at the conduit of the Upper Pool at the Launderer's Field road. 3 Eliaqim son of Hilqiah who was over the house, Shebna the scribe, and Joah son of Asaph the recorder, went out to meet him. 4 The Rabshaqeh said to them, "Will you say to Hezekiah: 'The Great King, the king of Assyria has said this: "What is this trust that you have? 5 I have said [to myself], 'Yes, the word on the lips [equals] a plan and might for battle!' Now, on whom have you trusted, that you have rebelled against me? 6 There, you have trusted in this broken reed of a staff, in Egypt, which goes into the palm of the person who leans on it, and pierces it. Such is Pharaoh, the king of Egypt, to all who trust in him. 7 But if you say to me, 'Yahweh our God – we have trusted in him': is it not he whose high place and altars Hezekiah removed, and said to Judah and Jerusalem, 'Before this altar you are to bow down'? 8 Now, do make a bargain with my lord the king of Assyria. I will provide you with two thousand horses if you can provide yourself riders for them. 9 How could you turn away a single governor among my lord's least servants? But you trust for yourself in Egypt for chariotry and horsemen. 10 And now, is it without Yahweh that I have come up to this country to destroy it? Yahweh himself said to me, 'Go up to this country and destroy it.'"'"

[11] Eliaqim, Shebna, and Joah said to the Rabshaqeh, "Do speak to your servants in Aramaic, because we are listening. Don't speak to us in Judahite in the ears of the people that is on the wall." [12] The Rabshaqeh said, "Was it to your lord and to you that my lord sent me to speak these words? Was it not to the individuals sitting on the wall, about [their] eating their excrement and drinking the water they have passed, along with you?" [13] The Rabshaqeh stood and said and called in a loud voice in Judahite and said, "Listen to the words of the Great King, the king of Assyria. [14] The king has said this: 'Hezekiah must not deceive you, because he won't be able to save you. [15] Hezekiah must not make you trust in Yahweh, saying, "Yahweh will definitely save us; this city won't be given into the hand of the king of Assyria."' [16] Don't listen to Hezekiah. Because the king of Assyria has said this: 'Make a [treaty of] blessing with me. Come out to me, and eat each his vine and each his fig tree, and drink each the water from his cistern, [17] until I come and take you to a country like your country, a country of grain and new wine, of bread and vineyards. [18] Don't let Hezekiah mislead you, saying "Yahweh will save us." Have the gods of the nations, any of them, saved his country from the hand of the king of Assyria? [19] Where were the gods of Hamat and Arpad? Where were the gods of Sepharvaim? And [is it the case] that they saved Samaria from my hand? [20] Who was it among all the gods of these countries that saved their country from my hand?'"'" [21] They were silent and didn't answer him a word, because it had been the king's command, "Don't answer him."

[22] Eliaqim son of Hilqiah who was over the house, Shebna the scribe, and Joah son of Asaph the recorder came to Hezekiah with their clothes torn and told him the Rabshaqeh's words.

[37:1] When King Hezekiah heard, he tore his clothes and covered himself in sackcloth. He came into Yahweh's house, [2] and sent Eliaqim, who was over the house, Shebna the scribe, and the elders of the priests, covered in sackcloth, to Isaiah son of Amoz. [3] They said to him, "Hezekiah has said this: 'This day is a day of trouble, reproof, and disgrace, when children come to birth but there's no strength for giving birth. [4] Perhaps Yahweh your God will listen to the words of the Rabshaqeh, whom the king of Assyria, his lord, sent to revile the living God, and will reprove the words that Yahweh your God has heard. So lift up a plea on behalf of the remains that are here.'" [5] When King Hezekiah's servants came to Isaiah, [6] Isaiah said to them, "Say this to your lord: 'Yahweh has said this: "Don't be afraid before the words you have heard with which the king of Assyria's young men have blasphemed me. [7] Here—I am putting a spirit in him. He will hear a report and will return to his country, and I will make him fall by the sword in his country."'" [8] The Rabshaqeh returned and found the king of Assyria fighting against Libnah, because [the Rabshaqeh] had heard that he had moved on from Lachish.

[9] The king of Assyria had heard concerning Tirhaqah the king of Sudan, "He has come out to fight with you." When he heard, he sent aides to Hezekiah, saying, [10] "You are to say this to Hezekiah, king of Judah: 'Your God whom you are trusting, saying "Jerusalem won't be given into the hand of the king of Assyria," must not mislead you. [11] There—you yourself have heard what the kings of Assyria have done to all the countries, by devoting them. And you will be saved? [12] Did the gods of the nations that my ancestors destroyed save them—Gozan, Haran, Reseph, the Edenites who are in Telassar? [13] Where is the king of Hamat, the king of Arpad, the king of Lair, Sepharvaim, Hena, and Ivvah?'"

[14] Hezekiah received the letter from the aides' hand, read it out, and went up to Yahweh's house. Hezekiah spread it out before Yahweh. [15] And Hezekiah pleaded with Yahweh: [16] "Yahweh Armies, Israel's God, you who sit over the cherubs: you are God alone, in relation to all the kingdoms of the earth. You are the one who made the heavens and the earth. [17] Yahweh, bend your ear and listen, open your eye and see, listen to all the words of Sennacherib that he sent to blaspheme the living God. [18] Of a truth, Yahweh, the kings of Assyria have devoted all the countries, and their country, [19] giving their gods to the fire, because they were not gods but the work of human hands, wood and stone, and they have destroyed them. [20] But now, Yahweh our God, deliver us from his hand, so that all the kingdoms of the earth may acknowledge that you alone are Yahweh."

When I was the principal of a seminary, I would get lots of mail. Usually my assistant would open it, but on Saturday I would do so, and thus would get first sight of the tricky pieces of correspondence, ones that raised worrying issues or asked questions to which I didn't know the answer or apprised me of an unwelcome decision. Maybe a ministerial selection board had not recommended a student who I thought was a fine candidate; or maybe they had recommended one who seemed to me to be implausible. I would stand in my office puzzling over such a letter.

I came to love the picture of Hezekiah taking his much trickier letter into the temple and standing in front of God as I would in my office, holding it out to God—"Have you seen this? It's monstrous! What shall I do?"

The situation really is tricky. The story avoids drawing our attention to the way Hezekiah is at least partly responsible for the mess he's in. His underlings' amusing plea to the Rabshaqeh (one of Sennacherib's senior aides) that he avoid speaking in a way that ordinary people can understand hints at their embarrassment. There are no untarnished heroes in the story. Many of the peoples on the **Assyrian** empire's western edge have rebelled against Assyrian authority, and Hezekiah seems to have joined in. Chapters 29–31 have related how **Judah** sought to get Egypt's support in resisting Assyria, how this wouldn't work because it ignored **Yahweh's** involvement in affairs, and how Yahweh threatened to go as near as it's possible to go in letting Jerusalem fall, short of actually doing so. In keeping with this threat, Sennacherib has devastated Judah's cities and looks about to devastate Jerusalem. In his own subsequent account of events in an inscription he declares, "because Hezekiah, king of Judah, would not submit to my yoke, I came up against him, and by force of arms and by the might of my power I took forty-six of his strong fenced cities; and of the smaller towns that were scattered about, I took and plundered a countless number . . . Hezekiah himself I shut up in Jerusalem, his capital city, like a bird in a cage, building towers around the city to hem him in, and raising banks of earth against the gates, so as to prevent escape."

This sequence of events is nearing its climax. Jerusalem is in the mountains and Sennacherib has initially focused on the cities in the lower land nearer the Mediterranean, whose capture is an easier task. He sends the Rabshaqeh to try to negotiate Jerusalem's surrender, so the king doesn't have to undertake a tricky and potentially lengthy siege. His speech on the king's behalf brings up just the right questions.

One theme is planning. Talk is one thing, but planning and executing an operation is another. If Hezekiah had the military hardware, does he have the personnel to operate it? Isaiah would agree that the question of planning is important, but the deeper reason is that Yahweh is the one who knows about planning and executing operations. Sennacherib almost makes that point, too, with his audacious claim to be coming as Yahweh's agent—which is truer than he means. Yahweh's being the one who plans and executes operations is a fact that is going to rebound on Sennacherib.

Another theme is trust, the issue Isaiah keeps raising. Is Hezekiah really so stupid as to trust in the Egyptians? Alternatively, is he in a position to trust in Yahweh, when he has been involved in destroying Yahweh's sanctuaries in Judah? The longer version of this story in 2 Kings confirms Sennacherib's words. It's a clever argument, though Isaiah would have approved of Hezekiah's action (the sanctuaries were inclined to unorthodox worship). But in speaking of trust, the Rabshaqeh later makes one mistake. It's a fatal one. He ends up questioning whether Yahweh can deliver Jerusalem, any more than other gods have delivered their cities (the observation that it didn't work with Samaria would be especially painful). Perhaps Hezekiah's aides are devastated out of fear, but Hezekiah is devastated because of the blasphemy. He knows there's a good chance that Sennacherib has tied a noose around his own neck. He knows it's a prophet's job to speak to God on the people's behalf as well as to speak to the people on God's behalf, and bids him do so. The same action will be good for God's name as well as for the "**remains**" of Judah, for the one city that is left.

The last two paragraphs repeat many of the story's themes. They may be an alternative version of it rather than a continuation. The new thing they add is the prayer, which models the way the most powerful prayer is one prayed "for your name's sake." They imply the awareness that God may indeed act to reclaim his holy name when it has been disparaged.

ISAIAH 37:21–38

Things That Shouldn't Happen, Yet Do

[21] Isaiah son of Amoz sent to Hezekiah saying, "Yahweh, Israel's God, with whom you pleaded concerning Sennacherib king of Assyria, has said this. [22] This is the word that Yahweh has spoken about him.

She has despised you,
> maiden Ms. Zion has mocked you.
Behind you Ms. Jerusalem
> has shaken her head.

[23] Whom have you blasphemed and reviled,
> against whom have you lifted your voice?
You have raised your eyes on high
> to Israel's holy one.

[24] By the hand of your servants
> you have blasphemed my Lord, and said,
'With the abundance of my chariotry
> I am the one who has gone up to the mountains' height,
> Lebanon's furthest parts.
I have cut down the tallest of its cedars,
> the choicest of its cypresses.
I have come to its ultimate height,
> its richest forest.

[25] I am the one who has dug and drunk water,
> and dried with the sole of my feet
> all Egypt's streams.'

[26] Have you not heard?—
> long ago I did it,
from days of old I formed it,
> now I have made it come about.
It has happened, causing fortified cities
> to crash into ruined heaps.

[27] Their inhabitants have been sapped of power,
> shattered and shamed.
They have become vegetation of the countryside,
> green herbage,
grass on the roof,
> something blasted before it grows up.

²⁸ Your staying, going out, and coming I know,
>   and how you raged at me.
²⁹ Because you raged at me,
>   and your confidence came up into my ears,
> I will put my hook in your nose,
>   my bit in your mouth,
>   and make you return by the way you came.

³⁰ This will be the sign for you [Hezekiah]:
> This year, eat the natural growth;
>   in the second year, the secondary growth.
> In the third year you can sew and reap,
>   and plant vineyards and eat their fruit.
³¹ The survivors of Judah's household that remain
>   will add root downwards and produce fruit above.
³² Because the remains will come out from Jerusalem,
>   and survivors from Mount Zion.
> The passion of Yahweh Armies
>   will do this.
³³ Therefore this is what Yahweh has said concerning the king
>   of Assyria:
> "He will not come into this city;
>   he will not shoot an arrow there.
> He will not draw near to it with a shield;
>   he will not construct a ramp against it.
³⁴ By the way that he came he will return;
>   into this city he will not come
>   (Yahweh's declaration).
³⁵ I will shield this city in order to deliver it,
>   for my sake and for the sake of David my servant."

³⁶ Yahweh's aide went out and struck 185,000 in the Assyrian camp. People got up in the morning—there, all of them were dead corpses. ³⁷ Sennacherib the king of Assyria broke camp and went. He returned and lived in Nineveh. ³⁸ He was bowing down in the house of Nisrok his god when Adrammelek and Sarezer his sons struck him with the sword. They escaped to the country of Ararat, and his son Esarhaddon became king instead of him.

As we woke this morning, the man in the apartment above had already set his washing machine going, and it was making a clunkier noise than usual. Indeed, at first I thought there was a helicopter hovering above the building. Was it about to crash into us? Was the washing machine about to crash through our ceiling? Then I heard a news item about a disc jockey from Brooklyn who was lying in bed in a hotel in Portland when a taxi crashed through the wall and pinned him under its wheels. "It's a random, absurd thing that shouldn't happen, but happened," he said.

I can imagine a commander-in-chief such as Sennacherib reacting in that way to the slaughter in his army that this story tells and reacting that way again if he had chance to do so when his sons raised their swords against him. **Assyrian** sources tell of Sennacherib's assassination by his sons. They don't tell of an army massacre. You may think the story is a legend. You may think there was a natural disaster—one or two later sources suggest there might have been an epidemic in the camp. You may think there was simply a supernatural event exactly as the story describes. Your view will probably be decided by the assumptions you bring to the story. I think there are lots of stories in Scripture where something happened but the story is told larger than life and that this is an example. So I find it easiest to believe that something like an epidemic happened in the camp and that it was indeed God's way of bringing judgment on the Assyrians—as indeed was the king's murder by his sons.

If this is so, it would help to explain Israel's concluding that Isaiah was a true prophet and thus keeping his prophecies in a book, when there were other prophets whose words were not preserved. Maybe the words of a true prophet have the ring of truth and we know they are true, though we might prefer not to acknowledge it because we don't like them. But two or three factors may have objectively distinguished Isaiah from other prophets and pushed Israel in that direction. His prophecies often came true, so that the ones that had not come true were worth holding onto against the day when they would. But false prophets can utter prophecies that come true; you can't believe every prophet. So another factor is the theological and moral integrity about

Isaiah's words. He talked about God in a believable way and one that you could live with. His God was not involved only with people's inner spiritual life and worship but also with the outside world. He was active in a way that combined commitment to Israel, David, and Jerusalem, and commitment to keeping his promises, with concern for the whole world to come to acknowledge Yahweh. Isaiah also insisted that Israel and the world had a responsibility to Yahweh and to justice and did not get away with it if they ignored such obligations. So in Sennacherib's case, the events that Isaiah describes are ones that shouldn't happen but do, yet they're not random. Another factor, I suspect, was that Isaiah was interesting, made you think, haunted you.

The prophecy he gives Hezekiah provides examples. He begins with Jerusalem mocking Sennacherib, a neat and bold picture. At the moment Jerusalem is doing nothing of the sort, but in his God-inspired imagination Isaiah has seen Jerusalem doing so, and he invites the city to start doing so even at the moment when it has no visible basis for it. Isaiah knows Sennacherib has signed his own and his army's death warrant by its scorn for the real God and its assumption about itself and its achievements.

The second paragraph in the message with its opening question about whether people have heard about these things provides another sort of example. It sounds as if it continues Sennacherib's self-account, but eventually it becomes clear that these are God's questions. You think you did these things Sennacherib? Think again. I was the one whose plans were being implemented. You were just a pawn in my hand. And you're going to pay for your arrogance.

The third paragraph makes outrageous promises to Hezekiah, further examples of the promises whose fulfillment will have led to Isaiah's words being held onto and preserved.

ISAIAH 38:1–39:8

The Ambiguous Hezekiah

38:1 In those days Hezekiah was deathly sick. Isaiah the son of Amoz, the prophet, came to him and said to him, "Yahweh has said this: 'Give orders to your household, because you're dying; you won't come back to life.'" ² Hezekiah turned his face to the wall and pleaded with Yahweh. ³ He said, "Oh, Yahweh, do be mindful of how I have walked before you in truth and with a whole mind, and have done what was good in your eyes." Hezekiah wept much. ⁴ Yahweh's word came to Isaiah: ⁵ "Go and say to Hezekiah: 'Yahweh, the God of your ancestor David, has said this: "I have listened to your plea, I have seen your tears. Now: I am adding to your lifespan fifteen years. ⁶ From the hand of the king of Assyria I will rescue you and this city, and I will shield this city." ⁷ This will be the sign for you from Yahweh that Yahweh will do this thing that he has spoken. ⁸ "Here, I am going to reverse the shadow on the steps that has gone down on the steps of Ahaz because of the sun, back ten steps."'" And the sun reversed ten steps by the steps that it had gone down.

⁹ A composition for Hezekiah, king of Judah, when he was sick and came back to life from his sickness.

¹⁰ I myself said,
   "In the midst of my days I shall go.
  I have been appointed to Sheol's gates
   for the rest of my years."
¹¹ I said, "I shall not see Yah;
   Yah is in the land of the living.
  I shall not look to humanity again,
   with the inhabitants of the world.
¹² My dwelling has pulled up and gone away from me
   like a shepherd's tent.
  I have rolled up my life like a weaver
   as he cuts me from the loom.
  While from day until night you requite me,
¹³   I have composed [myself] until morning.
  Like a lion, so he breaks all my bones,
   while from day until night you requite me.
¹⁴ Like a swift, a swallow, so I chirp;
   I murmur like a dove.
  My eyes have looked to the height, my Lord,
   it is oppression to me, make a pledge to me.
¹⁵ What shall I speak?—
   he said [this] about me, and he himself acted.

139

I will walk all my years
in the pain of my heart.
16 My Lord, in all [such pains] people will live,
and in all [the years] will be the life of my spirit;
may you restore me and bring me back to life."

17 There—as regards well-being,
it was tough for me, tough.
But you yourself loved [and took] me
out of the pit of nothingness,
because you threw all my offenses
behind your back.
18 Because Sheol does not confess you
[nor] death praise you.
People who go down to the Pit
don't expect your truthfulness.
19 The living person, the living person,
he confesses you this very day.
A father makes known to his children
your truthfulness.
20 Yahweh was here to save me,
and we will make our music,
all the days of our lives
at Yahweh's house.

(21 Isaiah had said, "They are to take a block of figs and apply it to the infection, and he will come back to life," and Hezekiah had said, "What will be the sign that I will go up to Yahweh's house?")

39:1 At that time, Merodak-baladan son of Baladan, king of Babylon, sent letters and a gift to Hezekiah; he had heard that he had been ill and had regained strength. 2 Hezekiah celebrated with them and showed them all his treasure house, the silver, the gold, the spices, and the fine oil, and his entire armory and all that was to be found in his storehouses. There was not a thing that Hezekiah did not show them in his house and his entire realm. 3 But Isaiah the prophet came to King Hezekiah and said to him, "What have these men said, and from where do they come to you?" Hezekiah said, "It's from a far country that they have come to me, from Babylon." 4 He said, "What have they seen in your house?" Hezekiah said, "They have seen everything in my house. There was not a thing that I didn't show them in my storehouses." [5] Isaiah said to Hezekiah, "Listen to the word of Yahweh Armies. [6] 'There: days are coming when everything in your house, and what your ancestors have stored up until this day, will be carried to Babylon. Not a thing will be left,' Yahweh says. [7] 'Some of your descendants who will have issued from you, whom you will father, will be taken and will become eunuchs in the palace of the king of Babylon.'" [8] Hezekiah said to Isaiah, "The word from Yahweh that you have spoken is good." He said, "Because there will be well-being and truth in my days."

The other week we heard a Los Angeles priest who works with ex-gang members tell of going to a university to talk about his work. He took with him an ex-gang member called Juan. During the day they went to classes and spoke to students and in the evening addressed a meeting of a thousand members of the student body. In the subsequent discussion, someone asked Juan what were his hopes or his advice for his son, who was about to enter his teens. Fighting back tears, Juan said he hoped his son wouldn't be like him. The questioner, who had heard Juan during the day, stood up again. "You're a gentle, caring, wise person. You should want your son to be like you." Our perceptions of ourselves are often skewed; we may be more honorable than we think, or less so. It's so partly because we ourselves are probably complicated; we have honorable and dishonorable features. We may not be able to make up our minds about ourselves or about other people.

The book of Isaiah can't quite make up its mind about Hezekiah, and neither can Hezekiah make up his mind about himself. He can appeal to God as one who has walked before God in truth and with a whole mind, and the story about him and Sennacherib has portrayed him in this way. On the other hand, his prayer made no claim to be undeserving of his illness (unlike most such prayers in the Psalms) and he recognizes that God had to throw a load of offenses behind his back in answering his prayer, which fits with its repeated reference to God's requiting him—presumably in making him sick. Further, Isaiah has

141

implicitly critiqued him in his earlier attacks on **Judahite** political policies. There's then an ambiguity in the story about the Babylonian envoys. What is the significance of his reaction to Isaiah's message about the coming **exile**? Is it a cynical contentment—though disaster is coming, it won't affect him personally? Or is it a proper appreciation of the fact that disaster can be postponed, with the implication that it's not inevitable?

Many biblical characters are described in ambiguous ways—it's true of Noah, Abraham, Joseph, Moses, and David. The stories recognize the complexity of people and the complexity of evaluating people. The point for readers isn't to try to make up our mind whether they're good guys. It's to let the ambiguity in their stories help us reflect on the ambiguity of our own.

It seems unlikely that God would have reworked the intricate movements of the planets to give Hezekiah his sign, and the account of the sign is also somewhat ambiguous. I assume it's likely to have been an unusual natural event. But maybe that conclusion shows I'm too rationalist. The expression of thanksgiving and testimony to **Yahweh's** act of deliverance is apparently composed for him by people such as the Levites, as one would expect—it's their job to compose such prayers. It parallels prayers in the Psalms in spending much time recalling the trouble he had been in. It had seemed inevitable that he would end up in **Sheol** (in the absence of antibiotics, an infected sore or wound could easily lead to septicemia). He had tried to submit himself to Yahweh, but it seemed that Yahweh had laid down what was to happen and that it was inevitable. But that fact doesn't mean you just have to accept what God says, and Hezekiah recalls how he had prayed for God to restore him. He then testifies to how God had delivered him. The footnote about the fig compress presumably indicates that Isaiah combined regular medical treatment with prayer.

The story about the **Babylonian** envoys conveys the usual double significance of references to Babylon in Isaiah's ministry. In Hezekiah's day Babylon was part of the **Assyrian** empire, interested in peoples such as Judah because it wants them to join in rebellion against their shared overlord. But a century later Babylon will realize its ambitions to take over Assyria's position as superpower. It thus also becomes the superpower against whom Judah rebels, and whereas Yahweh prevented Assyria from taking Jerusalem, a century later Yahweh finally says "That's it!" and lets Babylon finish the job that Assyria started. So in 597 and again in 587 the Babylonians attacked and captured Jerusalem and took off to Babylon key Judahite leaders, including people such as priests, prophets, and members of the administration such as kings and their families. There they languished for fifty years. The story appositely closes off Isaiah 1–39, because Isaiah 40 takes up the story from there.

ISAIAH 40:1–11

Comfort My People

¹ "Comfort, comfort my people,"
    says your God.
² "Speak to Jerusalem's heart,
    proclaim to it,
that its tour of duty is fulfilled,
    that its waywardness is paid for,
that it has received from Yahweh's hand
    double for all its offenses."

³ A voice is proclaiming,
"In the wilderness clear Yahweh's way,
    make straight in the steppe a highway for our God.
⁴ Every valley is to rise up,
    every mountain and hill is to sink.
The ridge is to become level,
    the cliffs a vale.
⁵ Yahweh's splendor will appear,
    and all flesh will see it together,
    because Yahweh's mouth has spoken."

⁶ A voice is saying, "Proclaim,"
    but someone says, "Proclaim what?
All flesh is grass,
    and all its commitment is like a wild flower's.
⁷ Grass withers, a flower fades,
    when Yahweh's wind blows on it."

143

"Yes, the people are grass;
8   grass withers, a flower fades—
       but our God's word stands forever."

9   Get yourself up onto a high mountain
       as a bringer of news to Zion.
    Raise your voice with power
       as a bringer of news to Jerusalem.
    Raise it, don't be afraid,
       say to Judah's cities,
    "There is your God,
10   there is the Lord Yahweh!"
    He comes as the strong one,
       his arm is going to rule for him.
    There, his reward is with him,
       his earnings before him.
11 Like a shepherd who pastures his flock,
       he gathers lambs in his arm.
    He carries them in his embrace,
       guides the nursing ones.

A week ago we had dinner with two clergy friends from England, one of whom commented in passing that on present trends the Church of England would be functionally nonexistent in twenty years. I discovered that the comment was echoing speeches at the Church of England's general synod, where it has been reported that the average age of people in its congregation is now sixty-one. Different people have varying explanations of the situation, regarding whose fault it is and regarding what needs to be done. Does doing something about it rest on us?

It's easy to imagine people in **Judah** asking similar questions in the situation that is the background to this section. It presupposes that Jerusalem's fall to the **Babylonians** happened some time ago. The five poems or prayers that comprise the book of Lamentations tell us what people were thinking in the aftermath of that event. They end with the thought, "unless you have utterly rejected us; you're so very wrathful with us . . ." They begin with a repeated lament about Jerusalem, the abandoned woman who "has none to comfort her," a lament repeated five times.

144

God now responds to that wondering and that lament, first with the commission to "comfort, comfort my people." The prophet doesn't say who the comforters are. They might include the prophet, but the verb is plural; it doesn't just refer to him. Perhaps he doesn't know who they are; he simply hears God commissioning them. The point lies in the fact that some comforting is commissioned. The first element in the message of comfort lies in the words that follow, "my people" and "your God." Another bit of background to the prophecy is the way Hosea had long ago reported God's words to Israel, "You are no longer my people and I am no longer your God." These words were a death knell. But God had also promised through Hosea that the moment would come when God would again say "my people" and "your God." The moment has arrived.

The reason is that God knows when enough is enough. The people resemble an army unit who have been on a demanding tour of duty; the tour is over. They needed to pay for their way-wardness, and they have done so. "Double for all your offenses" underlines the adequacy of the payment; the Babylonians have been tougher with Judah than was needed (the prophecy will later critique them for their heartlessness). Yet another bit of background is Ezekiel's description of God's splendor leaving Jerusalem on the eve of its fall to Babylon in 587. If God leaves the city, its protection is gone. But now God intends to return to the city, and in the second paragraph a voice thus commissions freeway contractors to carve out a highway to take God back.

The third paragraph relates the commission of another voice; the prophecy continues to be all voices, without our knowing who speaks or who is addressed. Someone is commissioned to preach. This time the verb is singular; it addresses one potential preacher. Maybe it's the prophet himself. But the preacher can't imagine preaching. How can he preach to people who are like plants withered by the hot desert wind? The commissioning voice reminds him of a factor he has left out of consideration. He is of course right that the people are like plants withered by the desert wind. But he has forgotten about the difference it makes when God declares the intention to do something. When God speaks, things happen. God had said way back that he would not simply abandon Israel as "not-my-people." Earlier chapters of Isaiah have declared that God won't finally abandon Jerusalem. God is saying now that the moment of comfort has come. When God says things, they happen.

The last paragraph reports another commissioning voice, restating the commission to preach. It's as if the preacher is to soar to the top of a mountain higher than **Zion** itself, higher than the Judahite mountains, a perspective from which he can see God coming along that highway. God isn't on his own. He has a flock of sheep, the flock of Israel, for whom he is caring with power and compassion as he brings them with him. The prophecy turns out to have in its mind not only Jerusalem and Judah and the people living there, praying those desperate prayers in Lamentations. It has in mind the people who were taken off to Babylon decades ago. They're coming back.

The prophet who speaks this prophecy evidently lives at the time when these events are about to take place and ministers his message of comfort to his contemporaries. It's not Isaiah the son of Amoz talking about something that will happen 150 years after his time—the prophecy doesn't say that "in that day" God will send a message along these lines. God is speaking to his people in the present. This is someone to whom God gives the mantle of Isaiah, who is called to say the kind of thing Isaiah would say if he were here now. He is a kind of Second Isaiah.

ISAIAH 40:12-31

Hope Means Energy

¹² Who has gauged the waters in his palm,
     surveyed the heavens with his span,
  measured earth's dirt by the gallon,
     weighed the mountains with a balance,
     the hills with scales?
¹³ Who has directed Yahweh's spirit,
     or as the person to give him counsel made it known to
       him?
¹⁴ With whom did he take counsel, so that he helped him
       understand,
     taught him the way to make decisions,

taught him knowledge,
    made known to him the way of understanding?
¹⁵ There, nations count like a drop from a pan,
    like a cloud on scales;
  there, foreign shores are like a fine cloud rising.
¹⁶ Lebanon—there's not enough to burn,
    its animals—there aren't enough for a burnt offering.
¹⁷ All the nations are like nothing over against him;
    they count as less than naught, emptiness, to him.

¹⁸ So to whom would you compare God,
    or what comparison would you put forward for him?
¹⁹ The image, which a craftworker casts?—
    a smith beats it out with gold,
    and a smith with silver chains.
²⁰ Is it sissoo fit for tribute,
    wood that doesn't rot, that someone chooses?
  He seeks for himself a clever craftworker
    to set up an image so it doesn't wobble.

²¹ Do you not acknowledge,
    do you not listen?
  Has it not been told you from the beginning,
    have you not understood earth's foundations?
²² There is one who sits above earth's horizon,
    its inhabitants like grasshoppers,
  one who stretches out the heavens like net,
    spreads them like a tent for sitting in,
²³ one who makes sovereigns nothing,
    makes earth's authorities pure emptiness.
²⁴ They're really not planted, really not sown,
    their stem is really not rooting in the earth,
  then he blows on them and they shrivel,
    and the whirlwind carries them off like straw.

²⁵ So to whom would you compare me,
    so I could be similar (says the holy one)?
²⁶ Lift your eyes on high and look—
    who created these?
  The one who brings out their army in full number
    summons all of them by name.

Because of the abundance of his power,
and as one mighty in strength, not one lags behind.

²⁷ Why do you say, Jacob,
why speak, Israel,
"My way has hidden from Yahweh,
a decision about me passes away from my God"?
²⁸ Have you not acknowledged,
or not listened?
Yahweh is God of the ages,
creator of earth's ends.
He doesn't get faint or weary;
there's no fathoming of his understanding.
²⁹ He gives strength to the faint,
and to the one who has no resources he gives much
energy.
³⁰ Youths may get faint and weary,
young men may totally collapse.
³¹ But people who look for Yahweh get new energy,
they grow pinions like eagles.
They run and don't get weary,
they walk on and don't faint.

Yesterday in church we were visited by the choir from a shelter for women who have been finding their way out of involvement with alcohol, drugs, and prostitution. Their first song was about the hope they have found in Christ, and that theme ran through the testimonies three of them gave as they told their overwhelmingly moving stories about experiences that lay behind the trouble they had got into, such as abandonment by a mother or abuse by a husband. I found it impossible to look at the choir as it sang, because of the overpowering way in which joy shone out of these faces that were lined by past troubles.

They were people who had surely cried out about how their way had been hidden from God and how God was not making any **decisions** about what happened to them. It was as if their lives had ceased to be lived within the purview of God's area of concern. It was as if there was an area of light over there, but where they lived was darkness outside that light; it's an image one of them used. But then they had found their way into the area of light, through the people at the shelter, and had begun to imagine that they could have a future.

Given how God had abandoned the **Judahites** when commissioning the **Babylonians** to destroy their capital city and had let them take many into **exile** and then let the people mark time at best in Judah or in **Babylon** for half a century, you couldn't blame the Judahites for crying out the same way. Yet the prophet does rebuke them for doing so, or at least wants them to see that the moment has arrived to stop.

He begins by bringing out into the open four other realities they are tempted to trust in or be overwhelmed by. The first is the empire itself, "the nations." You couldn't blame the Judahites for being impressed. The empire had, after all, defeated them, destroyed their capital, and exiled many of them. So the prophet begins with an outrageous assertion of how unimpressive the empire is. But everything depends on what you compare it with. Suppose you compare it with God, the God whose power is expressed in the world that he created and whose history he controls? The implication isn't that he doesn't care about the nations and Lebanon or its forests and animals. It's that they aren't a threat to him.

To whom else could you compare **Yahweh**? What about the images of gods that the Babylonians had, which would impress the exiles as they were carried about in procession in Babylon? Compare them with that pathetic destroyed temple in Jerusalem. Excuse me, says the prophet, have you thought about how images get made? They're made by human craftworkers, overlaid with gold and provided with silver chains so no one can steal them. It's embarrassing if someone steals your god. They start off as a piece of sissoo wood, a hard wood that's valuable enough for using to pay tribute to the king, wood that doesn't rot. It's embarrassing if your god rots. Their work complete, the craftworkers set up the image carefully to make sure it doesn't fall over. It's embarrassing if your god falls over.

What about the empire's rulers, the great succession of kings, and the rulers of the nations within the empire? Think again about the world Yahweh created, the prophet says. These sovereigns are no more impressive than the rest of the grasshopper-like creatures that God looks down on from the heavens. Again the prophet doesn't imply that God doesn't care about human beings. The point is that God doesn't have to be impressed by them. God can put them down in a moment if he chooses.

Fourth, what about the heavenly beings of whom the Babylonians took so much notice, the planets and stars that they saw as ruling what happens on earth. But who is in charge of them, the prophet asks. It's Israel's holy one. The planets and stars are the army of which he is the commander-in-chief. They obey his orders (for instance, in the way they bring day and night, and changes in seasons).

In light of all those considerations, it's foolish to entertain the idea that the people's destiny could have escaped God's purview and that they need to be afraid of or impressed by Babylon and its spiritual resources. Yahweh is about to act to put down the empire, restore Jerusalem, and bring the exiles home. Events you could watch unfolding on the television news were the ones in which Yahweh was involved in order to fulfill these intentions. If you know who God is and what God is going to do, so that you can look to those events that are coming, then it energizes you in the present.

ISAIAH 41:1–20

Don't Be Afraid

1 Be silent for me, foreign shores;
    peoples must renew their strength.
  They must draw near, then speak;
    together let us come forward for the making of a
      decision.
2 Who aroused someone from the east
    whom faithfulness summons to its heel?
  He gives up nations before him,
    enables him to put down kings.
  He makes them like dirt with his sword,
    like driven straw with his bow.
3 As he pursues them, he passes on in peace
    by a path on which he doesn't go straight.
4 Who acted and did it,
    summoning the generations from the beginning?

150

I am Yahweh, the first,
   and I myself am with the last.
5   Foreign shores have seen and become afraid,
      earth's ends tremble,
      they have drawn near and come.
6   One person helps his neighbor,
      and says to his brother, "Hold firm!"
7   Craftworker bids smith hold firm,
      one who flattens with a hammer [bids] one who strikes
         with a mallet.
   One who says of the joint, "It's good,"
      holds it firm with fastenings so it doesn't wobble.

8   But you as Israel are my servant,
      as Jacob you are the one that I chose.
   As the offspring of Abraham you are my friend,
9   the one of whom I took hold from earth's ends,
   summoned from its corners, and said to you,
      "You are my servant, I chose you, and did not spurn you."
10   Don't be afraid, because I am with you;
      don't be frightened, because I am your God.
   I am strengthening you, yes, helping you,
      yes, supporting you with my faithful right hand.
11   There—they will be shamed and disgraced,
      all who rage at you.
   They will become absolutely nothing, they will perish,
      the people who contend with you.
12   You will seek them and not find them,
      the people who attack you.
   They will become absolutely nothing, zero,
      the people who do battle against you.
13   Because I am Yahweh your God,
      who takes hold of your right hand,
   who says to you, "Don't be afraid,
      I myself am helping you."
14   Don't be afraid, worm Jacob,
      relics Israel.
   I am helping you (Yahweh's declaration),
      Israel's holy one is your restorer.
15   There—I am making you into a harrow,
      a new thresher fitted with points.

You will trample mountains and crush them,
>   and make hills like chaff.
16 You will winnow them and the wind will carry them,
>   the storm will scatter them.
And you yourselves will rejoice in Yahweh;
>   in Israel's holy one you will exult.

17 The lowly and needy are seeking water and there is none,
>   and their tongue is parched with thirst.
I Yahweh will answer them;
>   the God of Israel will not abandon them.
18 I will open up streams on the bare places,
>   springs in the midst of the vales.
I will make the wilderness into a pool of water,
>   dry land into water courses.
19 In the wilderness I will put cedar,
>   acacia and myrtle and oil tree.
In the steppe I will set juniper,
>   maple, and cypress, together,
20 so that people will see and acknowledge,
>   consider and understand together,
that Yahweh's hand did this,
>   Israel's holy one created it.

My wife's degree program requires her to take part this week in a day's silent retreat. Students are not allowed to bring their computers or other communication devices. Kathleen is looking forward to the event, but some of her classmates are freaking out about it. They don't think they can survive that many hours in silence without any electronic contact with the outside world. One guy is especially insistent that he has to bring his music resources and his earphones. Now if I were the student in question, I would be arguing that the Bible has no spirituality of silence. It pretty universally assumes that a relationship with God is noisy.

Isaiah 41 does assume a spirituality of silence, yet of a different kind from the one that is rightly advocated in the West where we are always surrounded by noise in a way that may not have been the case in the contexts out of which the Bible comes. When the Bible advocates silence, it's a silence before God that expresses submission to God, not a silence that amounts to listening to ourselves. In Isaiah 41 God both urges silence and urges nations to speak, but both exhortations make the same point. The silence will acknowledge that **Yahweh** is God. The exhortation to speak is ironic, because the prophecy presupposes that they will have nothing to say by way of response to the question Yahweh is asking.

The question concerns a conqueror who came from the east. Not naming him means he can be identified in two ways. He is both Abraham, whose military activity features in the story of his rescue of Lot in Genesis 14, and Cyrus, the Medo-Persian king who is rampaging through the Middle East to the north and across to Turkey before turning his attention to **Babylon** itself. Whose initiative lies behind the activity of both Abraham and Cyrus? Mine, says Yahweh. Do you have any other suggestions? Shut up then. Each of these conquerors was the agent of Yahweh's faithful purpose in the world.

The peoples of the Middle East, and even of the Mediterranean, are understandably panicking as they watch these events unfold on the television news. But what can they do? They can only think of making another image of a god to whom they can appeal. We know from the previous chapter how sensible is this ploy.

You couldn't blame the **Judahites** for reacting with the same anxiety as everyone else. But you could, because they should be able to look at things differently. You're my servant, my chosen, the offspring of the aforementioned Abraham, God reminds them. They could be forgiven for thinking God had abandoned them, but it's not so. They are, after all, God's servant. It's maybe the first time someone has described Israel as God's servant; certainly Isaiah 40–49 uses that description more often than anywhere else in Scripture. Many individuals have previously been described as God's servant–people such as Moses and David; it meant God was committed to them and had a purpose to achieve through them. It's a big privilege and security to be God's servant. It means your master is committed to you. Now that position is extended to the people as a whole. Their being God's servant means they don't have to fear what God is doing politically, as other peoples do. They don't have to fear other peoples attacking them—God will see they are protected. They may feel like a worm (speaking of them thus isn't God putting them down, but God's picking up their self-perception), but God can turn them into a more impressive earth mover that can deal with whatever mountains they have to face.

The last paragraph again picks up the way they speak of themselves; this imagery also comes from the Psalms. They are like thirsty people with nothing to drink. But God has the capacity to transform desert into flourishing, fertile land. Indeed, God intends to do so. They're going to come to life again as a people. People will see it and recognize that Yahweh is God and has done something amazing. The people are not limited to Israel, but what the prophet has to say will be amazing to Israel. The point finds expression in the twofold recurrence of the description of Yahweh as the holy one. Earlier in Isaiah, Yahweh's being Israel's holy one was worrisome—it meant Yahweh intended to chastise Israel for its waywardness. In Isaiah 40–55 that logic is turned on its head. Because Yahweh is the holy one *of Israel*, he is bound to act in a way that recognizes the demands placed upon him by that relationship.

He will do so by acting as Israel's **restorer**. This further image maybe comes here for the first time in the Bible and certainly appears much oftener in these chapters than anywhere else. A restorer is someone within your family who has resources that you don't have and who accepts an obligation to use those resources on your behalf when you get into trouble: for instance, if your harvest fails, you get into debt, and you are in danger of losing your livelihood and/or your land. This person enables you to be restored to a viable life. The story of Boaz, Naomi, and Ruth provides an example. The Old Testament then portrays God as treating Israel as a member of his family to whom he works out a commitment of that kind.

ISAIAH 41:21–42:17

Good News for People Who Are Broken and Flickering

41:21   "Bring your case forward,"
      Yahweh says.

154

"Bring near your strong points,"
    says Jacob's King.
22 They should bring them near
    and tell us what will happen.
The previous events—tell us what they were,
    so we may apply our mind and recognize their outcome.
Or inform us of the coming events,
23   tell us things that will arrive after,
    so we may acknowledge that you are gods.
Yes, do good or do evil,
    so we may bow low and see together.
24 There, you're less than nothing,
    your action is less than a sigh;
    it's an outrage that someone chooses in you.
25 I aroused one from the north and he arrived,
    from the rising of the sun one who was to call on my
        name.
He came on viceroys as if they were mire,
    as if he was a potter who treads clay.
26 Who told of it from the beginning so we might acknowl-
        edge him,
    beforehand so we might say "He was right"?
No, there was no one telling of it;
    no, there was no one informing about it;
    no, there was no one hearing your words.
27 The first for Zion (there, there they are),
    for Jerusalem, I give a bringer of news.
28 Were I to look, there was no one;
    of them, there was no consultant,
    who could respond with a word if I asked them.
29 There, they are all a bane, their acts are zero,
    their images are a breath, emptiness.

42:1 There is my servant whom I support,
    my chosen whom I myself favor.
I am putting my breath on him;
    he will issue my decision to the nations.
2 He won't cry out and he won't raise
    or make his voice heard in the streets.
3 A broken cane he won't snap,
    a flickering lamp he won't snuff.

For the sake of truthfulness he will issue the decision;
4   he won't flicker or break,
until he sets the decision in the earth,
    as foreign shores wait for his teaching.

5   The God Yahweh has said this,
        the one who created the heavens and stretched them out,
        the one who beat out the earth and its produce,
    the one who gave air to the people on it,
        breath to those who walk on it:
6   I am Yahweh, I summoned you in faithfulness,
        took hold of your hand.
    I formed you and gave you as a covenant for the people,
        a light for the nations,
7   by opening blind eyes,
        by bringing out the captive from the dungeon,
        from the prison house people who live in the dark.
8   I am Yahweh, that is my name;
        my splendor I do not give to another,
        nor my praise to images.
9   The previous events—there, they came about;
        and I am telling of new events—
        before they grow, I inform you.
10   Sing Yahweh a new song,
        his praise from the end of the earth,
    you who go down to the sea, and its throng,
        foreign shores and those who live in them.
11   The wilderness and its cities are to shout,
        the villages where Qedar lives.
    The people who live in Sela are to resound,
        to yell from the top of the mountains.
12   They are to give glory to Yahweh,
        to tell of his praise on foreign shores.

13   Yahweh goes out like a warrior,
        like a man of battle he arouses his passion.
    He shouts, yes roars,
        acts as a warrior against his enemies.
14   "I have been quiet from of old;
        I have been being still and restraining myself.

156

Like a woman giving birth I will shriek,
  I will devastate and crush together.
¹⁵ I will waste mountains and hills,
    wither all their growth.
  I will turn streams into shores,
    wither wetland.
¹⁶ I will enable blind people to go by a way they have not
      known,
    lead them on paths they have not known.
  I will make the darkness in front of them into light,
    rough places into level ground
  These are the words that I am performing for them,
    and I will not abandon them.
¹⁷ They are turning back, they are utterly shamed,
    the people who trust in an image,
  who say to an idol,
    "You are our God."

In a movie we recently watched called *Stuck between Stations*, the protagonists, a man and a woman, tell each other stories that explicate something of who they are. The man is a U.S. soldier in Afghanistan who has watched one of the men in his unit blown up trying to help another man who has been shot. Such experiences had a devastating effect on other members of his unit, but somehow (in the movie at least) he survived in one piece as a person; in a way he feels guilty that he has done so. The woman had been with a friend when they accepted a lift from two men who announced the intention to rape them. The woman knew her friend wouldn't survive this experience without its having a devastating effect and destroying her life, so she told both the men to rape her instead of her friend. She knew she would survive, and (in the movie at least) she did.

There are people who flicker and break and people who don't. The servant whom this section describes is the latter kind, someone commissioned to minister to people who are flickering and breaking but someone who won't be overwhelmed by their weaknesses. The fact that God has breathed on him makes all the difference.

His ministry is to tell them about a **decision** God has made. The first paragraph indicates the nature of that decision, continuing the declarations in the previous section. God is involved in freeing the world from **Babylonian** domination, and resumes the questioning from that previous section. There the question was, whose decision-making lies behind the rise of the conqueror from the east? Here the related question is, who can give a plausible explanation of this event and tell people what else is going to happen? **Yahweh** can do so because he is the one who makes these things happen. He brought both Abraham and Cyrus from the east (or from the north, the direction from which Abraham actually arrived in Canaan and from which Cyrus will arrive in Babylon). He can show how they're part of his plans for the world. Yahweh's capacity to explain events to people in Jerusalem and declare the events that are going to happen is further evidence that he is God. The Babylonian gods can't make sense of these events, partly because they can't do anything (anything good or bad).

So the decision Yahweh's servant will speak of is the plan Yahweh has been implementing by means of Abraham and Cyrus. It will be good news for peoples that are as depressed as the Israelites about the way things are in the world (not least under Babylon's authority). Now we know from the previous section that it's Israel who is Yahweh's servant. The way this prophecy speaks fits. Yahweh is giving his servant to the nations as a covenant or a light. In other words, Yahweh's servant embodies what it means to have Yahweh in covenant relationship with you, embodies what it means to have Yahweh's light (that is, Yahweh's blessing) shine in your life. That covenant and light are not designed just for Israel but for the nations; Yahweh's plan was to embody them in Israel as something also available to the nations. Thus the nations that were blind and captives would find illumination and freedom. No wonder the new song they can join in! (Passages such as 42:1–4 have been called "servant songs," but it's a misleading description, and 42:10–12 is the song here.)

So whereas that previous section focused on the master's commitment to the servant, this section focuses on the other side of the coin, the servant's commitment to the master, in announcing what Yahweh is doing. It's Israel's vocation as Yahweh's servant. But one can see this is a hopeless project. Yahweh's servant has a ministry to the blind and captives, the broken and the flickering. But Israel is itself blind and in captivity, broken and flickering, worried about Yahweh's decision-making in the world as it affects its own destiny. It's in no position to give a confident announcement about Yahweh's decision-making. It's thus significant that the prophet's description of Yahweh's servant doesn't repeat the designation of Israel as Yahweh's servant, as the one to fulfill the servant's task. It's not realistic. The section sets up a problem that the prophecy is going to have to solve.

Meanwhile, the last paragraph announces the good news for Israel. With justification Israel can lament that Yahweh has been so inactive for the past fifty years, but that time is now over. Yahweh is going to assert himself in political events and put the empire down and thus lead the blind and the people in darkness into light and freedom. It won't just be good news for Israel.

ISAIAH 42:18–43:21

What Will We Do When God's Servant Is Deaf and Blind?

42:18 Listen, you deaf people;
    you blind people, look and see!
19 Who is blind except my servant,
    as deaf as my aide that I send?
  Who is as blind as the one in a covenant of well-being,
    as blind as Yahweh's servant?
20 While seeing many things, you don't pay heed;
    while opening ears, he doesn't listen.
21 Yahweh wishes, for the sake of his faithfulness,
    that he should magnify the teaching, glorify it.
22 But that is a people plundered and spoiled,
    trapped in holes all of them,
    and they are confined in prisons.
  They have become plunder with no rescuer,
    spoil with no one saying, "Give it back!"
23 Who among you will give ear to this,
    will attend and listen for the future?

²⁴ Who gave Jacob as spoil, Israel to plunderers?—
    was it not Yahweh, against whom we had committed
        offense?
  They were not willing to walk in his ways,
    they didn't listen to his teaching.
²⁵ So he poured wrath upon it,
    his anger and warring power.
  It blazed upon it all around, but it didn't acknowledge;
    it burned it, but it doesn't take it into its thinking.

^{43:1} But now Yahweh has said this,
    your creator, Jacob, your former, Israel:
  "Don't be afraid, because I am restoring you;
    I summon you by name, you are mine.
² When you pass through water I will be with you,
    and through rivers they will not overwhelm you.
  When you go in the middle of fire you will not burn,
    and into flames, they will not consume you.
³ Because I am Yahweh your God,
    Israel's holy one, your deliverer.
  I gave Egypt as your ransom,
    Sudan and Seba in place of you.
⁴ Because you were valuable in my eyes;
    you were honorable and I myself loved you,
  so that I would give people in place of you,
    nations in place of your life.
⁵ Don't be afraid,
    because I will be with you.
  From the east I will bring your offspring,
    from the west I will gather you.
⁶ I will say to the north, 'Give,'
    and to the south, 'Don't restrain.
  Bring my sons from far away,
    my daughters from the end of the earth,
⁷ everyone called in my name and for my honor,
    whom I created, formed, yes made.'"

⁸ Bring out the people that is blind though it has eyes,
    those who are deaf though they have ears.
⁹ All the nations must assemble together,
    the peoples must gather.

Who among them could tell of this,
    inform us of the earlier events?
They must provide their witnesses so that they may prove
      right,
    so that people may listen and say, "It's true."
10 You are my witnesses (Yahweh's declaration),
    and my servant whom I chose,
so that you may acknowledge and believe in me,
    and understand that I am the one.
Before me no god was formed,
    and after me there will be none.
11 I myself, I am Yahweh,
    and apart from me there is no deliverer.
12 I am the one who announced and delivered;
    I informed, and there was no stranger among you.
You are my witnesses (Yahweh's declaration);
    I am God.
13 Yes, from this day I am the one,
    and there is no one rescues from my hand;
    I act, and who can reverse it?

14 Yahweh has said this,
    your restorer, Israel's holy one.
  "For your sake I am sending to Babylon,
    and I will bring down all of them as fugitives,
    the Kaldeans into their boats with a shout.
15 I am Yahweh, your holy one,
    Israel's creator, your King."
16 Yahweh has said this,
    the one who made a way in the sea,
    a path in powerful waters,
17 who brought out chariot and horse,
    army and powerful one, altogether.
(they lie down, they don't get up;
    they were extinguished, they went out like a wick):
18 "Don't be mindful of the earlier events,
    don't think about previous events.
19 Here am I, doing something new;
    now it is to grow—do you not acknowledge it?
Yes, I will make a way in the wilderness,
    streams in the desert.

> ²⁰ The wild animals will honor me,
>   jackals and ostriches,
>   because I am giving water in the wilderness,
>   streams in the desert,
>   to give drink to my people, my chosen,
> ²¹   the people that I formed for myself;
>   they will declare my praise."

One of our bishops came to visit our church last Sunday. She recently moved to California from Maryland, and I asked her whether she missed the East Coast. Basically, she said, she was too busy enjoying the new things here, but there were a few things she missed, such as red crabs. It reminded me of my feelings on first visiting England after some years and being entranced by green meadows and villages snuggling in dales with their spired churches pointing heavenward. Coming to the United States meant giving up England and giving up proximity to my mother and my newly married sons, not to say easy access to Indian food, British candies, British tea, and Cornish Cream. To gain one thing, you give up other things.

"I gave up Egypt for you," God says to Israel, "along with Sudan and Seba, because you were valuable to me." It's as if the exodus involved God in a choice: either Egypt along with its neighbors or Israel. It's the language of love and commitment. Isaiah 19 has made clear that God cares about Egypt and intends it to come to worship him; his reminder about his love for Israel at the exodus is designed to encourage Israel when it has understandable reason for wondering whether it really is the object of God's love. It's reminiscent of the way we may tell another person that he or she has "all our love" when we also have other love commitments. As God once made a priority of bringing Israel out of Egypt into Canaan, so God is making a priority in the present of bringing back to Canaan the Israelites now scattered around the Middle Eastern and Eastern Mediterranean world. It's as if they have gone through fire and water, and God doesn't promise that fire and water won't threaten them again (on the journey home or afterwards), but does promise they won't be consumed by the fire or overwhelmed by the water. Fire and water have been images for

God's judgment in earlier chapters, which adds an extra level of reassurance to the promise, though also an implicit element of threat. Calamity may come again, but God will never let his people be consumed or overwhelmed. Both elements of this prospect have been realities in the Jewish people's subsequent history, not least in the twentieth century.

There's extra significance in this promise in light of what precedes it in the opening paragraph about blindness and deafness. The two preceding sections of Isaiah (chapters 41–42) have implicitly raised a question. Israel is God's servant; God's servant has a role to play; but what we know of Israel makes it an implausible candidate for the fulfilling of that role. The paragraph about blindness and deafness makes the question explicit. God's servant is to be the means of blind people coming to see the truth about God and deaf people coming to hear what God has to say, coming to hear God's teaching about the way current events are an expression of God's faithfulness. But God's servant is himself deaf and blind. Only ironically can he be urged to look to what God is doing in the world. He can see many things, events such as the fall of Jerusalem and the rise of Cyrus, but he can't really "see" them. He doesn't understand their significance. Once again one can hear the protests of Israel's prayers behind the prophet's words—"you have let us be plundered by the nations and taken into captivity by them." "Yes, I have," says **Yahweh**, "and still you don't understand why!"

Obviously what Yahweh will do is give this servant the sack and employ another. But the trouble with being a master like Yahweh is you can't work by the rules of the market place. Israel's not having kept its side of the master-servant relationship doesn't mean Yahweh can abandon his side—hence the reminder about Yahweh's love and commitment that go back to the exodus. Instead, Yahweh intends to bring the servant out of his prison and thus provide the nations with another embodiment of what God's power and faithfulness look like. Yahweh's servant will be in a position to give an even more spectacular testimony to that power and faithfulness. The closing paragraph thus speaks for the first time concretely about the deliverance Yahweh intends to perform. Forget about the Reed Sea deliverance and the journey through the wilderness to Canaan (what an extraordinary exhortation!). I'm doing something equivalent in the present for you!

A further result will be to give Israel itself an even more spectacular experience of Yahweh's faithfulness and power, with the capacity to bring Israel itself to a renewed acknowledgment of Yahweh. There's no guarantee that Yahweh's plan will work. Yahweh intends Cyrus to come to acknowledge him, but Cyrus will do so only in a formal way. Yahweh intends Israel to come to acknowledge him, but Israel will do so only in a partial way.

ISAIAH 43:22–44:23

There Is to Be No Forgetting

43:22 Now it's not me you have called on, Jacob,
  because you have been weary of me, Israel.
23 You have not brought me sheep as your whole offerings,
  nor honored me with your sacrifices.
 I have not made you serve me with an offering,
  nor made you weary with incense.
24 You have not gained me cane with silver,
  nor soaked me with the fat of your sacrifices.
 Actually you have made me serve with your offenses,
  wearied me with your wayward acts.
25 I, I am the one,
  who wipes away your acts of rebellion for my sake,
  and your offenses I will not keep in mind.
26 Remind me; let's decide together—
  you give an account, so you may prove to be in the right.
27 Your first ancestor—he offended,
  and your interpreters—they rebelled against me.
28 So I profane the holy officials,
  give Jacob to being "devoted," Israel to taunts.

44:1 But now listen, Jacob my servant,
  Israel whom I chose.
2 Yahweh your maker has said this,
  your former from the womb who will help you:
 Don't be afraid, my servant Jacob,
  Jeshurun whom I chose.

3   Because I will pour water on the thirsty,
        streams on the dry ground.
    I will pour my spirit on your offspring,
        my blessing on those who issue from you.
4   They will grow like a grassy tamarisk,
        like willows by water channels.
5   One will say, "I am Yahweh's,"
        one will proclaim in Yahweh's name.
    One will write on his hand "Yahweh's,"
        take as his name "Israel."

6   Yahweh, Israel's King, has said this,
        your restorer, Yahweh Armies:
    "I am first and I am last;
        apart from me there is no God.
7   Who is like me?—he must proclaim it,
        announce and lay it out for me.
    Who has made known coming events from of old?—
        they must announce for us what will happen.
8   Don't fear or take fright,
        didn't I make it known to you in time past, and
            announce it?
    And you are my witnesses:
        is there a God apart from me?—
        but there is no crag, I do not acknowledge one.

9   People who form an image—
        all of them are emptiness,
        and the objects of their delight are no use.
    They are their witnesses—
        they don't see and they don't acknowledge,
        so that they may be shamed.
10 Who forms a god or casts an image
        so that it may be of no use?
11 There, all his associates will be shamed;
        craftworkers are but human.
    If all of them gather and stand up,
        they will be afraid, shamed, together.
12 A craftworker in metal with a cutter
        works in the fire.

He shapes it with hammers,
    works it with his strong arm.
Should he get hungry, he would have no strength;
    should he not drink water, he would be faint.
13 A craftworker in wood stretches a line,
    outlines it with a chalk.
He makes it with squares,
    outlines it with a compass.
He makes it in the image of a person,
    with the majesty of a human being, to live at home.
14 In cutting himself cedars,
    getting ilex or oak,
he secures it for himself among the trees of the forest,
    plants a pine so that the rain may make it grow,
15 so it may be fuel for someone,
    and he takes some of them and gets warm.
He both lights it and bakes bread,
    and also makes a god and bows down to it,
He makes an image and prostrates himself to it
16   while half of it he burns in the midst of the fire.
Over the half of it he eats meat,
    he makes a roast and is full.
He also gets warm and says,
    "Ah, I'm warm, I see a flame."
17 The rest of it he makes into a god, into his image,
    to which he will bow down and prostrate himself.
He will plead with it and say,
    "Rescue me, because you are my god."
18 They don't acknowledge,
    they don't understand,
because their eyes are smeared so that they don't see,
    their minds so that they don't discern.
19 He doesn't bring back to his mind,
    there's no knowledge nor understanding to say,
"Half of it I burned in the midst of the fire,
    also I baked bread on the coals.
I roasted meat and ate,
    and the rest of it I will make into an outrage.
I will bow down to a lump of wood"—
20   feeder on dirt!

166

A deluded mind has directed him,
    and he cannot rescue himself.
He cannot say,
    "Isn't it a falsehood in my hand?"

21 Be mindful of these things, Jacob,
    Israel, that you are my servant.
I formed you as a servant, you are mine;
    Israel, there is to be no forgetting.
22 I am wiping away your rebellions like a cloud,
    your offenses like thundercloud.
Return to me,
    because I am restoring you.
23 Resound, heavens, because Yahweh has acted;
    shout, depths of the earth.
Break out in sound, mountains,
    forest and every tree in it.
Because Yahweh has restored Jacob,
    and shown his majesty in Israel.

Yesterday we dropped by a bakery and coffee shop because we were early for a meeting. I was confused by there being two counters and lines, one for coffee and one for pastries, and asked one of the servers what the system was. Kathleen thought my tone was brusque (I know I can sound brusque when I don't mean to be), and she apologized to the server on my behalf. It was a reasonable action, but I didn't like it, so we got into an argument. We sorted the matter out over coffee (I never got the pastry, though), and Kathleen soon put the spat out of mind, but I have a hard time doing so. I keep going over the incident in my mind for twenty-four hours, as if it has generated something like adrenalin, and I have to wait till it has drained away.

God is keen on Israel forgetting certain things, letting go of them, and remembering other things, keeping them in mind, holding onto them. He has already urged Israel not to be mindful of previous events, which might mean the exodus, or Israel's own waywardness and the fall of Jerusalem in which it issued or the things that Cyrus has done so far. Whatever the reference, it's quite an exhortation. In the first paragraph here, he declares the intention not to keep in mind Israel's offenses, which is quite a commitment. God has more control of his memory than me. In the last paragraph he urges Israel to keep in mind its own position. Of that fact there's to be no forgetting. Yet that last expression is ambiguous. It suggests no forgetting of Israel on God's part as well as no forgetting of God on Israel's part.

Linked with God's commitment to keeping Israel in mind is God's wiping away Israel's wrongdoings like a cloud. This May morning we had cloud cover for some hours, but a few minutes ago it disappeared; the sun had melted it away. It's a feature of the May weather pattern in our area. The prophecy uses such a phenomenon as an image for the ease with which God can wipe away wrongdoing, so that his sun shines directly onto his people. It provides half of the basis for the appeal to Israel that follows. There's the fact that Israel is God's servant— it's Israel's raison d'être; and there's the fact that God wipes away wrongdoing. Both facts are the basis for the appeal, "return to me, because I am **restoring** you." The logic isn't, "Return to me and then you will be my servant and I will forgive you and restore you." It's "You're my servant and I am forgiving you and restoring you—so return to me." Israel doesn't have to worry about whether God will have it back. God is already taking it back.

The last paragraph thus repeats one aspect of the first paragraph. Initially that first paragraph reworks the theme of the earlier berating of Israel for its blindness and deafness. During the **exile** Israel didn't have to bring God costly offerings. Either people were in Babylon, where was no temple, or they were in Jerusalem, where the temple had been destroyed. Instead of serving God in that way, they've been making God serve them, making him carry their wrongdoings. They've been complaining at God's treating people such as their priests as if there was nothing sacred about them and about God's "devoting" the people themselves. It's quite a verb, the one used in the Old Testament to describe what Israel was supposed to do to the Canaanites—annihilating as a way of giving them to God. Israel didn't actually annihilate them, which may indicate they knew God didn't mean it literally; here, too, the expression isn't meant literally. Nevertheless, using it involves some chutzpah. God reminds them that they have no basis for complaining at how they've been treated. Yet in the midst of this frank exchange ("You've ill-treated us"—"Yes, and you deserved it") is the declaration about God's wiping away waywardness. In the context of this argument, even that declaration has an edge to it. "It's for my sake that I am wiping away your waywardness." It's because of who I am, and because of what I want you to be for me. **Yahweh's** action (the second paragraph then declares) will result in God's blessing and increasing Israel, and drawing Israel into acknowledging once more the God to whom it belongs.

The long paragraph about making images is the longest lampoon on images in Isaiah. At great length it simply says, "Just think about what is involved in making an image. Can't you see that it's ridiculous to be impressed by the images made by the people among whom you live? Are you really tempted to follow their example rather than committing yourself to the God who speaks and acts?"

ISAIAH 44:24–45:8

God the Creator of Evil

44:24 Yahweh, your restorer, has said this—
      your former from the womb:
   "I am Yahweh,
      maker of everything,
   who stretched out the heavens on my own,
      who spread out the earth by myself,
25   frustrates the signs of soothsayers,
      makes fools of diviners,
   turns the wise back,
      makes nonsense of their knowledge,
26   establishes his servant's word,
      fulfills his aides' plan—
   who says to Jerusalem, 'It will be inhabited,'
      and to Judah's cities, 'They will be built up,'
      and 'I will raise its wastes,'
27   who said to the deep,
      'Be wasted—I will dry up your streams,'
28   who says to Cyrus, 'My shepherd,
      he will fulfill my every wish,'

by saying of Jerusalem, 'It will be built up,'
  and to the palace, 'Be founded.'"

45:1 Yahweh has said this:
  to his anointed, to Cyrus,
"the one whom I took by the right hand,
  putting down nations before him,
  undoing the belt of kings,
opening doors before him,
  so that gates might not shut:
2   I will go before you and level walls;
  I will break up bronze doors, cut up iron bars.
3   I will give you dark treasuries
  and hidden hordes,
so you may acknowledge that I am Yahweh;
  Israel's God is the one who summons you by your name.
4   For the sake of my servant Jacob,
  Israel my chosen,
I summoned you by your name,
  I designate you though you have not acknowledged me.
5   I am Yahweh and there is no other;
  apart from me there is no God.
I gird you, though you have not acknowledged me,
6   so that people may acknowledge
  from the rise of the sun and from the setting
that there is none apart from me;
  I am Yahweh and there is no other,
7   forming light and creating dark,
  making well-being and creating evil.
I am Yahweh,
  doing all these things."

8   Rain, heavens above;
  skies are to pour down faithfulness.
Earth is to open so that deliverance may fruit,
  faithfulness is to burst out all at once;
  I Yahweh have created it.

My wife used to lead a women's Bible Study where some women
who came for a while would commonly give the existence of evil
as their reason or excuse for not believing in God and not staying.

Her comment is that the existence of evil surely makes it more important that God is real and is there to be turned to. Who created evil? Where does it come from? Was it under God's control, so that God is responsible for it? Or was it not under God's control, so that God is not really sovereign? What about the disasters that happen in the world—the wars and tsunamis and earthquakes? Is God in control of them, so is he responsible? Or does he just let them happen—in which case is he still responsible? Or do they happen against his will, so he isn't really sovereign?

God here declares himself to be the one who makes **well-being** and creates evil. He doesn't thereby provide a complete answer to those questions (the Bible never does so) but does provide a partial answer. The Hebrew word for "evil" or "bad" is ambiguous, like those English words. We can say "I did a bad thing" or "I did an evil thing," meaning I did something morally wrong. We can also say "Something bad happened to me" or "This tastes evil," and denoting something painful or unpleasant but not morally wrong. When **Yahweh** challenged the other so-called gods to "do good or do evil" (41:23) he meant "Do anything"—do something nice or something nasty, show you're capable of doing *something*. Here Yahweh affirms that he is able to act. He is alive. He is the one who can bring about well-being, blessing, good things for people. He is about to do so in freeing **Judah** and other peoples from **Babylonian** domination. He is also one who can bring about trouble, calamity, bad things for people. Letting the Babylonians conquer Jerusalem meant people died. Yahweh's act of liberation will mean calamity for Babylon; it will mean people die. Yes, Yahweh makes bad things happen and makes good things happen. Yahweh makes this affirmation in articulating the claim to be the only God. If there's more than one God, then there can be a good cop and a bad cop among the gods. In reality Yahweh is the only God, and as the one God accepts responsibility (indeed claims responsibility) for acts of judgment and of blessing. (The claim doesn't in itself solve all the questions with which we started. Yahweh isn't here talking about responsibility for disasters that don't count as acts of judgment. That's another story.)

The prophet's point isn't merely that there's only one God as opposed to there being many gods. It's that Yahweh is the one

God and that the other so-called gods don't deserve to be taken seriously as gods. The evidence is that Yahweh is one who can declare an intention and then put it into effect. It's not merely that Yahweh can *prophesy* the future, having superior knowledge. It's that Yahweh can *announce* the future, being the one who decides it. The Babylonians had their experts who would say what was going to happen; they had vast data collections on the basis of which to make their scientific predictions. But Yahweh can frustrate their predictions, because he is the one who decides what happens.

It's in that capacity that he is announcing that Cyrus will indeed take control of the Babylonian empire and then let the Judahites go home and rebuild their cities and their temple. He acted in that way at the Reed Sea and will act that way again. In this connection he can call Cyrus "my shepherd." The term was a common one in the Middle East to describe the king as the one exercising authority over and caring for his people, his "sheep" (Westerners might find it demeaning to be called sheep, but people in traditional societies wouldn't take this view). Yahweh declares that Cyrus is "my shepherd," one acting in his capacity under a higher sovereignty. More astonishingly, Yahweh describes Cyrus as his "anointed." It is the word transliterated as "Messiah." In light of what the word came to mean, it's extraordinary that Yahweh uses it to describe the pagan king. It's never used in the Old Testament to describe a coming king, only the present king (or priest). A person such as Saul or David is "my anointed." Yet in its own way, applying to a pagan king this term for Israel's king is just as extraordinary. It indicates in the strongest way that God intends to use Cyrus to fulfill his purpose for Israel. It's no obstacle that the leader of the superpower doesn't acknowledge Yahweh.

ISAIAH 45:9-25

The People Who Know What's Best

9   Hey, one who contends with his shaper,
       a pot with earthen pots!

172

Can clay say to its shaper, "What do you do,"
    or can your work say, "It has no handles"?
¹⁰ Hey, one who says to a father, "What do you beget?"
    or to a woman, "What do you give birth to?"
¹¹ Yahweh has said this—
    Israel's holy one and its shaper:
"Ask me about things to come for my children—
    you can give me commands about the work of my hands!
¹² I'm the one who made the earth
    and created humanity upon it.
I—my hands stretched out the heavens,
    I commanded their entire army.
¹³ I'm the one who aroused him in faithfulness
    and level all his ways.
He is the one who will build up my city
    and send off my exiles,
not for payment, not for inducement,"
    Yahweh Armies has said.

¹⁴ Yahweh has said this:
"Egypt's toil, Sudan's profit,
    the Ethiopians, people of stature,
will pass over to you and will be yours,
    they will follow behind you.
They will pass over in fetters and will bow low to you,
    to you they will make their plea:
'God is in you only,
    and there is no other, no God.
¹⁵ Certainly you are the God who hides,
    God of Israel who delivers.'
¹⁶ They are shamed, yes, they are humiliated, all of them at
    once,
    they have gone in humiliation, the people who craft
    forms.
¹⁷ Israel has found deliverance in Yahweh,
    everlasting deliverance.
You will not be shamed or humiliated
    to everlasting ages."

¹⁸ Because Yahweh has said this,
    the creator of the heavens, he is God,

the former of the earth and its maker—
he established it, he did not create it an emptiness,
   he formed it for inhabiting:
"I am Yahweh
   and there is no other.
¹⁹ It was not in hiddenness that I spoke,
   in a place in a dark country.
I did not say to Jacob's offspring,
   'Inquire of me in emptiness.'
I am Yahweh, speaking of faithfulness,
   announcing what is right.
²⁰ Gather, come, draw near together,
   survivors of the nations.
Those who carry their wooden images have not
      acknowledged,
   the people who plead with a god who does not deliver.
²¹ Announce, bring near,
   yes, consult together.
Who informed of this beforehand,
   announced it of old?
Was it not I, Yahweh?—
   and there was no other God apart from me,
the faithful God and deliverer;
   there is none except me.
²² Turn to me and find deliverance, all the ends of the earth,
   because I am God and there is no other.
²³ By myself I have sworn,
   faithfulness has gone out from my mouth,
   a word that will not turn back:
to me every knee will bend,
   every tongue swear.
²⁴ 'Only in Yahweh (of me it is said)
   are faithful acts and strength.'"
To him they will come and be shamed,
   all who rage at him.
²⁵ In Yahweh all Israel's offspring
   will be faithful and will exult.

I have been a student or a professor in four seminaries. One
thing that students and faculty have in common is that they
often think they know more about how to run the seminary

than its head or the board of governors. For most of this time I was either student or faculty, and therefore I knew that we were right. Why were the people in power making such stupid decisions about degree programs, appointments, finance, building plans, or other policy questions? Of course I felt different when I was the head of the seminary, but then I would say that if the seminary wasn't attracting students and faculty who thought they could run it better than me, we weren't attracting the really able people. Now I'm back in the blessed position of not being in charge, I just roll my eyes when I hear people talking as if the people running the seminary are idiots.

God is often on the receiving end of such attitudes on our part. I expect sometimes he rolls his eyes, but on this occasion he gets steamed up about it. The **Judahites** are evidently appalled at the idea of **Yahweh** designating Cyrus as his anointed, as if he were someone who could stand in David's line. If God had made a commitment to David and his line, how could God do such a thing? What about descendants of David such as Jehoiachin (who had been king but had been deposed by the **Babylonians**), or his son Shealtiel, or Shealtiel's son Zerubbabel (who did later become governor of Jerusalem)?

Who do you think you are (Yahweh asks) to tell me what to do with the pots I make, when you yourselves are just pots? Or to behave like someone confronting parents about their children ("Your baby's not very pretty, is it")? Remember something I've been emphasizing: I'm the creator of the world. I do what I like, even if it makes no sense to you. So I reaffirm that I have summoned Cyrus as my agent in fulfilling my faithful purpose for Israel.

In the middle paragraph Yahweh addresses Jerusalem and restates points he has been making. When he acts in this way, peoples like the Egyptians, Sudanese, and Ethiopians, on the edge of the Babylonian empire, will heave a sigh of relief when the empire collapses, so they will come to acknowledge Yahweh as the one who has brought them freedom and/or security. They will be only too glad to bow down to the Judahites in Jerusalem as people who belong to Yahweh and to bring their offerings to Jerusalem as Yahweh's city. They acknowledge the

175

truth about Yahweh that Israel is also challenged to acknowledge—it's almost as if the Egyptians are preaching a sermon to Jerusalem. Yahweh is one who sometimes hides—the Israelites have complained about that characteristic of Yahweh, though they have themselves to blame because Yahweh's hiding is a response to their waywardness. But Yahweh is also the God who delivers. This moment is the one when Yahweh is turning from hiding to delivering. It means shame for people who make images to worship but an end to shame for the people Yahweh delivers.

The last paragraph pushes the point further. Yahweh isn't by nature one who hides. He's been living in an open relationship with Israel over the centuries and has not hidden from them even when they were in Babylon. He's been speaking to them, telling them what he intended to do in his faithfulness to them. Further, the response of Egypt, Sudan, and Ethiopia is but one example of a response Yahweh looks for. "The survivors of the nations" are invited, or rather challenged, to acknowledge Yahweh. The reference to "the nations" and their useless images suggests the Babylonians themselves. The fact that God is bringing calamity upon them doesn't mean he has written them off. They will need to be ashamed of their trust in their images, but they will now be able to find deliverance in Yahweh, like the Egyptians and the Israelites themselves. Because every knee is destined to bow to Yahweh, the only real God, and it will not be a humiliation or a drag but a relief and joy.

The Judahite people who held onto the promises in these paragraphs knew well that they hadn't been fulfilled. It's not that they hadn't been fulfilled at all; aspects of them came true. The fact that there was much else to be fulfilled was not reason to abandon them but reason to hold onto them.

ISAIAH 46:1-13

Gods You Have to Carry and the God Who Carries You

¹ Bel has bowed down, Nebo is stooping;
        their images have become for animals, cattle.

176

The things carried by you are loaded as a burden for weary
      ones;
2   they have stooped, they have bowed down together.
They could not rescue the burden;
    they themselves have gone into captivity.
3 Listen to me, Jacob's household,
    all the remains of Israel's household,
who have been loaded from birth,
    who have been carried from the womb.
4 Even until old age I will be the one;
    even until gray-headedness I will be the one who will bear.
I am the one who made, I am the one who carries;
    I am the one who bears, and I will rescue.
5 To whom can you compare me so that I should be similar,
    or liken me so that we are comparable?
6 People who lavish gold from a purse,
    or weigh out silver by the rod,
hire a smith so that he may make it into a god
    to which they may fall down, bow low.
7 They carry it on their shoulder, bear it,
    so they can settle it in its position and it can stand;
    from its place it won't move.
And someone can cry out to it, but it doesn't answer;
    it doesn't deliver him from his trouble.

8 Keep this in mind, be strong,
    bring it back to mind, you rebels,
9 keep in mind earlier events of old,
    because I am God and there is no other.
I am God and there is none like me,
10   announcing the outcome from the beginning,
and from beforehand things that have not been done,
    saying "My plan will arise, all I wish I will do,
11 summoning from the east a shriek,
    from a far country the person in my plan.
I both spoke and will also bring it about;
    I formed and will also do it."
12 Listen to me, you strong of mind,
    you who are far away from faithfulness.
13 I have brought faithfulness near; it's not far away,
    and my deliverance won't delay.

177

> I will put deliverance in Zion,
>   my magnificence for Israel.

We had Mother's Day dinner yesterday with some Jews and some Roman Catholics and some agnostics. The agnostics thought that if you need the prop of faith in something in order to keep you going, fine, but if you can live your life without that prop, why bother with religion? My answer was that I wasn't involved with God because I needed it but because God is there; one can hardly ignore God if he is there. I was a bit offended at the idea that I need God as a prop, as if I would otherwise collapse, but I didn't say so. Maybe the Fatherless agnostics fear that if they let God prop them up, they will be disappointed as they are in their absent fathers.

Maybe the prophet would say there's nothing wrong with needing God as a kind of prop. The logic of his sarcastic prophecy is that either you stop God collapsing or God stops you collapsing, and he knows which faith is more impressive. He has a vision of **Babylon** about to fall to the **Persians**. When a city falls, its conquerors may destroy its divine images or may appropriate them and take them back to their own capital as a sign of their defeat by the conquerors' gods. In the vision the Babylonians are hastily removing the images from the city to forestall that possibility. Here is a moment of crisis in Babylon's life, a moment when it needs a deity that can stop it collapsing, but instead of its gods carrying and protecting their people, the people are having to carry and protect their gods. What's the use of a God you have to carry, instead of the God carrying you, **Yahweh** asks. I've carried you since the beginning of your life and I'll carry you until you're old, Yahweh promises, with another sarcastic dig at the process whereby the images that represent the gods come into being. These images correspond to no reality; the sad implication is that when you cry out to them in a crisis like the one coming to Babylon, you get no answer.

The second paragraph resumes the exhortation to keep in mind how Yahweh has shown he is the only real God also by declaring what was going to happen and then doing it. It was he who summoned the screaming Cyrus from the east, and it's he who will see that Cyrus completes Yahweh's work. The trouble is that the **Judahites** are strong-minded—they know what they think and it's hard to change their mind. They are thus "far away from **faithfulness**"—far away from being ready to profit from Yahweh's intention to show his faithfulness to them by what he does though Cyrus. They're in danger of never being able to recognize Yahweh's act when it happens. This act of faithfulness and deliverance is near, but they could fail to see it. Yahweh's glorious, magnificent presence is returning to **Zion**, but they could miss it.

ISAIAH 47:1–15

The Unexpected Fall of the Superpower

1   Get down, sit in the dirt, young Ms. Babylon,
    sit on the ground without a throne, Ms. Kaldea.
  Because you will not again have people call you
    sensitive and delightful.
2   Get the millstones and grind meal,
    expose your hair.
  Uncover your tresses, expose your leg,
    cross streams.
3   Your nakedness will be exposed,
    yes, your disgrace will be visible.
  I will take redress,
    no one will intervene.
4   (Our restorer: Yahweh Armies is his name,
    Israel's holy one.)
5   Sit in silence, enter into darkness,
    Ms. Kaldea.
  Because you will not again have them call you
    mistress of kingdoms.
6   I was angry with my people, I profaned my own,
    I gave them into your hand.
  You did not show compassion to them;
    upon the aged you made your yoke very heavy.
7   You said, "I will be here forever,
    mistress always."
  You did not bring these things to mind;
    you were not mindful of its outcome.

8 So now listen to this, charming one,
      who sits in confidence,
   who says to herself,
      "I and none else am still here,
   I will not sit as a widow,
      I will not know the loss of children."
9 The two of these will come to you,
      in a moment, on one day.
   The loss of children and widowhood
      in full measure will have come upon you.
   In the multiplying of your chants
      and in the great abounding of your charms,
10 you have been confident in your evildoing;
      you said, "There's no one looking at me."
   Your wisdom, your knowledge,
      it turned you.
   You said to yourself,
      "I and none else am still here."
11 But evil is going to come upon you
      whose countercharm you won't know.
   Disaster will fall upon you
      that you won't be able to expiate.
   There will come upon you suddenly
      desolation that you won't know about.
12 Do stand in your charms and in the multiplying of your chants,
      in which you have labored from your youth.
   Perhaps you will be able to succeed,
      perhaps you will terrify.
13 You're collapsing in the multiplying of your plans;
      they should indeed stand up and deliver you,
   the people who observe the heavens,
      who look at the stars,
   who make known for the months
      some of what will come upon you.
14 There, they have become like straw
      that fire burns up.
   They cannot rescue themselves
      from the power of the blaze.
   It's not a coal for warming,
      a flame for sitting before.

¹⁵ Such have they been for you,
   those with which you have labored,
   your charmers from your youth.
They have wandered, each of them his own way;
   there is no one delivering you.

I was born when the British Empire was about to fold. The tide
was turning in the Second World War as Britain and its allies
were about to defeat Nazi Germany and its allies. Yet in another
sense Nazi Germany won, because war left Britain and the
other European powers exhausted, never to recover in a way
that could hold onto imperial power in the world. The British
Empire was over. Now I live at a time that some people in the
United States see as an equivalent moment in its history as a
superpower, a moment when it's exhausted and in the midst
of being defeated, not merely by the effort involved in exercising power abroad but by collapse from within through the
commercialization of everything. Maybe that gloomy view is
wrong; we shall see.

Babylon is at the point Britain reached after the Second
World War. Hardly anyone would have realized Britain had
reached this point, and it took a prophet in Babylon to per-
ceive it about Babylon. Like any prophet, he finds it hard to get
anyone to believe him. Here, he continues trying to get people
to see that Babylon is about to fall, and that this event is good
news. As he tried to do in portraying the Babylonian gods
being taken out of the city, so he does by imagining and portraying the event actually taking place, addressing Ms. Babylon
as if she is a queen who has been deposed. A city such as Los
Angeles, New York, or London is somehow larger than the sum
total of its inhabitants, with a personality of its own. The same
was true of Jerusalem or Babylon. So the prophet can picture
Babylon as a young queen in the midst of being overthrown.

Instead of being someone with a staff to see to all the palace's
needs, she has become an ordinary woman fulfilling ordinary
tasks, no longer able to maintain the dignified dress of a queen
(nakedness doesn't imply she has no clothes at all, but that
she no longer wears the impressive garb of a woman at court).
There are two telling reasons for her losing her throne. One

is that she lacked compassion. It's a telling accusation against someone who is imagined as a woman, because the Hebrew word for compassion is related to the word for a womb. A woman instinctively has womb-like feelings. But Ms. Babylon has lacked these. She has been heartless in her treatment of her own people and of other nations (such as **Judah**). You would have expected her to care about older people, but she didn't do so. Like **Assyria** in earlier chapters of Isaiah, she has been **Yahweh's** agent in bringing calamity on Judah, but she has treated Judah far more heartlessly than Yahweh needed. God's expectation is that a superpower operates with compassion in relation to its own people and in relation to other peoples.

The other reason for her losing her throne is that she thought it would never happen. She thought she was like a god. Babylon would rule the Middle East forever. Superpowers can never imagine they will be overthrown; Babylon had vast resources to enable it to formulate policies to ensure it stayed as top dog forever. The prophet stops speaking as if the dethronement has actually taken place and moves to speaking of it as future: she is about to find that her resources will be useless when Yahweh brings about the catastrophe he intends.

ISAIAH 48:1–22

If Only . . .

1 Listen to this, Jacob's household,
      you who call yourselves by Israel's name,
   you who came out of Judah's waters,
      who swear by Yahweh's name,
   who invoke Israel's God—
      not in truthfulness, not in faithfulness—
2 because they call themselves by the holy city,
      lean on Israel's God,
      whose name is Yahweh Armies.

3 The earlier events I announced of old,
      from my mouth they came out so I could make them
         heard.

182

Suddenly I acted and they came about,
4   because of my knowing that you're hard.
Your neck is an iron sinew,
    your forehead bronze.
5   I announced them to you of old,
    before they came about I let you hear,
so you could not say, "My icon did them;
    my image, my idol commanded them."

6   You've heard—look at all of it;
    will you yourselves not announce it?
I'm letting you hear of new events right now,
    secrets that you didn't know.
7   Now they are created, not of old,
    or before today, and you have not heard of them,
so you could say, "There, I knew about them."
8   No, you haven't heard; no, you haven't known;
    no, of old your ear did not open up.
Because I knew you would be utterly treacherous;
    rebel from birth, you were called.

9   For the sake of my name I delay my anger,
    for the sake of my praise I muzzle it for you
    so that I don't cut you off.
10   There, I smelted you, and not in the silver [furnace];
    I chose you in the affliction furnace.
11   For my sake, for my sake, I act,
    because how can my splendor be profaned?—
    I will not give it to someone else.

12   Listen to me, Jacob,
    Israel whom I called.
I am the one, I am the first,
    yes, I am the last.
13   Yes, it was my hand formed earth;
    my right hand spanned the heavens.
I am going to summon them
    so that they stand together.
14   Gather, all of you, and listen—
    who among them announced these things?

One whom Yahweh loves will effect his wish on Babylon,
    and his arm [on] the Kaldeans.
¹⁵ I, I am the one who spoke,
    yes, I summoned him,
    I brought him and he will succeed in his journey.
¹⁶ Draw near to me,
    listen to this.
Not from the first did I speak in hiddenness;
    from the time it came to be, I was there.

Now Lord Yahweh
    has sent me, with his spirit.
¹⁷ Yahweh has said this, your restorer,
    Israel's holy one.
"I am Yahweh your God,
    the one who teaches you to succeed,
who directs you in the way you should go—
¹⁸   if only you had paid heed to my commands.
Your well-being would have been like a river,
    your faithfulness like the waves of the sea.
¹⁹ Your offspring would have been like the sand,
    the people who came out from you like its grains.
Your name would not be cut off,
    not be destroyed, from before me."

²⁰ Go out from Babylon,
    flee from Kaldea.
Announce with resounding voice,
    make it heard.
Send it out to the end of the earth,
    say, "Yahweh is restoring his servant Israel."
²¹ They were not thirsty
    as he made them go through wastes.
He made water flow from the crag for them,
    he split the crag and water gushed out.

²² There is no well-being
    (Yahweh has said) for faithless people.

I was talking this week to a student who told me that his wife
had left him. They had been married for five years and she had

discovered he was addicted to porn; I don't know how he had kept it secret for so long. I don't know, and he doesn't know, if this is the end of the line for their marriage or whether they may be able to find a new start as he faces up to the issues and changes and as she finds healing. At the moment it's just a situation filled with "If only you hadn't . . ." and "You shouldn't have . . ." A friend of mine says that "You shouldn't have . . ." is the most destructive expression in the English language. "You shouldn't . . ." is okay—you can do something about the yet-to-be-committed act in question. "You should . . ." is even better. "You shouldn't have . . ." is simply negative in its implications. You can't undo what you did. And there may be no way of undoing the results of what you did.

God lives with a huge "if only" in his relationship with Israel. Maybe at some level God knew whether there was going to be a change in Israel's longstanding inclination to ignore his expectations, but if so, he hasn't told the prophet, and this address to Israel resonates with an agonized poignancy and uncertainty about what stance Israel will take in the future. It's both the most agonized and the most confrontational of the addresses, and it brings a major section of the book of Isaiah to a close.

The first paragraph gives a quite straightforward and uncontroversial description of what Israel is and how it sees itself—except for that shocking, upsetting phrase "not in truthfulness, not in faithfulness," which sabotages the positive significance of the rest of the description. The second paragraph manifests a similar dynamic as it includes several further descriptions of how **Yahweh** has often told Israel beforehand about actions he intended to take, which is evidence for the fact that he is God—but here he adds a different reason for doing so, that it meant Israel could not attribute events to the other gods that Israel often worshiped. The third paragraph speaks again of how Yahweh is now revealing new things—but here with the disdainful explanation that Israel always needs to hear new things, otherwise it gets bored.

It's enough to make you wonder why Yahweh doesn't abandon Israel. The fourth paragraph notes that it's not as if Yahweh gained much from his involvement with Israel. Israel had not turned out to be valuable silver when it emerged from the furnace from which Yahweh had extracted it. The reason he doesn't abandon his people is that he would look stupid—it's the argument Moses used to keep God committed to Israel.

It's a noteworthy aspect of the relationship between Yahweh and Israel that each party feels free to speak so straight with the other. Yahweh's stance here matches Israel's stance in the Psalms. It's quite clear that there's a real relationship between these two parties. They can sure fight. It's a sign of how deep the relationship is. The paragraphs that follow reflect how the tough stance that Yahweh takes in those opening paragraphs is not all there is to his attitude to them. Having tried to whack them to their senses, Yahweh once again reverts to appeal. The appeal becomes most explicit when the prophet speaks about Yahweh's sending him with his spirit to reach out to them, speaks again of how Yahweh is the **restorer**, and comes to his "If only . . ." If only they had lived lives committed to Yahweh. Then they would have known **well-being**. Then they would have experienced Yahweh's **faithfulness** in a more unadulterated form instead of a form necessarily mixed with chastisement.

In the closing lines the prophet again speaks as if **Babylon's** fall is happening before people's eyes. They have to be ready to leave when the moment comes, to seize their opportunity, encouraged by the memory of God's looking after their ancestors when they "got out" and "fled" from another place that was not really their home. They also have to bear in mind the implications of that "if only." It's not the gloomy kind of "if only" that accompanies "you should have," the kind that indicates there's no hope. There is hope. But there does have to be a change from faithlessness to obedience if Israel is to experience the well-being it has missed.

When my sister and I pestered my mother about something, she would say, "There's no peace for the wicked." I don't think she realized she was quoting the book of Isaiah.

ISAIAH 49:1–13

The Servant's Servant

¹ Listen, foreign shores, to me;
    give heed, peoples far away.

Yahweh summoned me from the womb,
    from my mother's insides he made mention of my name.
2 He made my mouth like a sharp sword,
    in the shadow of his hand he hid me.
He made me into a burnished arrow,
    in his quiver he concealed me.
3 He said to me, "You are my servant, Israel;
    in you I will show my majesty."
4 But I myself said, "It was to no end that I toiled,
    to emptiness and purposelessness that I used up my
        strength."
Yet a decision for me is with Yahweh,
    my earnings are with my God.
5 Now Yahweh has said—
    the one who formed me from the womb as a servant for
        him,
by bringing Jacob back to him,
    so that Israel might not withdraw;
and I have found honor in Yahweh's eyes,
    and my God has become my strength—
6 he has said, "It's slight, your being a servant for me
    to raise Jacob's clans and bring back Israel's shoots.
I will make you into a light of nations,
    to be my deliverance to the end of the earth."

7 Yahweh has said this—
    Israel's restorer, its holy one—
to one despised in spirit, loathed by nations,
    to a servant of rulers.
"Kings will see and rise,
    leaders, and they will fall prostrate,
for the sake of Yahweh, who is trustworthy,
    Israel's holy one—he chose you."
8 Yahweh has said this:
    "In a time of favor I'm answering you,
    on a day of deliverance I'm helping you.
I will guard you and make you
    into a covenant for people,
by raising up the country,
    by sharing out the desolate shares,

⁹ by saying to captives, 'Go out,'
    to people in darkness, 'Appear.'
Along the roads they will pasture,
    on all the bare places will be their pasture.
¹⁰ They will not hunger and not thirst;
    khamsin and sun won't strike them down.
Because the one who has compassion on them will lead
        them,
    and guide them by springs of water.
¹¹ I will make all my mountains into a road;
    my highways will rise up.
¹² There—these will come from afar;
    there—these from the north and the west,
    and these from the country of Sinim."
¹³ Resound, heavens, and rejoice, earth;
    mountains, break into sound.
Because Yahweh is comforting his people;
    he will have compassion on his lowly ones.

A few weeks ago I had to preach at the ordination of a friend. She asked me to choose a passage as a Scripture reading from which I would preach. She laughed when I told her it would be the first of these two paragraphs, because (she commented) everyone knew that her mouth was a sharp sword; but that was not what drew me to the passage. I believe that God called her from before she was born and had been involved with her through the thirty years that had passed, including the tough times, which had been tough indeed. God had given her the sharp sword of a tongue that pastors need if they are to confront as well as comfort. God calls her to be a servant, with the protection as well as the subservience that means. God calls her to embody what it means to be the people of God. He calls her to hang on in hope when things are discouraging. God calls her not to be surprised if she ends up with a vocation that is even bigger than anything we could imagine on the day of her ordination.

So it was for the Second Isaiah. The ministry he has been exercising to people in the context of the **exile** has brought him and God to an impasse. Israel is God's servant, God's servant has a role to fulfill, but Israel seems incapable of fulfilling it; yet

God cannot simply give Israel the sack. I wonder if the prophet has been wrestling with the question of what God can possibly do now, as Paul will later wrestle with the implication of his people's refusal to recognize Jesus as Messiah. Whether the prophet has been doing so or not, he becomes aware that God does have a Plan C (Plan A was Adam and Eve, plan B was Abraham and Israel).

His description of his call before he was born reminds us of Jeremiah's (whereas the original Isaiah lived before Jeremiah, this "Second Isaiah" lived after Jeremiah); Paul will take up the language again in Galatians 1, to describe his call. As Jeremiah's call designated him a prophet in relation to the nations, so this prophet addresses foreign shores and speaks of having a ministry that involves attack, presumably on the imperial power of **Babylon**. By declaring that Babylon is about to fall, he implements God's aggressive word, which will free the **Judahites** and thus manifest **Yahweh's** power, though the Judahites have to be wary about the possibility that resisting Yahweh's message could mean the sword recoiling on them.

His call also promised him protection, which links with his being designated Yahweh's servant. There's nothing so surprising about this designation; Yahweh had designated the original Isaiah "my servant." But the previous chapters' emphasis on Israel's being Yahweh's servant gives the designation new significance. It's in light of Israel's inability to function as Yahweh's servant that the prophet hears Yahweh saying to him, "You're my servant." Yahweh elaborates the point by adding that as servant he is the Israel in whom Yahweh will show his majesty. In a context in which Israel cannot function as Israel, he is called to do so, to be Israel's stand-in.

His problem is the related fact, implicit in preceding chapters, that he is a failure as a prophet; no one takes any notice of him. Yet he has summoned up the trust in Yahweh to believe that this won't be the end of the story. Indeed, he has received a more shattering revelation. He had seen that he had a role in relation to Israel, to seek to get them to turn back to Yahweh. He has not had much success with that commission. He now senses Yahweh giving him a bigger one. He is to be a light to nations, to bring Yahweh's deliverance to the end of the earth—hence (in part) his addressing foreign shores and peoples far away. Through proclaiming what Yahweh will do in putting Babylon down and freeing the Judahites to go home, the prophet will bring light and deliverance to the nations. Part of the evidence that he was not deluding himself in giving this account of his calling is the fact that we are reading his message now and being enlightened by it. (Paul also takes up this aspect of his account of his vocation in describing his own ministry in Acts 13.)

The promise to Israel that follows in the second paragraph again confirms that God hasn't finished with his original servant—the prophet's servanthood in this connection is a temporary expedient. At the moment Israel is the servant of rulers instead of the servant of Yahweh, but Israel is still destined to be a covenant for people, an embodiment of what it means to be in covenant with Yahweh that will draw people to acknowledge Yahweh and seek that relationship for themselves. It's the restoring of the Judahite community that will demonstrate that Yahweh is the God of compassion and comfort, which is good news for members of Israel scattered all over the world.

ISAIAH 49:14–50:3

Can a Mother Forget?

49:14 But Zion says, "Yahweh has abandoned me,
    my Lord has put me out of mind."
15 Can a woman put her baby out of mind
    so as not to have compassion on the child of her womb?
Yes, these may put out of mind,
    but I—I cannot put you out of mind.
16 There—on my palms I engraved you;
    your walls are in front of me continually.
17 Your children are hurrying your destroyers,
    your devastators will go out from you.
18 Lift your eyes around and look,
    they're all gathering, they're coming to you.
As I am alive (Yahweh's declaration),
    you will indeed put on all of them like jewelry,
    bind them on like a bride.

19 Because your wastes, your devastations,
 your country that was destroyed—
because now you will be too confined for your population,
 while the people who consumed you go away.
20 The children of your bereavement
 will yet say in your ears,
"The place is too confined for me,
 move over for me so I can settle."
21 You will say to yourself,
 "Who fathered these for me?
When I was bereaved and barren,
 gone into exile and passing away—
 these, who reared them?
There, when I remained alone,
 these—where were they?"

22 My Lord Yahweh said this:
 "There, I will raise my hand to the nations,
 to the peoples I will lift up my signal.
They will bring your sons in their embrace,
 carry your daughters on their shoulder.
23 Kings will be your foster fathers,
 their queens your nursing mothers.
Face to the ground they will bow low to you,
 they will lick up the dirt under your feet.
You will acknowledge that I am Yahweh;
 those who wait for me will not be shamed."

24 Can prey be taken from a warrior
 or the captives of a faithful one escape?
25 Because Yahweh has said this:
 "Yes, the warrior's captives may be taken,
 the prey of the violent may escape.
I myself will contend with the one contending with you,
 and your children I will deliver.
26 I will feed your oppressors with their own flesh;
 they will be drunk on their own blood as on grape juice.
All flesh will acknowledge
 that I am Yahweh your deliverer,
 Jacob's strong one, your restorer."

191

^{50:1} Yahweh has said this:
> "Where's the divorce paper belonging to your mother,
>   whom I sent off?
> Or who among my creditors was it
>   to whom I sold you?
> There—you were sold for your wayward acts,
>   and for your rebellions your mother was sent off.
> ² Why did I come and there was no one there,
>   did I summon and there was no one answering?
> Has my hand become far too short for redeeming,
>   or is there no strength in me to rescue?
> There, with my blast I can dry up the sea,
>   I can make rivers into wilderness.
> Their fish will smell because there's no water;
>   they will die of thirst.
> ³ I can clothe the heavens in black,
>   make sackcloth their covering."

At a party, I overheard a mother talking to her daughter who is soon to have a baby, about how it would be to look after the baby, and about how it had been for the mother herself in relation to her daughter. The mother had gone back to work soon after her daughter's birth but had continued to feed her baby, pressing her milk at midday and keeping it until she got home. You have to do it, because the accumulation of the milk becomes a physically painful reality for the mother. She can go to work but she can never forget she has a baby. Her body won't allow her to do so. It's a pain that's not letting her forget, as Israel would be a pain to **Yahweh**.

That experience lies behind Yahweh's response to Ms. **Zion's** protest that Yahweh has forgotten her. The personified city speaks like a woman who has been abandoned by her husband, reversing the way Yahweh uses this image elsewhere in the Prophets. There Yahweh pictures Zion as an unfaithful wife. Here with a further expression of the chutzpah that featured in chapter 44, Ms. Zion speaks as if the breakdown in the relationship issued from her husband's wanton abandonment, not her unfaithfulness.

Yahweh has several things to say in reply. Initially he holds back from the snorting reply that one might expect, by drawing that analogy with a mother. As a mother, Ms. Zion herself knows what it's like to be unable to put her baby out of mind. Maybe she could imagine a woman desperate enough to do so. If there is such a person, Yahweh says, then it's not me. It's said that Mary I, the queen of England before Elizabeth I, told people that when she died, they would find Calais—which the English had lost to the French—inscribed on her heart (it was not entirely a metaphor; the heart was sometimes removed after someone died, and buried separately, and this happened to Mary). Yahweh declares that he has Jerusalem engraved on his hands. Every time he looks at them, he sees its demolished walls. No, he cannot forget Zion.

He thus invites the city to picture its inhabitants encouraging its devastators out of the city and to imagine its former inhabitants, Zion's lost children, returning in such numbers that the city won't be big enough for them and that their mother won't be able to work out where they have all come from. The very imperial powers that lorded it over her and took them off into **exile** will bring them back and become her domestic servants (the description of their physical self-lowering could seem to imply a more abject humiliation than it actually indicates— it's not so different from actions attributed to people such as Abraham, Joseph, and Ruth on various occasions). If it seems implausible to imagine the empire surrendering its captives, then Ms. Zion needs to remember who its God is. Nothing is impossible for Yahweh. Yahweh can turn them into people fighting and killing each other. The result of it all will be the recognition of the real truth about Yahweh by Ms. Zion herself and by the world as a whole that looks on in amazement at Yahweh's capacity to put down the superpower and rescue Judah.

Yahweh's final response to Ms. Zion's complaint about being abandoned is much more confrontational or is confrontational in a different way. Yahweh now speaks to the children rather than their mother, in the way a couple who are in conflict may start trying to communicate through their children. It transpires that Yahweh does so because in reality it's Zion's "children"—the city's people—whom he needs to confront. Yahweh asks about his "wife's" divorce certificate, which relates to her protests about her abandonment. He wants to draw attention to the reasons it gives for the divorce. The subsequent question about the children will likewise take up her and their protests, to which Yahweh then gives his snorting reply. She and they speak as if Yahweh did the abandoning, when he has been seeking reconciliation and getting no response. Their stance again implies they have forgotten how Yahweh acted at the exodus.

ISAIAH 50:4–51:11

On Following God's Prompting

50:4 My Lord Yahweh gave me the tongue of disciples,
 so as to know how to aid someone who is faint.
With a word he wakens, morning by morning,
 wakens my ear so as to hear like the disciples.
5 My Lord Yahweh opened my ear,
 and I did not rebel, I did not turn away.
6 I gave my back to people striking me,
 my cheeks to people pulling out my beard.
I did not hide my face
 from deep disgrace and spit.
7 My Lord Yahweh helps me;
 therefore I have not been disgraced.
Therefore I set my face like flint,
 and knew I would not be shamed.
8 The one who shows that I am faithful is near;
 who will contend with me?—let us stand up together.
Who is the person with a case against me?—
 he should come forward to me.
9 There, my Lord Yahweh will help me—
 who is the one who will show that I am faithless?
There, all of them will wear out like clothing;
 moth will consume them.
10 Who among you is in awe of Yahweh,
 listens to his servant's voice?
One who has walked in darkness
 and has no illumination
must trust in Yahweh's name
 and lean on his God.
11 There, all of you who kindle fire,
 who gird on firebrands:

walk into your fiery flame,
　　into the firebrands you have lit.
This is coming about from my hand for you;
　　you will lie down in pain.

51:1 Listen to me, you who pursue faithfulness,
　　who seek help from Yahweh.
Look to the crag from which you were hewn,
　　to the cavity, the hole, from which you were dug.
2　Look to Abraham your ancestor
　　and Sarah who was laboring with you.
Because he was one when I summoned him
　　so I might bless him and make him many.
3　Because Yahweh is comforting Zion,
　　he is comforting all its wastes.
He is making its wilderness like Eden,
　　its steppe like Yahweh's garden.
Gladness and joy will be found there,
　　thanksgiving and the sound of music.
4　Pay heed to me, my people;
　　give ear to me, my nation.
Because teaching goes out from me,
　　my decision for the light of peoples.
In a flash 5 my faithfulness is near,
　　my deliverance is going out,
　　my arm will decide for peoples.
Foreign shores will look for me,
　　they will wait for my arm.
6　Lift up your eyes to the heavens,
　　look to the earth below.
Because the heavens are shredding like smoke,
　　the earth will wear out like clothing,
　　its inhabitants will die in like manner.
But my deliverance will be forever,
　　my faithfulness will not shatter.
7　Listen to me, you who acknowledge my faithfulness,
　　a people with my teaching in its mind.
Don't be afraid of human reproach,
　　don't shatter at their taunting.
8　Because moth will consume them like clothing,
　　grub will consume them like wool.

But my faithfulness will be forever,
    my deliverance to all generations.

9 Wake up, wake up, put on strength,
    Yahweh's arm.
Wake up as in days of old,
    generations long ago.
Are you not the one who split Rahab,
    pierced the dragon?
10 Are you not the one who dried up the sea,
    the water of the great deep,
who made the depths of the sea
    a way for the restored people to pass?
11 The people redeemed by Yahweh will return,
    they will come to Zion with resounding,
    with eternal gladness on their head.
Joy and gladness will overtake them;
    sorrow and sighing will flee.

We were at a singer-songwriter venue and the singer's last song was about her mother's death two or three years ago. The song title referred to the year of her mother's birth, which was the same birth year of someone who was with us. She later told us that she had felt prompted to go and give the singer a hug afterward on her mother's behalf but had resisted the prompting—what if the act was unwelcome? It reminded me of a story someone had told us. Her college professor was sitting in an airport and felt God telling her to go and talk about Jesus to a disheveled-looking fellow passenger. She, too, resisted the prompting, but then felt a crazier prompting, that she should go and comb his hair. She did, and he burst into tears and explained he was going to see his wife in a nursing home in another city; he was so grateful to be spruced up.

The prophet knows what it's like to be prompted by God and to be tempted to resist because he fears rebuff. His fear is justified but he has followed the prompting. He has the tongue of the disciples—it's the word that designated Isaiah's disciples in chapter 8 and points to the fact that Second Isaiah is a disciple of Isaiah ben Amoz (in a later century) and also a disciple of **Yahweh**, like them. He listens and can therefore speak. His rebuff means he experiences shame, but only in the short term; he knows he will be shown to be one who belongs to the **faithful** not the faithless, who will find themselves caught up in the fire they ignite for him. But for the time being he walks in darkness, without the brightness of life experience that people who belong to God expect; he has to live in trust in God.

He goes on once more to resume the message he has been prompted to give his people. They're people who pursue faithfulness, though not in the same sense as he does. They long for some expression of God's faithfulness to them—in this sense they're seeking help from Yahweh. But they can't see the signs of it that the prophet points them to. They can't believe that Yahweh can or will reverse their fortunes. Earlier the prophet has pointed them to Yahweh's power as creator, as evidence to build up their faith, and pointed them to Yahweh's act at the Reed Sea. Here he points them to what God did with Abraham and Sarah, that hopeless childless couple. Once again he asserts that through Yahweh's **decision** about what to do with them he will bring teaching and illumination to the entire world. It will be a decision that is good news for them as well as for **Judah**. It will be the deliverance they're looking for. The world is collapsing, but Judah and other peoples can come through the other side of these events because Yahweh will be faithful to his purpose in delivering them.

With some irony the prophet goes on to describe Judah as people who acknowledge Yahweh's faithfulness, who have Yahweh's teaching inscribed on their mind. There's some sense in which it's true; they acknowledge Yahweh and they're aware of Yahweh's teaching. Yet they're also people who are scared and torn. In a sense you can't blame them. The prophet continues to seek to buttress up this faint people to whom he has been prompted to minister by continuing to remind them of Yahweh's profile as the faithful God who does deliver.

The last words have the same aim but seek to achieve it in a different way by allowing the people to overhear words addressed to Yahweh's arm. It was Yahweh's arm that had been raised at the Reed Sea to deliver the Israelites from the Egyptians (Rahab is a mythic character that appeared as a figure for Egypt in Isaiah 30, and the dragon is another term for the same power asserted against God and his people.) Here it's commissioned to lift itself up again. To underline the commission, it repeats the last verse of Isaiah 35, as if to underline the challenge and thus underline the good news it constitutes.

ISAIAH 51:12–52:12

Beautiful Feet

51:12 I, I am the one who is comforting you—
    who are you to be afraid,
  of a mortal who dies,
    of a human being who is treated like grass?
13 You have put Yahweh your maker out of mind,
    the one who stretched out the heavens and founded the
      earth.
  You are fearful constantly, all day,
    of the fury of the oppressor,
    as he is applying his mind to destroying.
  But where is the fury of the oppressor?—
14   the one stooping is hastening to be released.
  He won't die in the pit,
    he won't lack his bread.
15 I am Yahweh your God,
    one who stills the sea when its waves roar—
    Yahweh Armies is his name.
16 I have put my words in your mouth,
    and covered you with the shade of my hand,
  in planting the heavens and founding the earth,
    in saying to Zion "You are my people."

17 Wake yourself up, wake yourself up,
    get up, Jerusalem,
  you who drank from Yahweh's hand
    his fury cup.
  The chalice, the shaking cup,
    you drank, you drained.
18 There was no one guiding her,
    of all the children she bore.
  There was no one taking her by the hand,
    of all the children she brought up.

¹⁹ There were two things befalling you
  (who was to mourn for you?),
destruction and devastation, famine and sword
  (who was I to comfort you?).
²⁰ Your children were overcome,
  they lay down at the entrance to all the streets
  like a snared oryx,
the people full of Yahweh's fury,
  of your God's blast.
²¹ Therefore do listen to this, lowly one,
  drunk but not with wine.
²² Your Lord Yahweh has said this,
  your God who contends for his people:
"There, I'm taking from your hand
  the shaking cup,
my chalice, the fury cup,
  which you will not ever drink again.
²³ I will put it into the hand of your tormentors,
  the people who said to your neck,
  'Bow down, and we will pass over,'
and you made your back like the earth,
  like the street for them to pass over."

⁵²:¹ Wake up, wake up,
  put on your strength, Zion!
Put on your majestic clothes,
  Jerusalem, holy city!
Because the uncircumcised or taboo person
  will never again come into you.
² Shake yourself from the dirt,
  get up, sit down, Jerusalem!
They are loosening the bonds from on your neck,
  captive Ms. Zion.
³ Because Yahweh has said this:
  "For nothing you were sold;
without silver you will be restored,"
⁴   because my Lord Yahweh has said this:
"My people went down to Egypt at the beginning
  to sojourn there,
  but Assyria oppressed them to no purpose.

⁵ Now what was there for me here (Yahweh's declaration),
   that my people were taken for nothing?
Its rulers boast (Yahweh's declaration),
   and constantly, all day, my name stands reviled.
⁶ Therefore my people will acknowledge my name,
   therefore on that day [they will acknowledge]
   that I'm the one who speaks—here I am."

⁷ How lovely on the mountains are the feet of one who brings
      news,
   one who announces "All is well,"
one who brings good news, who announces deliverance,
   who says to Zion, "Your God has begun to reign!"
⁸ A voice!—lookouts are lifting voice,
   together they resound!
Because with both eyes
   they see Yahweh returning to Zion.
⁹ Break out, resound together,
   wastes of Jerusalem.
Because Yahweh is comforting his people,
   he is restoring Jerusalem.
¹⁰ Yahweh is baring his holy arm
   before the nations' eyes.
All the ends of the earth
   will see our God's deliverance.

¹¹ Depart, depart, get out from there,
   don't touch what is taboo.
Get out from its midst, purify yourselves,
   you who carry Yahweh's things.
¹² Because you won't get out in haste,
   you won't go in flight.
Because Yahweh is going before you,
   and Israel's God is bringing up your rear.

My feet went all nasty a few years ago in Jerusalem. Visiting Jerusalem was the only occasion when I got to wear sandals continually for two weeks, and the skin on my heels frayed. One result was that it became impossible to keep them clean. They looked horrible. I was ashamed of them. After that summer, the fraying and the nastiness never really went away. Yet their nastiness was nothing compared with the regular nastiness of people's feet when cities lacked sewers, donkeys or horses rode through them, and streets ran with filth and you couldn't avoid your feet getting filthy. Imagine what it was like to have people come into your home off the street. Imagine what it was like to wash someone's feet.

The declaration that a messenger's feet are beautiful is therefore implausible. Yet they're beautiful because of the message they bring. Today was the day of a marathon in our city (we left home in the car, waited in vain for fifteen minutes at one of the places that was supposed to be a crossing point, then went back home to get our bikes for the ride to church). Marathons commemorate the legendary run of a messenger called Pheidippides from Marathon to Athens to tell the Athenians that their army had defeated the **Persians**. There's no doubt that he had feet that were beautiful as well as dirty. The prophet imagines such a messenger arriving in Jerusalem. Ironically, he would be announcing a Persian army's victory over the **Babylonians**. It would mean that Jerusalem was free from Babylonian rule and **Judahites** in Babylon would be free to come home.

It would mean **Yahweh** was reigning. There's some sense in which God reigns all the time. Nothing happens that God doesn't allow to happen. Yet God's control of the world often looks like the governor's control of a prison during a riot. There's a limit to what the prisoners can do, but the governor's will isn't exactly being implemented there. Yet from time to time God makes something happen that really fulfils his will. Jesus' coming was the greatest such occasion, when he declared that God's reign had come, though one look at our world shows that this reigning was only partial. God's putting Babylon down was an earlier such occasion. It was the occasion when Yahweh returned to the Jerusalem that he had walked out on fifty years previously. The prophet imagines Jerusalem's lookouts watching Yahweh nearing the city and telling its people what they can see.

Yahweh won't return alone; he will bring the Judahites from Babylon with him. The prophet thus also imagines telling these Judahites to get going when the moment of freedom arrives. They must avoid contact with things that would bring uncleanness back to Jerusalem with them. The great objects of uncleanness were the Babylonian images that attracted Judahites there.

201

The Judahites couldn't stroll into Yahweh's presence when the taint of their worship of Babylonian gods infected them. They need to purify themselves, especially as they're going to take back with them the articles that the Babylonians had appropriated from the Jerusalem temple as trophies when they return to rebuild the temple. It will be appropriate for them to waste no time about leaving, but in another sense they needn't hurry. There will be no need for panicked flight, as if they may get recaptured. They will be going with Yahweh. He will go ahead and he will bring up the rear.

This exhortation addressed to the Judahites in Babylon is also meant for the people in Jerusalem. It appeals to their imagination too. Conversely the earlier part of the section that addresses the city would also be good news for the Judahites in Babylon. The "you" that is told not to be afraid and that is accused of putting Yahweh out of mind is the city ("you" is feminine singular in Hebrew). Its people are afraid of their rulers, but in the prophet's imagination the oppressor has been defeated: his victims are about to be released.

So Jerusalem can stop lying prostrate and demoralized. It had been victim of Yahweh's wrath as well as victim of Babylonian aggression, but a statute of limitation applies to both. Yahweh has said "Enough is enough." It's time to punish the oppressor instead of the victim. There's more to it. She isn't just going to be liberated. She's going to be made beautiful again. She's going to be cleansed; before the uncleanness brought upon Judahites in Babylon because they had associated themselves with Babylonian gods, there had been uncleanness brought upon Jerusalem itself by the Babylonian feet that had trampled their way through the temple and devastated it. It won't happen again, says Yahweh, at least not in this generation's lifetime. (It will happen again in four hundred years' time, but Yahweh will rescue the city again.)

ISAIAH 52:13-53:12

The Man Who Kept His Mouth Shut

52:13 There, my servant will thrive,
    he will rise and lift up and be very high.

14 As many people were appalled at you,
  so his appearance is anointed beyond anyone,
  his look beyond that of [other] human beings.
15 So he will spatter many nations;
  at him kings will shut their mouths.
Because what had not been told them they will have seen,
  and what they had not heard they will have understood.
53:1 Who believed what we heard,
  and upon whom did Yahweh's arm appear?
2 He grew before him like a sucker
  or a root out of dry ground.
He had no look and no majesty so that we should look at him,
  no appearance so that we should want him.
3 He was despised and the most frail of human beings,
  a man of great suffering and acquainted with weakness.
As when people hide their face from someone,
  he was despised and we didn't count him.
4 Yet it was our weaknesses that he carried,
  our great suffering that he bore.
But we ourselves had counted him touched,
  struck down, by God, and afflicted.
5 But he was the one who was wounded through our
      rebellions,
  crushed through our wayward acts.
Chastisement to bring us well-being was on him,
  and by means of his being hurt there was healing for us.
6 All of us like sheep had wandered,
  each had turned to his own way.
Yahweh—he let fall on him
  the waywardness of all of us.
7 He was put down, but he was one who let himself be afflicted,
  and wouldn't open his mouth.
Like a sheep that is led to slaughter
  or like a ewe that is silent before its shearers,
  he wouldn't open his mouth.
8 By the restraint of authority he was taken;
  who would complain at his generation?
Because he was cut off from the land of the living;
  through my people's rebellion the touch came to him.
9 He was given his tomb with the faithless,
  his burial mound with the rich person,

because he had done no violence
    and no deceit with his mouth.
10 While Yahweh desired the crushing of the one he
    weakened,
    if with his whole person he lays down a reparation
    offering,
he will see offspring, he will prolong his life,
    and Yahweh's desire will succeed in his hand.
11 Out of his personal trouble, when he sees he will be sated;
    by his acknowledgment my servant will show many that
    he is indeed faithful,
    when he bears their wayward acts.
12 Therefore I will give him a share with the many;
    he will share out the powerful as spoil,
in return for the fact that he exposed his person to death
    when he let himself be numbered with the rebels,
when he was the one who carried the offense of many
    people
    and was appealing for the rebels.

I just came across a comment someone made when my first wife died five years ago. "We are forever grateful that she paid the price of her discipleship." She "stands tall" among people who have "worked for our comfort and edification . . . Her direct contribution to our ministry is, without a doubt, one of the greatest gifts we have ever received." The phrase "paid the price of her discipleship" struck me. It's the kind of phrase you might use of someone who faced persecution or volunteered for some dangerous mission. Ann didn't volunteer or do something of that kind. She was totally disabled with multiple sclerosis. For the last decade or so, she couldn't even speak. Yet somehow she exercised a ministry to people.

This vision of **Yahweh's** servant gives me a possible clue to the way she "paid the price of her discipleship." It speaks of the servant "laying down a reparation offering"; maybe the way Ann handled her disability was a kind of offering to God. Lots of details in this passage are difficult to interpret (it's one of the trickier passages in Hebrew in the Old Testament), but the big picture is clear. Someone has gone through extreme suffering. Mostly if not entirely it's suffering at the hands of other people, which makes it different from being ill, but a common feature is that the person has to face the question of what to do with the experience, how to handle it. I almost described the person as the "victim" but then I realized that one aspect of the question is whether you agree to be a victim. The servant in the vision could decline to be a victim and instead could turn his experience into a kind of offering to God, which makes him an active agent instead of a mere victim. That's the way he pays the price of his discipleship.

Specifically, he has the opportunity to turn his experience into a reparation offering. This kind of sacrifice was one you made when you needed to make amends for something you had done. The vision makes clear that the servant himself has no need to make amends for anything. He has lived a life of dedication to his Master. Yet he lives among a people who have desperate need to make amends to God. The people are there in **exile** because of the way they have turned to other gods, trusted in politics rather than God, and let people with power and resources take advantage of people without power and resources. For the most part the generation that lives in exile has continued the same pattern. They have desperate need to make amends to God, though as far as we can tell they don't yet see that point.

Suppose someone who didn't have that need were to offer his obedient life to God on behalf of the exiles to see whether God would accept his offering of his life, with its extraordinary commitment and dedication to God and to other people, as a compensation for their lives that lacked such commitment. In one sense it's an implausible idea: How could one person's offering make up for many people's failure? Yet literal Old Testament sacrifices didn't work on that logical basis—there was no correlation between the sacrifice's size and its effectiveness. So maybe it could work and be the means whereby the servant would fulfill the commission to bring Israel back to God, of which he spoke in chapter 49. This would fit with this vision's associating God with the servant's experience: God lets everyone's waywardness fall on him; God desires his crushing.

It's Israel that is the "we" who speak in the main part of the vision. They took his being ignored and despised as a sign of his being punished by God. You could say they took him to be a false prophet. Eventually they realized they had the picture upside down. It was because of *their* wrongdoing that he was suffering, not his. He was sharing their experience of exile when he didn't deserve it, as they did. And he was ill-treated and persecuted by them. He was being punished, but not by God. It was a chastisement he accepted as the price of seeking to bring them **well-being** and healing. What enabled them to come to see how they were wrong and to see the picture right was the way he coped with his suffering. He simply accepted it and didn't complain. That's not what people usually do. It's not even what the Psalms expect you to do. It raised the question, "Who is this man?" and eventually they saw the answer (in the vision, that is; in the real world there's no such movement yet).

The commission in Isaiah 49 spoke of being a light for the nations, and this note reappears in the vision. The vision starts from the promise that the servant who has been afflicted will be exalted. As the one God anoints, he will then be in a position to spatter nations so as to cleanse them.

This vision of what God might achieve through his servant helped the New Testament to understand what Jesus was about and to understand the church's vocation. It has helped the Jewish people to understand their own suffering.

ISAIAH 54:1–17a

A Time to Cry and a Time to Whoop

1   Resound, infertile one, you who have not given birth;
        break out into sound and whoop, you who have not
            labored!
    Because the children of the desolate are many,
        more than the married woman's children
        (Yahweh has said).
2   Enlarge your tent space;
        people must stretch your dwelling curtains, don't hold
            back.
    Lengthen your ropes, strengthen your pegs,
3   because you will spread out right and left.

Your offspring will dispossess the nations,
    they will inhabit the desolate cities.
⁴ Don't be afraid, because you will not be shamed;
    don't be humiliated, because you will not be disgraced.
Because you will put out of mind the shame of your youth,
    you will no more be mindful of the disgrace of your
        widowhood.
⁵ Because your maker will be the one who marries you;
    Yahweh Armies is his name.
Israel's holy one is your restorer;
    he calls himself "God of all the earth."
⁶ Because it's as a wife abandoned,
    and distressed in spirit, that Yahweh is calling you,
the wife of his youth when she has been spurned,
    your God has said.
⁷ For a short moment I abandoned you,
    but with great compassion I will gather you.
⁸ In a burst of anger
    I hid my face from you for a moment,
but with lasting commitment I am having compassion for you
    (your restorer, Yahweh, has said),
⁹   because this is Noah's waters to me.
In that I swore that Noah's waters
    would not pass over the earth again,
so I am swearing
    not to be angry with you or to blast you.
¹⁰ Because mountains may move away, hills shake,
    but my commitment will not move away from you,
My covenant of well-being will not shake,
    the one who has compassion for you, Yahweh, has said.

¹¹ Lowly, tossing, not comforted—
    here I am, resting your stones in antimony.
I will found you with sapphires,
¹²   make chalcedony your pinnacles,
your gates into sparkling stones,
    your entire border into delightful stones.
¹³ All your children will be Yahweh's disciples;
    great will be your children's well-being.
¹⁴ In faithfulness you will establish yourself;
    you can be far from oppression

because you will not be afraid,
　　and from ruin, because it will not come near you.
¹⁵ So: someone need be in dread
　　of nothing from me.
Who contends with you?—
　　he will fall to you.
¹⁶ So: I am the one who created the smith
　　who blows into the fire of coals,
and who brings out a tool for his work,
　　and I am the one who created the destroyer to ravage.
^{17a} Any tool formed against you will not succeed;
　　you will show to be faithless every tongue
　　that arises with you for a judgment.

We had dinner with a young couple a few months ago and were delighted to discover that they were expecting their first baby. It was not their first pregnancy; the wife had had a miscarriage last year. I remember how distressing it was when my first wife had a miscarriage, but that would have been our second baby, and I imagine it's much more anxiety-making when it's your first. Will I miscarry again? And again? No doubt the doctors assure you that there's no reason why it should be so, but you have that thought sitting in the back of your head. Yesterday we received the joyful news. Evangeline has arrived! Evangeline the bearer of good news! The origin of the name is a word equivalent to the prophet's term in chapter 40 for the one who brings news to **Zion** that its God is on his way back. As Ecclesiastes might have put it, the happy couple have been through a time to cry and they now have a time to whoop.

So it is for Ms. Jerusalem. For fifty years she has seemed like a woman who couldn't have children, whose husband has left her or died, and who faces old age alone. When the prophet speaks of the disgrace of widowhood, the implication isn't that losing your husband is shameful in itself, but in a patriarchal society losing your husband puts you in a vulnerable position, especially if you're also childless. You may have to choose between being a beggar and a prostitute. It might be hard to imagine how you could have a viable life again (the story of Naomi and Ruth would be wonderful in the eyes of a person in this position).

208

Suddenly Ms. Jerusalem's position is transformed. She has a huge family to look after her, so huge she needs a larger house. The representatives of other nations who have occupied her land are gone. Her husband is back. Yes, God admits having abandoned her; the prophet doesn't here draw attention to the fact that she can hardly complain at his action. Like a woman who can forget the pains of giving birth when she has her baby in her arms, Ms. Jerusalem will be able to forget that her husband had gone for fifty years; you could say it was indeed only a moment in the context of her lifespan as a whole. The compassion and commitment and **well-being** that she will experience again will make it possible to put the separation out of mind. The city is to be rebuilt in wondrous splendor. Its people will be transformed into **Yahweh's** disciples and it will establish itself in faithfulness; gone will be the rebelliousness against its teacher and the faithlessness of its community life, which were what had made Ms. Jerusalem's husband depart. In association with that fact, its well-being will include peace and security; the domination by a superpower that it has known over decades won't recur. Yahweh is, after all, the one who created the destroyer, and thus he is sovereign over the destroyer.

Over coming decades Yahweh will indeed return to Jerusalem, taking some of its **exiles** with him. Its people will rebuild the temple and the walls. They will commit themselves to living by the Torah in a way they didn't before. Yet the picture is all marvelously larger than life. That commitment will have its blind spots, the city will remain a backwater, it will be underpopulated, it will turn out to have replaced one superpower-domination by another, and the couple's marital problems are not over. But we should give them the chance to rejoice in the potential of this new beginning, even though we know with hindsight that they will have to go this way again and that even today Ms. Jerusalem grieves. The chapter is another typical expression of the promises of Old and New Testament that picture a reality way beyond what the people of God typically experience, inviting us to rejoice in what we do experience and to hope and pray for what we don't experience.

ISAIAH 54:17b–55:13

Our Ideas and Plans, and God's

54:17b This is the possession of Yahweh's servants,
    their faithfulness from me (Yahweh's declaration).
55:1 Hey, anyone who is thirsty,
    come for water!
Whoever has no silver, come,
    buy and eat!
Come, buy without silver,
    wine and milk without cost!
2 Why weigh out silver for what is not bread,
    and your labor for what is not filling?
Listen hard to me and eat what is good;
    you can delight your appetite with rich food.
3 Bend your ear, come to me;
    listen, so that you may come to life.
I will seal for you a covenant in perpetuity,
    the trustworthy commitments to David.
4 There, I made him a witness for peoples,
    a leader and commander for peoples.
5 There, you will call a nation that you don't acknowledge,
    and a nation that doesn't acknowledge you will run to
        you,
for the sake of Yahweh your God,
    and for Israel's holy one, because he is glorifying you.

6 Inquire of Yahweh while he is making himself available,
    call him while he is near.
7 The faithless person must abandon his way,
    the wicked person his plans.
He must turn to Yahweh so he may have compassion on
        him,
    to our God because he does much pardoning.
8 Because my plans are not your plans,
    your ways are not my ways (Yahweh's declaration).
9 Because the heavens are higher than the earth;
    so are my ways higher than your ways,
    my plans than your plans.
10 Because as the rain or snow
    falls from the heavens,

and doesn't return there
  but rather soaks the earth,
and makes it bear and produce,
  and give seed to the sower and bread to the eater,
[11] so will my word be that
  goes out from my mouth.
It will not return to me futile,
  but rather do that which I wished,
  achieve that for which I sent it.
[12] Because you will go out with joy,
  and be brought in with well-being.
The mountains and hills
  will break out before you in resounding.
All the trees in the countryside
  will clap their hands.
[13] Instead of the thorn a cypress will come up,
  instead of the briar a myrtle will come up.
It will be a memorial for Yahweh,
  a sign in perpetuity that will not be cut down.

This morning we had the last regular seminary chapel of the year, the last regular seminary chapel ever for people who were graduating. The preacher was an eighty-year-old retired professor who told us stories about his experience at that stage of his life—how he graduated from Bible College with no clue what he was going to do and drifted from one ministerial involvement to another as a result of chance meetings. It was eventually as a result of one such chance meeting he came to be a professor of preaching. I imagine many of the students who were listening were frustrated because they like to have a plan for their lives—to discern their goal and work out what steps to take to get there. The trouble is that God seems to work the first way at least as often as the second way.

God's ideas and God's plans are often different from ours. The **Judahites** will have had some idea about God's plan for them. Jeremiah, for instance, had told them that after some decades of **exile** God would be restoring them. But the chapters in Isaiah that we have been reading suggest they couldn't imagine that God was going to fulfill his purpose by means of a wild Persian conqueror. They need to submit themselves to God's ideas about how to fulfill his purpose. God is making himself available to them, is near to them, is about to act among them in restoring them and fulfilling his promises to them. They need to be looking to him, calling him—elsewhere we translate this word "summon him." They're being invited to urge **Yahweh** to come and act in the way he has announced. Instead, they're discussing whether he really should be doing the thing he intends to do. They have to give up their formulation of how they should be restored, give up their plans, and believe that the word of promise and commission that God has issued will indeed produce its fruit in their restoration as a people. They don't have to hesitate about doing so; God will be quite happy to pardon them.

The first paragraph's talk about free food and drink and food that isn't worth buying makes the same point in a different way. We know from the Psalms that their prayers will have often spoken about thirst and hunger, as they look to God for healing and deliverance and the restoration of their fortunes. Okay, then, says God, come and find it; and I will tell you its real nature. Its nature is expounded in the lines that compare and contrast them and David. Way back, God had entered into a special covenant relationship with David. It didn't mean God was more real to David than to the average Israelite; the Psalms show us how real God was to ordinary Israelites. But God did work through David in ways that didn't apply to every Israelite. It meant David had special experiences of God's trustworthiness and God's commitments. As a result of these, David was a leader and commander for the peoples over whom God gave him victory. He was thereby a witness to these peoples to the reality of the God who worked through him. Now God intends to democratize the special Davidic covenant and commitment. They will apply to the whole people. They will be God's witnesses—it's an expression these chapters have used before. They will summon other nations to acknowledge Yahweh as a result of what Yahweh does in restoring them.

The section's opening declares that this is how they will come into possession of their land again; this is how God will show his faithfulness to "his servants." Whereas previous chapters have mostly spoken of Israel and of the prophet as God's servant, from now on the book will speak only of the people in the plural as God's servants, reverting to the Bible's more common usage. The singular reminds the people that they're altogether; the plural reminds them that this position and vocation applies to all of them.

ISAIAH 56:1–8

An Ambiguous "Because"

1 Yahweh has said this:
  Guard the exercise of authority,
      act [in] faithfulness,
  because my deliverance is near to coming,
      my faithfulness to appearing.
2 The blessings of the person who does this,
      the individual who holds onto it,
  guarding the Sabbath rather than profaning it,
      and guarding his hand rather than doing any evil.
3 So the foreigner who attaches himself to Yahweh
      is not to say,
  "Yahweh will quite separate me
      from among his people."
  The eunuch is not to say,
      "Here am I, a dry tree."
4 Because Yahweh has said this,
  "To the eunuchs who guard my Sabbaths,
      and choose what I want, and hold onto my covenant—
5 I will give to them,
      within my house and within my walls,
  a memorial and name
      better than sons and daughters.
  I will give to him a name in perpetuity,
      one that will not be cut off.
6 And the foreign people
      who attach themselves to Yahweh, to minister to him
  and to give themselves to Yahweh's name,
      to be his servants,
  anyone who guards the Sabbath rather than profaning it,
      and holds onto my covenant,
7 I will bring them to my holy mountain,
      and let them celebrate in my prayer house.

213

Their burnt offerings and their sacrifices
    will be for favor on my altar.
Because my house will be called
    a prayer house for all the peoples."
8   A declaration of my Lord Yahweh,
    the one gathering the scattered people of Israel:
    "I will gather yet more toward it, to its gathered ones."

At Yad Vashem, the Holocaust memorial in Jerusalem, is a room dedicated to the million and a half children who were murdered in the Holocaust. It's a hollowed out cavern with some candles whose light is reflected on the ceiling by hundreds of mirrors so that they shine like countless stars, and the names of the children killed are read out continuously. There's nowhere more moving in Jerusalem. In Hebrew Yad Vashem means "A Memorial and a Name," more literally, "A Hand and a Name." Yad Vashem exists in order to ensure that the millions who perished in the Holocaust will always be remembered.

The expression comes from this passage in Isaiah, which promises eunuchs that they will be remembered. People who have sons and daughters have people to remember them, to think about them, to keep them in mind, to thank God for them. Eunuchs cannot have children and therefore have no one to do so. The eunuchs in mind are presumably people who have been castrated in accordance with Middle Eastern and Greek practice to make members of the king's staff incapable of sexual involvement with women at court. Isaiah 39 envisaged this fate for young men in **exile**. Being incapable of having children also meant being incapable of contributing to Israel's future and therefore being viewed as useless by themselves and by other people; but not by God.

Foreigners could likewise be viewed as having no place in Israel, by themselves and by other people; but not by God. Here the question is whether they have attached themselves to **Yahweh**, like the foreigners whose stories are told in the Old Testament—people like Jethro, Rahab, Ruth, and Uriah. The question for eunuchs and for foreigners is whether they're prepared to commit themselves to Yahweh's covenant. Here, the cutting edge of the covenant's expectations is whether they keep the Sabbath. It's not a question of whether they need a day of rest. It's whether they're prepared to recognize that Yahweh has claimed this day, so they should guard it rather than profane it. In their context, the idea of observing a Sabbath is under pressure, as it is in the West where workaholism and consumerism rule.

The concern with eunuchs, foreigners, and the Sabbath suggest a different atmosphere from Isaiah 40–55, and indications will accumulate through the closing eleven chapters of Isaiah that the prophecy is addressing a different situation. Whereas Isaiah 1–39 addressed the situation of **Judah** two centuries previously, and Isaiah 40–55 addressed the concerns of people in **Babylon** and/or in Jerusalem when Babylon was about to fall, Isaiah 56–66 addresses more concrete, ongoing concerns of life in Jerusalem in subsequent decades—the period whose story is told in the books of Ezra and Nehemiah. We know from those books that Sabbath observance and the position of foreigners were live issues in their time. Ezra and Nehemiah witness to the importance of not being too open to foreigners, as if it's fine to "marry out" whether or not your partners have "attached themselves" to Yahweh. Isaiah 56 witnesses to the importance of not being too closed to foreigners if they have so attached themselves. They're destined to join in ministry to Yahweh, to be able to pray and offer their sacrifices in the temple. Israel was never destined simply to be an ethnic community, and it's still not so destined.

The chapter's opening thus marks the transition from the work of the "Second Isaiah" to that of a "Third Isaiah." It does so by means of a neat summary of key aspects of the significance of the book's earlier parts. "Guard **decision-making**, act [in] **faithfulness**" summarizes much of Isaiah 1–39 (the First Isaiah). "My deliverance is near to coming, my faithfulness to appearing" summarizes much of the message of Isaiah 40–55 (the Second Isaiah). The last chapters will reaffirm both emphases. In Isaiah 40–55 God had promised to return to Jerusalem and take its people back, and Jerusalem has experienced something of Yahweh's deliverance, but Yahweh has not yet fulfilled the promises of Second Isaiah in a full way, and these closing chapters reaffirm them. By now, there's some evidence of people's renewed commitment to Yahweh, but the community as a whole has not taken to heart the message of First Isaiah, and the closing chapters reaffirm his challenge.

Their opening line also makes a link between these two themes, though it does so in a neatly allusive way. People must pay attention to the exercise of decision-making in a way that reflects the faithfulness of the community to one another because they're excited at the fact that Yahweh is going to fulfill his promises. People must pay attention to the exercise of decision-making in a way that reflects the faithfulness of the community to one another because otherwise they can hardly hope that Yahweh will fulfill his promises. Both implications are true.

ISAIAH 56:9–57:21

High and Holy, but Present with the Crushed and Low in Spirit

56:9 All you animals of the wild, come and eat—
    all you animals in the forest!
10 Its lookouts are blind,
    all of them; they don't know.
All of them are dumb dogs, they cannot bark;
    they're lying snoozing, loving to doze.
11 But the dogs are strong of appetite;
    they don't know being full.
And these people—they are shepherds
    that don't know how to discern.
All of them have turned to their own way,
    each to his loot, every last bit of it.
12 "Come on, I'll get wine,
    we'll swill liquor.
Tomorrow will be like this,
    exceedingly, very great!"
57:1 The faithful person has perished,
    and there was no one giving it a thought.
Committed people are gathered up,
    without anyone discerning
that it is from the presence of evil
    that the faithful person has been gathered up.

² He goes in peace (while they rest on their beds),
    the one who walks straight.

³ But you people, draw near here,
    children of a diviner.
Offspring of an adulterer and a woman who acts immorally,
⁴   in whom do you revel?
At whom do you open your mouth wide,
    put out your tongue?
Are you not rebellious children,
    the offspring of falsehood,
⁵ you who inflame yourselves among the oaks,
    under any flourishing tree,
who slaughter children in the washes,
    under the clefts in the crags?
⁶ Among the deceptions in the wash is your share;
    they are your allocation.
Yes, to them you have poured a libation,
    you have lifted up an offering:
    in view of these things, should I relent?
⁷ On a high and lofty mountain
    you have put your bed.
Yes, you have gone up there
    to offer a sacrifice.
⁸ Behind the door and the doorpost
    you have set your memorial.
Because from me you have gone away, you have gone up,
    you have opened wide your bed.
You have sealed things for yourself from them,
    you have given yourself to their bed,
    you have beheld their love.
⁹ You have appeared to the King in your oils,
    you have multiplied your perfumes.
You have sent off your envoys afar,
    you have made them go down to Sheol.
¹⁰ When you grew weary with the length of your way,
    you didn't say, "It's futile."
You found life for your strength;
    therefore you haven't weakened.
¹¹ For whom have you felt reverence and awe,
    that you lie?

You have not been mindful of me;
  you have not given thought to me.
Have I not been still, yes from of old,
  but you are not in awe of me?
[12] I myself will announce your faithfulness,
  and your acts—they will not avail you.
[13] When you cry out, your abominable gatherings can save
      you;
  but a wind will carry them all off,
  a breath will take them.
But the person who relies on me will receive the country as
      his own,
  will possess my holy mountain.

[14] Someone has said, "Build up, build up, clear a way,
  lift high the obstacles from my people's way!"
[15] Because the one who is high and lofty
  has said this,
the one who dwells forever,
  whose name is "Holy one":
"I dwell on high and holy,
  but with the crushed and low in spirit,
bringing life to the spirit of the people who are low,
  bringing life to the heart of the crushed.
[16] Because I will not contend forever,
  I will not be perpetually irate.
Because before me the spirit would faint,
  the breathing beings I made.
[17] At the waywardness of [Israel's] looting I was irate;
  I hit it, hiding—I was irate.
It lived turning to the way of its own mind;
[18]   I have seen its ways, but I will heal it.
I will lead it and return all comfort to it;
  for its mourners [19] creating as the fruit of lips well-being,
well-being for one far away and one near
  (Yahweh has said), and I will heal it.
[20] But the faithless—they are like the sea tossing,
  because it cannot be still.
Its waters toss muck and mud;
[21]   there is no well-being (my God has said) for faithless
      people."

In a recent sermon in our seminary I told students that Jesus isn't their buddy. I'm told the air went out of the room when I said it. A friend subsequently gave me a "Buddy Christ" statuette, which I could put on my dashboard or on my computer console or anywhere else where I may be tempted by sin or plagued with self-doubt. Buddy Christ has his origin in the movie *Dogma*, where he represents a church's attempt to be more user-friendly. He winks, smiles, and gives a thumbs-up. More recently I discovered the Church of Buddy Christ, a group who follow Our Lord, Savior, and Buddy Jesus Christ in the conviction that he is the Messiah, the Son of God, and our bestest mate in the entire universe. To join, all you have to acknowledge is that Jesus is your friend. If it seems a blasphemy, one needs to recall how easily Jesus is portrayed as our life coach, financial guru, fitness trainer, career counselor, sex therapist, or wellness instructor.

The sermon's text came from the last paragraph of this section of Isaiah, which describes God as high and lofty and holy. Its important statement about God also applies to Jesus. But the statement's importance lies also in what it goes on to say, that the one who dwells on high and holy also dwells with the crushed and low in spirit, bringing life to the spirit of the people who are low, to the heart of the crushed. Either part of the statement on its own is disastrously misleading (as First Isaiah or Second Isaiah on its own would be misleading—hence Third Isaiah brings them together). People who have returned to Jerusalem after the **exile** or had never left **Judah** found life tougher than they hoped. It was as if they were continuing to be objects of the divine wrath that had destroyed the city and deported many of its people. So **Yahweh** speaks in a way designed to make clear that this is not so, commissioning aides to clear the obstacles that separate the people from their destiny and assuring them that anger belongs to the past, not the present. God's lips are going to speak of well-being for this mourning people, people here in Jerusalem and still far way in **Babylon**.

They do need to be people who turn to Yahweh. In the absence of such turning, there will be no well-being for them; the warning repeats from chapter 48. It sums up the implications of the first two paragraphs in the section. The opening paragraph concerns the community's leadership, its lookouts or shepherds, who are more like dogs than shepherds—sleeping dogs, too. They're too busy indulging themselves to keep an eye open on their people's behalf. Thus the faithful and committed people, the people who walk straight, can lose their lives—perhaps to ruthless people who deprive them of their land and their livelihood—without anyone noticing or caring. The leaders who should be looking out for them are fast asleep, resting in their beds. Ironically, the prophecy adds, perhaps losing one's life, being gathered to one's ancestors, is a kind of deliverance from the events one would otherwise see and experience, the judgment that must come.

While the opening paragraph thus critiques the leaders, the middle paragraph critiques people in general. Both aspects of critique indicate that the situation in the community has changed little from the time of Isaiah ben Amoz or Jeremiah. People are continuing in the traditional religious practices of the country, which the Old Testament associates with the Canaanites but also makes clear were commonly characteristic of Israel's religious life. The immorality they describe is the people's unfaithfulness to Yahweh; they're involved in religious adultery. On the top of Mount **Zion** in the temple they were offering the proper sacrifices to Yahweh, but on other occasions they were down in the ravines below the city or taking part in observances at other elevated sanctuaries, making offerings designed to facilitate contact with dead family members to get guidance or help from them. In making these offerings, people might not see themselves as being unfaithful to Yahweh. They were not exactly making the offerings to the family members or to other gods. If they were making offerings to the king of death, they might see him as Yahweh's underling, not a rival. But even if they rationalized their practices in that way, they were engaged in religious observances that clashed with real relationships with Yahweh and real commitment to Yahweh, all the more so when the offering involved sacrificing children.

They think they can combine commitment to Yahweh with adherence to these traditional practices. Actually they have to make a choice. They will find that the entities they're turning to cannot save them. They have to turn to Yahweh to the exclusion of these practices. It would be tempting to doubt whether they can ever be in secure possession of the land again, and thus truly be a people. The promise declares that it is possible.

ISAIAH 58:1–14

(Un)spiritual Practices

¹ Call with full throat, don't hold back,
    lift your voice like the horn.
Tell my people about their rebellion,
    Jacob's household about their offenses.
² They inquire of me day by day
    and want to acknowledge my ways,
like a nation that has acted [in] faithfulness,
    and not abandoned its God's decision-making.
They ask me for faithful decisions,
    they want to draw near to God.
³ "Why have we fasted and you have not seen,
    we have humbled ourselves and you have not
        acknowledged?"
There—on your fast day you find what you want,
    but you oppress the people who toil for you.
⁴ There—you fast for contention and strife,
    and for hitting with faithless fist.
You don't fast this very day
    in such a way as to make your voice heard on high.
⁵ Will the fast that I choose be of this very kind,
    a day for a person to humble himself?
Will it be for bowing one's head like a bulrush,
    and spreading sackcloth and ash?
Is it this that you call a fast,
    a day favored by Yahweh?
⁶ Won't this be the fast I choose:
    loosing faithless chains,
untying the cords of the yoke,
    letting the oppressed go free,
    and tearing apart every yoke?
⁷ Won't it be dividing your food with the hungry person
    and bringing home the lowly, downtrodden?

221

When you see the naked, you will cover him,
    and not hide from your fellow flesh and blood?
⁸ Then your light will break out like dawn,
    and your restoration will flourish speedily.
Your faithfulness will go before you;
    Yahweh's splendor will gather you.
⁹ Then you will call and Yahweh will answer;
    you will cry for help and he will say, "Here I am."
If you do away with the yoke from your midst,
    the pointing of the finger and wicked speech,
¹⁰ and offer yourself to the hungry person,
    and fill the need of the humble person,
your light will shine in the darkness,
    your gloom will be like midday.
¹¹ Yahweh will guide you continually,
    and fill your appetite in scorched places.
He will renew your frame
    and you will be like a watered garden,
like a spring of water
    whose waters do not deceive.
¹² People of yours will build up the ruins of old;
    you will raise the foundations from past generations.
You will be called "Breach-repairer,
    restorer of paths for living on."
¹³ If you take back your foot from the Sabbath,
    doing the things you want on my holy day,
and call the Sabbath "Reveling,"
    and Yahweh's holy thing "Honorable,"
and honor it rather than acting [in] your ways,
    or finding what you want, and speaking your word,
¹⁴ then you will revel in Yahweh
    and I will let you ride over the heights of the earth.
I will let you eat the possession of Jacob your father;
    because Yahweh's mouth has spoken.

I was talking with a friend about the way Christians in our culture have got interested in "spiritual practices" such as meditation, silence, and fasting. This development is taking place in a context where Christians don't have as much sense of God as they used to have, and they're trying to encourage one another's "spiritual formation." As it happens, tomorrow will be Pentecost, and a generation ago churches had experiences of God acting not unlike Pentecost and its aftermath—people spoke in tongues, prophesied, saw people healed, and saw demons cast out. There's not so much of that experience around nowadays, and one point about spiritual practices is to fill that vacuum. It's to reach God when God isn't reaching out to us. My concern was that people are trying to manipulate God or are really just seeking personal development. My friend's suspicion was that God was more interested in the kind of spiritual practice represented by Martin Luther King Jr., taking action to ensure that people are treated more fairly in our country.

People in Jerusalem were particularly interested in the spiritual practice of fasting and were puzzled as to why it didn't work. It's obvious why to the prophet, and it fits my friend's suspicion. There was a mismatch between people's spiritual practice and the rest of their lives. Actually no one in the Bible would call fasting a spiritual practice. In the Bible, spiritual practices or following the guidance of the Spirit involves the kind of action the prophet talks about. I read yesterday that in the United States we have 5 percent of the world's population but 25 percent of its prison population. It may be a myth that there are more African American men in prison than there are in college, but the myth isn't much of an exaggeration of the facts. Losing chains that put so many people in prison might be a good spiritual practice. So might dividing our food with the hungry person instead of throwing it away and bringing home the lowly downtrodden instead of giving them our change and otherwise hiding from our fellow flesh and blood.

The word "want" recurs in the prophecy. People want to acknowledge God's ways and want to draw near to God, but on their fast day and on the Sabbath they're doing what they want. Doing what they want includes treating their workers just as toughly as they do on other days. Spiritual practices raise questions about what we really want and whether all our wants are compatible and whether we are capable of doing something regularly that we don't "want" or "feel like" doing. Someone once said that you can't be mean to people just because you are having a bad hair day. But people justify their behavior based on how they feel or how they think it might make them feel.

So the chapter offers another take on the reason why the community isn't experiencing **Yahweh's** restoration of the city. The previous section implied one reason; people were worshiping Yahweh and seeking guidance in ways incompatible with who Yahweh is, so that in effect they were having recourse to some god other than Yahweh. This chapter makes the same point on a different basis. If you're seeking Yahweh in a way that involves serious self-discipline but you're behaving in the way the prophecy describes, you're again showing that you don't understand who Yahweh is. It's as if you are fasting before some God other than Yahweh; Yahweh cares so much about **decisions** being taken in **faithful** fashion in the community.

People's reluctance to keep the Sabbath has something in common with their instinct to ill-treat their employees. The one thing that matters is to be doing okay economically. It doesn't make sense to work only six days or let one's staff work only six days. Once again the concern of the comment about the Sabbath focuses on who Yahweh is as well as on the needs of people. Yahweh has claimed the Sabbath. Observing it is a sign that one takes seriously Yahweh's claim on time. It looks like an act that will incur economic loss. The prophecy challenges people to believe that Yahweh will honor such restraint. It will even pay off economically.

ISAIAH 59:1–21

Three Ways a Prophet Speaks

1 There—Yahweh's hand has not become too short to deliver,
   his ear has not become too heavy to listen.
2 Rather, your wayward acts have become separators
   between you and your God.
   Your offenses have hidden his face
   so as not to listen to you.
3 Because your hands—they have become polluted with
      blood,
   your fingers—with waywardness.
   Your lips—they have spoken deceit,
   your tongue—it talks of wrongful action.

224

⁴ There's no one summoning in faithfulness,
  there's no one calling for the exercise of authority with
    trustworthiness.
Relying on nothingness and speaking emptiness,
  conceiving trouble and giving birth to wickedness!
⁵ They've broken open a serpent's eggs,
  they spin a spider's webs.
Someone who eats of their eggs—he will die,
  and one that is smashed—an adder breaks out.
⁶ Their webs won't become a garment,
  they won't cover themselves in the things they make.
The things they make are things made of wickedness;
  the doing of violence is in their hands.
⁷ Their feet run for evil,
  they hurry to shed innocent blood.
Their plans are wicked plans,
  destruction and smashing is on their highways.
⁸ The way of well-being they have not acknowledged,
  and there's no exercise of authority on their tracks.
They've made their paths crooked for themselves;
  no one who walks in it acknowledges well-being.

⁹ Therefore the exercise of authority is far from us,
  faithfulness doesn't reach us.
We look for light but there, darkness;
  for brightness, whereas we walk in gloom.
¹⁰ We grope like blind people along a wall,
  like people without eyes we grope.
We have fallen over at midday as if it was dusk,
  among sturdy people as if we were dead.
¹¹ We rumble like bears, all of us,
  and murmur on like doves.
We look for the exercise of authority but there is none,
  for deliverance that is far from us.
¹² Because our rebellions are many in your sight,
  and our offenses have testified against us.
Because our rebellions are with us,
  and our wayward acts—we acknowledge them.
¹³ Rebelling, being treacherous against Yahweh,
  and turning back from following our God,

speaking deceit, conceiving lies,
and talking words of falsehood inside.
[14] So the exercise of authority has turned away,
faithfulness stands far off.
Because truthfulness has fallen over in the square,
and uprightness cannot come in.
[15] Truthfulness has gone missing;
the one who turns from evil is despoiled.

Yahweh saw and it was evil in his eyes
that there was no exercise of authority.
[16] He saw that there was no one,
he was devastated that there was no one intervening.
But his arm brought deliverance for him;
his faithfulness—it sustained him.
[17] He put on faithfulness like a coat of mail,
and a deliverance helmet on his head.
He put on redress clothes as clothing,
he wrapped on passion as a coat.
[18] In accordance with deserts,
as the one on high he will pay back fury to his foes,
deserts to his enemies,
deserts to foreign shores, he will pay back.
[19] They will be in awe of Yahweh's name from the west,
and of his splendor from the sunrise.
When an adversary comes like the river,
Yahweh's wind raises a banner against him.
[20] He will come to Zion as restorer,
to the people who turn from rebellion in Jacob
(Yahweh's declaration).

[21] "And me—this is my covenant with them (Yahweh has said).
My breath that is on you, and my words that I have put in your
mouth will not be missing from your mouth and from the
mouth of your offspring and from the mouth of your offspring's
offspring (Yahweh has said) from now and in perpetuity."

It's Pentecost Sunday. I came home from church with some
mixed feelings. There were fewer people in church than usual
(it happens also to be a holiday weekend), but the day had a
sense of celebration, including red balloons flying from the

pews. People sang with enthusiasm of their commitment to pray when the Spirit said pray, and they called for the Holy Spirit to fall on them afresh. As part of our preparation for a confirmation service in three weeks, I preached on the basics of Christian faith as the Creed expresses them, led a related discussion with some adults, and had a session with the teenagers who are also preparing for confirmation. It was the preaching and the discussions that left me less enthusiastic. Did I achieve anything? Did anyone get it?

Later in the day as one of the red balloons flies above our patio I'm encouraged by the promise with which this section closes, encouraged to continue to live in hope. The prophet speaks of promises God made to him. He knows that he himself isn't what counts; it's the people of God who count. The way God relates to the prophet is part of the covenant God makes with the people. His spirit rests on the prophet, and he puts his words in the prophet's mouth, and it will continue to be so for the people's sake—not only in the person of this prophet but in the person of other prophets who will be his spiritual children and grandchildren. I'm not a prophet, but my position as a preacher overlaps a bit with the prophet's, and I may ask God to put his Spirit on me so as to give me the words for the adults and the young people—not for my sake but for theirs, because he has made a commitment to them.

The section as a whole illustrates three ways in which the prophet had to fulfill his ministry, by means of challenge, prayer, and promise. The first paragraph concludes the challenge that dominated the previous section. **Yahweh's** words again likely pick up the people's prayers—they had been asking Yahweh whether there was something wrong with his hands or ears that made him fail to act on their behalf or listen to them. No, there's nothing wrong with his body parts. The problem lay with them. The serpent and spider imagery suggests that their actions are poisonous but also useless. To judge from what follows, it's themselves as much as other people that they're poisoning. They think they're behaving in a way that will serve themselves, but they have no clue where their **well-being**, their self-interest, lies.

In the second section the prophet turns around. Instead of speaking to the people on God's behalf, he speaks to God on their behalf. By letting them overhear the way he's praying, in effect he's inviting them to join in, to say "Amen" to his prayer, but unless something dramatic has happened, the people he's been confronting are unlikely to be doing so. In leading worship, I have recently started kneeling in the midst of the congregation when we confess our sins instead of kneeling at the front; I thus make clear I'm one with them in acknowledging my need for God's forgiveness. This prophet goes one step further. He has no need to identify with his people in their sinfulness. While he is a sinner like everyone else, he's not the kind of rebel they are. But he identifies with them, like the servant in Isaiah 53. He asks God not to forgive "them" but to forgive "us." Once more he speaks of the absence of the **faithful** exercise of **authority**, only now he refers to the fact that God isn't acting in this way toward his people, not to their not acting in this way toward one another. There is a link between the two, but implicitly the prophet reminds Yahweh of the commitment to the community that he cannot get out of. He is bound to act faithfully even if his people fail to do so.

In the third section the prophet speaks of Yahweh's response. It implies that the ploy has worked. Here Yahweh, too, speaks of the faithful exercise of authority, not within the community but toward it. A few chapters previously, Cyrus the Persian was the unwitting agent of faithful exercise of authority toward the community. A few chapters earlier, a Davidic king was to be the agent. Here, there's no one so acting. The prophet has a vision of Yahweh therefore acting in person. It's as if Yahweh puts on a warrior's armor and fights the battle himself. The results of his determining to do so lie in the future; "he *will* come to **Zion** as **restorer**." But the prophet has had a dream. In a vision he has seen something happening. Yahweh is set on taking action. It's up to people in Judah to turn from rebellion in order to find themselves on the right side when he comes.

ISAIAH 60:1–22

An Invitation to Imagination and Hope

¹   Get up, be alight, because your light is coming,
      Yahweh's splendor has shone on you!

2 Because there—darkness covers the earth,
    gloom the peoples.
But on you Yahweh will shine;
    his splendor will appear over you.
3 The nations will come to your light,
    the kings to your shining brightness.
4 Raise your eyes around and look,
    all of them are gathering, they're coming to you.
Your sons will come from afar,
    your daughters will support themselves on the hip.
5 Then you will see and glow,
    your mind will be in awe and will swell.
Because the sea's multitude will turn to you,
    the wealth of the nations will come to you.
6 A mass of camels will cover you,
    dromedaries from Midian and Ephah;
    all of them will come from Sheba.
They will carry gold and frankincense,
    and bring news of Yahweh's great praise.
7 All the sheep of Qedar will gather to you,
    rams of Nebayot will minister to you.
They will go up with favor on my altar,
    and I will add majesty to my majestic house.
8 Who are these that fly like a cloud,
    and like doves to their hatches?
9 Because foreign shores will look for me,
    Tarshish ships at the first,
to bring your sons from afar,
    their silver and their gold with them,
for the name of Yahweh your God,
    for Israel's holy one, because he has made you majestic.
10 Foreigners will build your walls,
    kings will minister to you.
Because in wrath I struck you,
    but with favor I'm having compassion on you.
11 Your gates will open continuously,
    day and night they will not shut,
to bring you the nations' wealth,
    with their kings being led along.
12 Because the nation or kingdom that doesn't serve you—
    they will perish, and the nations will become a total waste.

¹³ Lebanon's splendor will come to you,
  juniper, fir, and cypress together,
to add majesty to my holy place,
  so I may honor the place for my feet.
¹⁴ They will walk to you bending down,
  the children of the people who humbled you.
They will bow low at the soles of your feet,
  all the people who despised you.
They will call you "Yahweh's city,
  the Zion of Israel's holy one."
¹⁵ Instead of being abandoned,
  repudiated with no one passing through,
I will make you an object of pride in perpetuity,
  a joy generation after generation.
¹⁶ You will suck the nations' milk,
  suck the kings' breast.
And you will acknowledge that I am Yahweh;
  Jacob's champion is your deliverer and your restorer.
¹⁷ Instead of copper I will bring gold,
  instead of iron I will bring silver,
instead of wood, copper;
  instead of stone, iron.
I will make well-being your oversight,
  faithfulness your bosses.
¹⁸ Violence will not make itself heard any more in your
    country,
  destruction and smashing in your borders.
You will call deliverance your walls,
  praise your gates.
¹⁹ The sun will no longer be light for you by day,
  and as brightness the moon will not be light for you.
Because Yahweh will be light for you in perpetuity;
  your God will be your majesty.
²⁰ Your sun will not set any more,
  your moon will not withdraw.
Because Yahweh will be light for you in perpetuity;
  your mourning days will be complete.
²¹ Your people, all of them, will be faithful ones,
  who will possess the country in perpetuity.
They will be the shoot that I plant,
  the work of my hands, to demonstrate majesty.

²² The smallest will become a clan,
   the least a strong nation.
I am Yahweh;
   I will speed it in its time.

I was exchanging messages with a Pentecostal friend yesterday, the Feast of Pentecost, and was amused when he observed that oddly "we don't really celebrate Pentecost in the Assemblies of God." I don't know whether his Pentecostal church has the things happen to which I referred in connection with Isaiah 58 (healing and so on); if they do, maybe they don't need to celebrate Pentecost as other churches need to. Churches like mine need to do so to remind ourselves of the reality of the church described in the New Testament and to gain a vision of what life was like in those churches when God was involved in it. It doesn't mean you can then make that reality happen; it's God who has to do so. But you can pray for it to happen. You can lay the fire, but God has to ignite it.

Like many of our churches, the Jerusalem community lived with an everyday experience that fell far short of God's promises. Isaiah 56–59 has focused on what the community needed to do in this situation if it was to expect God to act. The next three chapters turn to what God promises to do. Jerusalem is still in the devastated state to which the **Babylonians** had reduced it. Some descendants of its former inhabitants have returned to their ancestral city; most have not done so. The chapters lay an astonishing prospect before it. Everything seemed dark there. Indeed, the vision pictures darkness enveloping not only Jerusalem but the entire world. It then pictures the sun dawning over the city. The city can therefore climb to its feet with a bright smile on its face. One practical reason for the smile emerges from what follows. The whole dark world is naturally attracted to this bright city; one concomitant of its being drawn here is that it will bring with it the city's own sons and daughters who are dispersed around it.

The world brings not only these descendants but vast resources. The city and the people who belong there are able to believe in its significance because it's not any old city but the city that had been the paramount place of worship of **Yahweh**, the place where Yahweh made his presence known in its sanctuary. So the world comes to its light not just to see the light and not just to bring its children back but to worship Yahweh. The world's resources come here for Yahweh's sake.

Christopher Columbus quoted the whole of Isaiah 60 in connection with his voyage to the Americas and explained to the King and Queen of Spain that his aim was to bring the resources of countries across the seas for Jerusalem's restoration. He said that he wasn't really guided in his journey by intelligence, mathematics, or maps. His journey was simply the fulfillment of what Isaiah had prophesied. The chapter's imagery and hyperbole make clear that it's not giving a literal picture of political and economic events to transpire in Jerusalem in the decades that will follow or in days to come a couple millennia later. It's an invitation to imagination and hope. There's a Jewish story told in connection with the chapter. A man was out walking at dusk, and several people lit a light for him to illumine his way, but each time, the light went out. Eventually the man concluded that henceforth he would simply wait for the dawn. The parable stands for Israel, which saw Moses' light go out, and Solomon's, but from now on waits only for God's light. Yet it's also an invitation to see events in Jerusalem such as the rebuilding of the temple or the rebuilding of its walls as little embodiments of the fulfillment of God's promises.

ISAIAH 61:1–9

Blown Over and Anointed

1   My Lord Yahweh's breath is on me,
      because Yahweh has anointed me.
   He has sent me to bring news to the lowly,
      to bind up the people broken in spirit,
   to proclaim release to captives,
      the opening of eyes to prisoners,
2   to proclaim a year of Yahweh's favor,
      our God's day of redress,
   to comfort all the mourners,
3   to provide for the people who mourn Zion—

to give them majesty instead of ash,
  festive oil instead of mourning,
a praise garment
  instead of a flickering spirit.
They will be called faithful oaks,
  Yahweh's planting, to demonstrate majesty.
4   People will build up perpetual ruins,
  raise up the ancestors' desolations.
They will renew ruined cities,
  desolations from generation after generation.
5   Strangers will stand and pasture your sheep,
  foreigners will be your farmworkers and vinedressers.
6   You yourselves will be called "Yahweh's priests,"
  you will be termed "our God's ministers."
You will eat the nations' wealth
  and thrive on their splendor.
7   Instead of your shame, double;
  [instead of] disgrace, people will resound at the share
    you have.
Therefore in their country they will possess double;
  joy in perpetuity will be theirs.
8   Because I am Yahweh, one giving himself to exercising
    authority,
  who repudiates robbery in wrongdoing.
I will give them their earnings in truthfulness;
  a covenant in perpetuity I will seal for them.
9   Their offspring will gain acknowledgment among the
    nations,
  their descendants in the midst of the peoples.
All who see them will recognize them,
  that they are offspring Yahweh has blessed.

This week I'm meeting with a young man considering ordination in the Episcopal Church who wants to "seek my advice regarding my vocation." There are aspects of the Episcopal Church about which he is uneasy—how will he cope with those? Should he ask his rector to set going the process whereby his local church seeks to "discern" whether ordination is something that the Holy Spirit has put into his heart? The way he puts the question (which corresponds to the way churches put the question) presupposes that a "call" to ordained ministry is something like a prophet's call.

The accounts of the commission of prophets in the Bible don't fit very well with that assumption. This particular account starts with the sense of **Yahweh's** spirit or breath or wind being on the prophet. It's unlikely to have been a gentle experience or one hard to discern. Yahweh's breath blows you over and leaves you without options. The additional talk of being anointed makes one think of the prophet as a bit like a priest or king— anointing isn't usually linked with being a prophet. Anointing was a sign of being commissioned and given **authority**.

Both those claims, to have been bowled over by Yahweh's wind and to have been anointed, buttress the message that follows. We are again reminded that the people to whom he ministers are lowly and broken in their inner being. They're like people in prison (it's as if they're still in **exile**). They're mourning **Zion**—mourning its own broken state. Their spirit is flickering. Their city lies in ruins, as it has done for years. They live with shame at the way their devastated state reflects their downfall to **Babylon** and their abandonment by God that lay behind that disgrace.

The prophet's commission doesn't involve his doing anything. Characteristically, all a prophet does is preach. This prophet's task is to bring news, declare that their release is imminent, that God's year of favor and day of redress is here. These are two sides of a coin. God's action will mean that redress against Israel is replaced by favor and that God's using the superpower's instinct for destruction is replaced by bringing judgment on its destructiveness. It's by bringing this message that the prophet will bind up the people, bring them comfort, make it possible for them to give up the clothes of mourning and put on celebration garments. God's purpose for them will be fulfilled. Instead of being humiliated they will be able to take on their proper role as priests looking after the worship of Yahweh. Other peoples will support their work by looking after the shepherding and farming and otherwise providing for them, as within Israel the clan of Levi look after the worship and the other clans support their work. The other peoples will thus come to be astonished at God's blessing of Israel instead of being astonished at their shame.

There's nothing new about the message of this section. Its significance is that it has a prophet's authority behind it. Sometimes a prophet's account of his call precedes his account of his message—that was so in Isaiah 40 (as in the books of Jeremiah and Ezekiel). Sometimes it comes in the middle of the message, as was so in Isaiah 1–12 and is so here. You want to know whether the promises that have appeared in Isaiah 56–60 have any authority behind them, the book asks? Here's the answer.

Jesus takes up the opening lines as a description of his ministry as he comes to bring good news to the lowly Jewish community of his day, living as they were under Roman overlordship.

ISAIAH 61:10–63:6

People Who Won't Let Yahweh Rest

61:10 I will rejoice ardently in Yahweh,
    my whole being will joy in my God.
Because he is clothing me in deliverance clothes,
    wrapping me in a faithfulness coat,
like a groom who behaves priestly in majesty,
    or like a bride who adorns herself in her things.
11 Because as the earth brings out its growth
    and as a garden makes its seed grow,
so my Lord Yahweh will make faithfulness and praise grow
    before all the nations.

62:1 For the sake of Zion I will not be silent,
    for Jerusalem's sake I will not be quiet,
until its faithfulness goes out like brightness,
    its deliverance like a torch that blazes.
2 The nations will see your faithfulness,
    all the kings your splendor.
You will be called by a new name,
    which Yahweh's mouth will determine.
3 You will be a majestic crown in Yahweh's hand,
    a royal diadem in your God's palm.

4   You will no longer be termed "Abandoned,"
        your country will no longer be termed "Desolate."
   Rather, you will be called "My-Delight-Is-In-Her,"
        and your country "Married."
   Because Yahweh delights in you
        and your country will be married.
5   Because a youth marries a girl;
        your sons will marry you.
   With a groom's rejoicing over a bride,
        your God will rejoice over you.

6   Upon your walls, Jerusalem,
        I'm appointing guards.
   All day and all night
        they will never be silent.
   You who remind Yahweh,
        there's no stopping for you.
7   Don't give him stopping, until he establishes,
        until he makes Jerusalem an object of praise in the earth.
8   Yahweh has sworn by his right hand,
        by his strong arm:
   "If I give your grain again
        as food for your enemies,
   if foreigners drink your new wine,
        for which you have labored . . .
9   Because the people who harvest it will eat it,
        and praise Yahweh.
   The people who gather it will drink it
        in my sacred courtyards."

10   Pass through, pass through the gates,
        clear the people's way!
   Build up, build up the ramp,
        clear it of stones!
   Raise a banner over the peoples—
11   there, Yahweh has let it be heard to the end of the earth.
   Say to Ms. Zion,
        "There, your deliverance is coming!
   There, his reward is with him,
        his earnings before him!"

12 People will call them
   "The holy people, ones restored by Yahweh."
You will be called
   "Sought out, a city not abandoned."

63:1 Who is this coming from Edom,
      marked in clothes from Bosrah,
   this person majestic in attire,
      stooping in his mighty strength?
   "I am the one speaking in faithfulness,
      mighty to deliver."
2   Why is your attire red,
      your clothes like someone treading in a wine trough?
3   "I trod a press alone;
      from the peoples there was no one with me.
   I tread them in my anger,
      trample them in my fury.
   Their spray spatters on my clothes;
      I have stained all my attire.
4   Because a day of redress has been in my mind,
      my year of restoration has arrived.
5   But I look, and there's no helper;
      I stare, and there's no support.
   So my arm has effected deliverance for me;
      my fury—it has supported me.
6   I trample peoples in my anger, make them drunk in my
      fury,
      bring down their eminence to the earth."

I mentioned earlier the work calling that my wife's daughter
and son-in-law have been following for several years to stir up
concern for the people of Darfur who are refugees in Chad. The
effort is hard work for little effect. Over the past year my wife
and I have felt drawn to pray one of the psalms of lament and
protest for these people every dinnertime that we are home;
these psalms make much more sense when you're praying
them for people in that kind of situation than if you're trying to
make sense of them in a context where we have food to eat and
a roof over our heads.

I could describe this impulse as the sense of a challenge to be people who issue reminders to **Yahweh**, along the lines of the people this prophecy speaks of. Previous sections of Isaiah have been promising a great act of restoration by Yahweh, but it has not materialized. What do you do when that disappointment happens? The Western instinct is to work to further the kingdom of God; we might (for instance) seek to advocate for people who are poor and oppressed. These chapters of Isaiah suggest two different responses. One that has appeared in preceding chapters is that the people need to look at their own community life. The other is that they need to pray.

Presumably the "I" that speaks in this section continues to be the prophet, yet the talk of deliverance clothes and a **faithfulness** coat also makes one think of Israel itself—it's the people that will be wearing such clothes. They will dress in a fashion that indicates their rejoicing in God's faithful act of deliverance. The prophet speaks as an embodiment of the people he belongs to, one who believes the message he has been giving them and puts his clothing where his mouth is. It's a common feature of Old Testament prayer, as the Psalms illustrate, that you begin praising God for answering your prayer when you have *heard* the answer, even if you have not yet *seen* it. So the prophet begins to give praise for what God is going to do.

The Psalms also show that having heard but not yet seen is also reason for continuing to pray; indeed, having heard gives more impetus and conviction to your prayers. In the second paragraph the prophet thus declares his determination to keep praying until he and his people *see* God's faithfulness expressed in God's act of deliverance. Alongside this commitment is his commissioning of others to join him as people who issue reminders to Yahweh. Behind this idea is the image of the heavenly King's cabinet as the place where decisions are taken and of prayer as our taking part in the meeting of this cabinet and pressing it to take action. With any such body there can be delay between the making of a decision and the implementing of it. There may even be slippage. The people issuing reminders are people making sure there's no slippage. It's as if they stand on Jerusalem's walls continually pointing out the situation about which action needs to be taken.

The fourth paragraph constitutes another indirect declaration that Yahweh's promises will be fulfilled. Perhaps the prophet is addressing heavenly highway contractors, but the point of the words lies in the encouragement they offer to the people in Jerusalem itself. Their presupposition can seem surprising if we assumed that all the **Judahites** in **Babylon** had returned to Jerusalem when the Persians conquered Babylon. The Old Testament makes clear that many didn't do so; the prophecy both presupposes that the desolate city still needs its people and promises that it will receive them.

The terrifying conversation that closes the section constitutes another such promise. The visions in Isaiah 60–62 have focused on the positive side to Judah's restoration, but the rescue of the victim requires the putting down of the tyrant. It had once seemed that **Persia's** victory over Babylon would constitute that deliverance, but history tells the story of how yesterday's deliverer is today's despot. One implication of the vision is that the people's situation is now worse than it was a few years previously. Then, Cyrus was on the horizon; now, there's no deliverer within sight. Yet the vision doesn't refer to Cyrus or Persia, and even Edom looks like not the victim of Yahweh's act of redress but simply the direction from which Yahweh comes to Jerusalem—as happens in other Old Testament passages. By not referring to a particular tyrant and not envisaging a particular deliverer, the vision points to a recognition of that fact that history is the story of a sequence of tyrannical superpowers that will need to be brought to an end by Yahweh's own action—which the vision promises.

ISAIAH 63:7–64:12

On Grieving God's Holy Spirit, and the Consequences

63:7 I will recount Yahweh's acts of commitment,
   Yahweh's praises,
in accordance with all that Yahweh bestowed on us,
   the great goodness to Israel's household,

that which he bestowed on them in accordance with his
    compassion
and the greatness of his acts of commitment.
8 He said, "Yes, they are my people,
    children who will not be false."
He became their deliverer;
9   in all their trouble it became troublesome to him.
His personal aide—
    he delivered them, in his love and pity.
He was the one who restored them, lifted them up,
    and carried them all the days of old.
10 But they—they rebelled
    and hurt his holy spirit.
So he turned into their enemy;
    he himself made war against them.
11 But he was mindful of the days of long ago,
    of Moses, of his people.

Where is the one who brought them up from the sea,
    the shepherds of his flock?
Where is the one who put in its midst
    his holy spirit,
12 the one who made his majestic arm go
    at Moses' right hand,
dividing the waters in front of them
    to make himself a name in perpetuity,
13 enabling them to go through the depths like a horse in the
    wilderness,
    so they would not collapse,
14 like a beast in the vale that goes down,
    so that Yahweh's spirit would give them rest?
In that way you drove your people,
    to make a majestic name for yourself.
15 Look from the heavens,
    see from your holy and majestic height!
Where are your passion and your acts of power,
    the roar from inside you and your compassion?
In relation to me they have withheld themselves,
16   when you are our Father.
When Abraham wouldn't acknowledge us,
    Israel wouldn't recognize us,

240

you Yahweh are our Father;
   "Our restorer from forever" is your name.
17 Why do you let us wander from your ways, Yahweh,
      let our mind be hard so as not to be in awe of you?
   Turn for the sake of your servants,
      the clans that are your very own.
18 As something small they dispossessed your holy people;
      our foes trampled your sanctuary.
19 Forever we have become people over whom you have not
      ruled,
      who have not been called by your name.

64:1 Oh that you had torn apart the heavens and come down,
      that mountains had quaked before you,
2 like fire lighting brushwood,
      so that the fire boils water,
   to cause your name to be acknowledged by your adversaries,
      so that the nations might tremble before you!
3 When you did wonders that we did not look for,
      you came down and mountains quaked before you.
4 Never had people heard or given ear,
      eye had not seen,
   a God apart from you,
      who acts for one who waits for him.
5 You met with the one who was rejoicing and doing what
      was faithful,
      the people who were mindful of you in your ways.
   Now: you yourself got angry,
      and of old we offended in relation to them, but we were
      delivered.
6 We became like something taboo, all of us,
      and all our faithful deeds like menstrual clothing.
   We withered like leaves, all of us,
      and our wayward acts carry us off like the wind.
7 There's no one calling on your name,
      stirring himself to take hold of you.
   Because you've hidden your face from us,
      and made us fade away at the hand of our wayward acts.

8 But now, Yahweh, you are our Father;
      we are the clay, you are our potter—

241

> the work of your hand, all of us.
> ⁹ Don't be so very angry, Yahweh,
>   don't be mindful of waywardness.
> Now: do look at your people, all of us;
> ¹⁰   your holy cities became a wilderness.
> Zion became a wilderness,
>   Jerusalem a devastation.
> ¹¹ Our holy and majestic house,
>   where our ancestors praised you,
> became something consumed by fire,
>   and all that we valued became a ruin.
> ¹² At these things do you restrain yourself, Yahweh,
>   do you remain still and let us be humbled so much?

The Episcopal Daily Devotions that we use each morning include prayers from Psalm 51 asking God to renew a right spirit within us, to sustain us with his bountiful spirit, and not to take his holy spirit from us. Using that prayer implies that God might take away his spirit, though someone recently observed to me how encouraging it is that God wouldn't take the Holy Spirit away from us as he did from Saul, and as Psalm 51 presupposes he might. I reflect on the question all the more during this Pentecost season. The New Testament indeed doesn't refer to the possibility of God taking his Holy Spirit from us, but neither does it say he couldn't; and if he has done so, it would explain some facts about the church. What the New Testament does say is that it's possible to lie, to test, resist, and grieve the Holy Spirit, and it wouldn't be surprising if some of those actions led to God withdrawing his Holy Spirit.

The idea of grieving or hurting God's Holy Spirit (Ephesians 4) comes from this prayer in Isaiah. It's a passage that makes clear that God's spirit was indeed active in Israel. There, as in the church's life, one can see moments when God's spirit is especially active and times when it's dormant (the pouring out of the Holy Spirit at Pentecost was then a moment of great activity).

The prayer forms a kind of response to the promises of preceding chapters. Like a psalm, it begins by recalling God's past acts. God got personally involved with Israel in Egypt and imagined they would be responsive to him. But they rebelled and grieved his holy spirit (I won't use capitals, Holy Spirit, because that risks us reading in too much New Testament thinking). God's holy spirit was with the people, not just with its leaders, but therefore they could hurt and antagonize God's spirit and could find God chastising them, though also being mindful of them—as God is at Sinai and in many later contexts.

The present problem (the second paragraph suggests) is that God is indeed chastising but has given up the mindfulness part. At the exodus and the Reed Sea God had put his holy spirit in their midst, but where is God now? God's action in bringing them through the Reed Sea so they could relax on the other side was a spectacular act of power and passion—but where are the power and passion now? God is supposed to be their Father, so why is he not showing the concern and commitment expected of a father or **restorer**? Their physical fathers/ancestors, Abraham and Jacob-Israel, would hardly recognize the "family" in its diminished state—hence perhaps the appeal to God's fatherhood, rare in the Old Testament. The paragraph goes on to embody the chutzpah that has appeared elsewhere in Isaiah. They grant that they have wandered from **Yahweh's** ways but come close to blaming Yahweh for their wandering— couldn't he have stopped them?

The third paragraph restates those themes, again expressing a longing for Yahweh to intervene and again suggesting some chutzpah as it implies that the people had offended in relation to Yahweh's ways (that is, failed to live by them) as a result of Yahweh's getting angry with them. Maybe Yahweh was justified in getting angry, but the result was that they sinned the more. The sin is described in terms of their abandoning a life of **faithfulness** for a life characterized by the kind of actions that made them taboo in Yahweh's eyes—something that couldn't be brought into Yahweh's presence. The prayer goes on also to acknowledge that people have not been seeking Yahweh, but the chutzpah receives yet further expression in the claim that the reason is that Yahweh had turned his face away. There was no point in seeking him.

The prayer's close constitutes a final appeal to God's being their Father and also their potter. Chutzpah features yet again, as this last image is one God has used more than once in Isaiah to put them in their place; they turn the image back onto God. Is Yahweh really going to continue doing nothing?

What will be the reply?

ISAIAH 65:1–25

Straight-Talking Meets Straight-Talking

1   I was available to people who didn't ask,
     I was accessible to people who didn't seek help from me.
I said, "I'm here, I'm here,"
     to a nation that was not calling on my name.
2   I spread my hands all day
     to a rebellious people,
who walk in a way that is not good,
     following their own plans.
3   The people are ones who provoke me,
     to my face, continually.
sacrificing in the gardens,
     burning incense on the bricks,
4   ones who sit in tombs,
     spend the night in secret places,
who eat swine's flesh,
     with a broth of desecrating things in their bowls,
5   who say, "Keep to yourself, don't come near me,
     because I'm too sacred for you."
These people are smoke in my nostrils,
     a fire burning all day.
6   There: it is written before me,
     I will not be still, rather I am repaying,
I will repay into their lap 7 your waywardness
     and your ancestors' waywardness together
     (Yahweh has said).
The people who burnt incense on the mountains,
     who reviled me on the hills:
I am counting out their earnings
     first of all into their lap.

8   Yahweh has said this:
"As the new wine can be found in the cluster,
     and someone will say 'Don't destroy it,

244

because there's a blessing in it,'
so I will act for my servants' sake,
    so as not to destroy everything.
9 I will bring out offspring from Jacob,
    and from Judah one who is going to possess my
        mountains.
My chosen ones will possess it,
    my servants will dwell there.
10 Sharon will become pasture for sheep,
    the Vale of Achor a resting place for cattle,
    for my people who have sought from me.
11 But you who abandon Yahweh,
    who disregard my holy mountain,
who set a table for Luck,
    who fill a mixing chalice for Destiny:
12 I will destine you to the sword,
    all of you will bow for slaughter.
Because I called but you didn't answer,
    I spoke but you didn't listen.
You did what was evil in my eyes,
    and what I didn't delight in, you chose."

13 Therefore my Lord Yahweh has said this:
"Now: my servants will eat,
    but you will be hungry.
Now: my servants will drink,
    but you will be thirsty.
Now: my servants will celebrate,
    but you will be shamed.
14 Now: my servants will resound
    from happiness of heart,
but you will cry out from pain of heart,
    from brokenness of spirit you will howl.
15 You will leave your name
    as an oath for my chosen ones,
'So may my Lord Yahweh kill you,'
    but for his servants he will proclaim another name,
16 so that the person who prays for blessing in the country
    will pray for blessing by the God who says 'Amen.'
Because the earlier troubles will have been put out of mind,
    and because they will have been hidden from my eyes.

¹⁷ Because here I am, creating
   new heavens and a new earth.
The earlier ones will not be recollected;
   they will not come into mind.
¹⁸ Rather, be glad
   and rejoice forever in what I am creating.
Because here I am, creating Jerusalem as a joy
   and its people as a rejoicing.
¹⁹ I will rejoice in Jerusalem
   and be glad in my people.
There will not make itself heard in it any more
   the sound of weeping or the sound of a cry.
²⁰ There will no longer be from there any more
      a baby of [few] days
      or an old person who doesn't fulfill his days.
Because the youth will die as a person of a hundred years,
      and the sinner will be humiliated as a person of a hun-
         dred years.
²¹ They will build houses and dwell [in them],
   they will plant vineyards and eat their fruit.
²² They won't build and another dwell;
   they won't plant and another eat.
The days of my people will be like a tree's days;
   my chosen ones will use up the work of their hands.
²³ They won't toil with empty result;
   they won't give birth with dismaying outcome.
Because they will be offspring blessed by Yahweh,
   they and their descendants with them.
²⁴ Before they call, I myself will answer;
   while they're still speaking, I myself will listen.
²⁵ The wolf and the lamb will graze together,
   the cougar, like the ox, will eat straw,
   but the snake—dirt will be its food.
People won't do evil, they won't destroy,
   in all my holy mountain (Yahweh has said)."

I sometimes have a hard time persuading people that prayer is an act of communication between us and God and that there's a mutuality about this communication. The idea has got around that prayer is really more like a form of reflection and meditation, designed to change us not to change God. There are several reasons why this idea has got around. People are puzzled and hurt by the experience of God not granting their prayers. When they pray, they don't have a feeling of communicating with someone who is listening. They understand God to be wise and unchanging, and the idea of God having a change of plan as a result of a suggestion from us seems to make no sense. Another reason is that we pray out loud less than previous generations.

Christians at the same time often think God must be more real to them than he was to Israel, when the impression one gets from the Old Testament is that the opposite is the case. These chapters in Isaiah offer a spectacular example. They also suggest another reason for hesitating about the idea that prayer might involve mutual communication. Much human communication gets fraught and fractious. It involves confrontation and argument. In the West, we are uneasy when that happens. It will seem more worrying for communication with God to take that form, but the Old Testament assumes it can do so. Yet being able to argue is a sign of strength in a relationship. It means the relationship won't break because you have a disagreement.

God here talks straight in response to the straight-talking in the previous section. Israel has had the nerve to complain at **Yahweh's** inaction, his hiddenness, his absence, and to blame Yahweh for its own waywardness. "Excuse me," Yahweh says. "You're saying that I have been hiding? You've got a nerve. You're the ones who have been hiding." Yahweh begins with an extraordinary piece of self-description. He has been standing with his hands open toward Israel, in the manner of a suppliant. He has been appealing to them and they have been treating him like a master who is ignoring his servant.

Yahweh thus sees the self-portrait of the people praying in the previous section as ingenuous. Even if they are loyal worshipers of Yahweh, many of their fellows are not. They are engaged in religious observances that deny any **faithfulness** to Yahweh. Maybe these people see themselves as worshipers of Yahweh. They certainly see themselves as deeply committed to their faith (hence the line about their warning people to be wary of coming too near to them because of their consecrated state). But their expression of their faith is totally unacceptable to Yahweh.

They will pay for it. But Yahweh allows more explicitly than usual for the possibility of distinguishing between the faithful and the faithless in the community. The latter have surrendered any right to be designated "my servants." That expression applies only to people who dissociate themselves from the faithless. When judgment comes, it will distinguish between the two groups. The prophecy's aim is thus to encourage the faithful and also to push the faithless to changing their ways so that the judgment that comes doesn't fall on them. It could still be the case that judgment needs to fall on no one.

Yes, Yahweh is to intervene positively in Jerusalem's life in the way that prayer urged. The last paragraph offers a picture of the result of that intervention. Its "new heavens and new earth" doesn't denote a new cosmos. There's nothing wrong with the cosmos. The later lines in the paragraph make clear that creating a new heavens and new earth is an image for creating a new Jerusalem where the problems about human life in the present Jerusalem are put right. At the moment most babies die in infancy and most people who survive to grow to adulthood die by middle age. Then the person who might have died as a youth will live to a hundred and the sinner who lives to a hundred, instead of dying young as he should, will still die and be humiliated. People will build houses and live in them and plant vineyards and live in them, instead of leaving the houses and the vineyards to the next generation. Flocks will be safe from wild animals and people will be safe from attackers. Life will be more the way God intended from the beginning. And communication with God will be real instead of being short-circuited.

ISAIAH 66:1–24

Choose Your Ending

¹ Yahweh has said this:
    "The heavens are my throne,
    the earth is my footstool.

Wherever would be the house that you would build for me,
    wherever would be the place that would be my abode?
2 All these things my hand made (Yahweh's declaration),
    and to this person I look:
to the lowly, to the broken in spirit,
    someone who trembles at my word.
3 One who slaughters an ox is one who strikes a person
       down;
    one who sacrifices a lamb is one who strangles a dog.
One who lifts up an offering—it's pig's blood;
    one who makes a memorial of incense—he worships a
       bane.
They for their part have chosen their ways,
    their soul delights in their abominations.
4 I for my part will choose caprices for them,
    and bring upon them what they dread.
Because I called and there was no one answering,
    I spoke and they didn't listen.
They did what was evil in my eyes,
    and what I didn't delight in, they chose."

5 Listen to Yahweh's word,
    you who tremble at his word.
"Your brothers have said, people who repudiate you,
    who exclude you for the sake of my name,
'May Yahweh be severe, so that we may see your
       celebration'—
    they will be shamed."
6 The sound of uproar from the city,
    a sound from the palace,
the sound of Yahweh
    dealing out retribution to his enemies.

7 Before she labors she has given birth,
    before pain comes to her she delivers a boy.
8 Who has heard something like this,
    who has seen things like these?
Can a country be brought through labor in one day,
    or a nation be born in one moment?
Because Zion is laboring
    and also giving birth to her children.

9   "Will I myself make a breach
      and not bring to birth? (Yahweh says).
    Or will I myself bring to birth
      and close [the womb]? (your God says)."

10 Celebrate with Jerusalem, rejoice in her,
      all you who give yourselves to her.
    Be glad with her in joy,
      all you who mourned over her,
11 so you may nurse and be full
      from her comforting breast,
    so you may drink deeply and delight yourself
      from her splendid bosom.
12 Because Yahweh has said this:
      "Here I am, extending to her
      well-being like a stream,
    like a flooding wash
      the splendor of the nations,
    so you may drink of it as you're carried on her side
      and dandled on her knees.
13 Like someone whom his mother comforts,
      so I myself will comfort you.
    You will be comforted in Jerusalem,
14   you will see, and your heart will rejoice,
      and your limbs will flourish like grass."
    Yahweh's hand will cause itself to be acknowledged among
          his servants,
      and he will rage among his enemies.
15 Because there—Yahweh will come in fire,
      his chariots like a whirlwind,
    to return his anger in fury,
      his blast in fiery flame.
16 Because Yahweh is going to exercise authority with fire,
      with his sword, among all flesh;
      the people slain by Yahweh will be many.
17 "The people who sanctify themselves and purify themselves
          for the gardens,
      following after one in the midst,
    people who eat the flesh of pig, reptile, and mouse,
      will come to an end together (Yahweh's declaration).

¹⁸ But as for me, on the basis of their deeds and their intentions, the gathering of all the nations and tongues is coming. They will come and see my splendor. ¹⁹ I will set a sign among them and send off from them survivors to the nations—Tarshish, Pul, and Lud, the people who draw the bow, Tubal, Javan, the distant shores, which have not heard report of me and have not seen my splendor. They will tell of my splendor among the nations. ²⁰ They will bring all your family members from all the nations as an offering to Yahweh, by means of horses, chariotry, coaches, mules, and dromedaries, to my holy mountain, Jerusalem (Yahweh has said), as the Israelites bring the offering in a pure vessel to Yahweh's house. ²¹ Also from them I will take people as priests and Levites (Yahweh has said). ²² Because as the new heavens and the new earth that I'm going to make stand before me (Yahweh's declaration), so will your offspring and your name stand. ²³ New moon by new moon, Sabbath by Sabbath, all flesh will come to bow low before me (Yahweh has said). ²⁴ They will go out and look at the corpses of the people who rebel against me. Because their worm will not die and their fire will not go out. They will be a horror to all flesh."

There's a classic movie called *The French Lieutenant's Woman*, set in nineteenth-century England, that tells of a tortuous relationship in which a man is powerfully drawn to a woman who hardly belongs to his class and when he is already committed to marrying someone else. The novel on which the movie is based has two alternative endings, which in effect invite the reader to decide where the relationship goes in the end. The movie script cleverly takes the form of a movie about the making of a movie in which the leading actors are having an affair that mirrors the affair of the leading characters in the story. That provides an alternative way of having two endings and leaving the audience to choose between them.

The book of Isaiah ends in a comparable way. The next-to-last verses have people from Israel brought home and people from the nations joining them in worship and brought into the body of the people who lead worship and offer the sacrifices. They are even involved in missionary work to their kin. But the very last verse pictures them gazing at the bodies of people who have died through **Yahweh's** judgment as a result of their rebellion, thrown onto a heap in the canyon where **Judahites** used to offer their children as whole burnt offerings, which in effect becomes a graveyard for their parents. When this closing passage from Isaiah is read in synagogue worship, the next-to-last verse is repeated after the last verse to avoid the book closing on such a grim note, and Hebrew Bibles also repeat it in that connection. A saying in the Talmud (the collection of the sayings of rabbis from the early centuries of the Common Era) declares that the prophets were in the habit of concluding their addresses with words of praise and comfort, and it commends their example to us in connection with our everyday conversations. While the book of Isaiah looks a particularly spectacular exception, it may be less so than it seems. The last verses of the book offer their readers two alternative prospects for their own destiny. If the book's compilers had had the technology available, they might have ended the book with these closing verses in parallel columns, so that people can choose their column.

On one hand, then, there are the people whom the book has from time to time attacked throughout, people who worship Yahweh but do so in a way that conflicts with who Yahweh is or who also worship other deities. The prophet again speaks in terms of two-way communication, a reality that played an important role in the previous section. They claim they are calling out to Yahweh and he isn't answering, but the way they are calling out means Yahweh cannot answer. He is calling out to them about that fact, but they are not answering.

Then there are the people who tremble at Yahweh's word. They know that the community as a whole has deserved and continues to deserve Yahweh's judgment. Their own acceptance of this fact earns them the disapproval of other people and in some sense earns them their exclusion—perhaps they were priests who were debarred from ministry. The people in power mockingly welcome the idea that Yahweh may act in severe fashion. Admittedly even the people who count as Yahweh's servants need to be wary about their assumptions concerning Yahweh and worship. Since preceding chapters have been positive about the temple, the opening verses of this section can hardly be totally rejecting it, but they are reminding Judahites that there's a sense in which the idea of a temple for Yahweh is incoherent. They are also reminding them that a community that is broken in spirit and couldn't build a temple would not be thereby incapable of relating to Yahweh. The prophet again seeks to build up their conviction that Yahweh is going to restore Jerusalem. Yahweh doesn't bring a baby to full term and then not bring it to birth.

Readers of Isaiah have to choose which ending will apply to them.

GLOSSARY

Assyria, Assyrians
The first great Middle Eastern superpower, the Assyrians spread their empire westward into Syria-Palestine in the eighth century, the time of Amos and Isaiah. They first made **Ephraim** part of their empire, then when Ephraim kept trying to assert independence, they invaded Ephraim, destroyed its capital at Samaria, transported its people, and settled people from other parts of their empire in their place. They also invaded **Judah** and devastated much of the country but didn't take Jerusalem. Prophets such as Amos and Isaiah describe how Yahweh was thus using Assyria as a means of disciplining Israel.

authority, authoritative
English translations commonly translate the Hebrew *mishpat* by words such as judgment or justice, but the word suggests more broadly the exercise of authority and the making of decisions. It is a word for government. In principle, then, the word has positive implications, though it is quite possible for people in authority to make decisions in an unjust way. It is a king's job to exercise authority in accordance with **faithfulness** to God and people and in a way that brings deliverance. Exercising authority means taking decisions and acting decisively on behalf of people in need and of people wronged by others. Thus speaking of God as judge implies good news (unless you are a major wrongdoer). God's "decisions" can also denote God's authoritative declarations concerning human behavior and about what he intends to do.

Babylon, Babylonians
A minor power in the context of Isaiah ben Amoz, in the time of Jeremiah Babylon took over the position of superpower from **Assyria** and kept that for nearly a century until conquered by **Persia**. Prophets such as Jeremiah describe how **Yahweh** was using Babylon as a means of

disciplining **Judah**. Their creation stories, law codes, and more philosophical writings help us understand aspects of the Old Testament's
comparable writings, while their astrological religion also forms background to aspects of polemic in the prophets.

Day of the Lord

The oldest occurrence of the expression "the Day of the Lord," "**Yahweh's** Day," comes in Amos 5, which indicates that people saw it as a
time when Yahweh would bring great blessing on them. Amos declares
that the opposite is the case. Henceforth the expression always has sin-
ister connotations. Yahweh's Day is a day when Yahweh acts in decisive
fashion. It doesn't happen just once; there are various occasions that the
Old Testament describes as Yahweh's Day, such as Jerusalem's fall in 587
and **Babylon's** fall in 539. In Isaiah, Sennacherib's devastation of **Judah**
was such an embodiment of Yahweh's Day (22:5).

decision, see authority

Ephraim, Ephraimites

After the reign of David and Solomon, the nation of Israel split into
two. Most of the twelve Israelite clans set up an independent state in the
north, separate from **Judah** and Jerusalem and from the line of David.
Because this was the bigger of the two states, politically it kept the name
Israel, which is confusing because Israel is still the name of the people
as a whole as the people of God. In the prophets, it is sometimes difficult to tell whether "Israel" refers to the people of God as a whole or just
to the northern state. Sometimes the state is referred to by the name of
Ephraim as one of its dominant clans, so I use this term to refer to that
northern state to try to reduce the confusion.

exile

At the end of the seventh century, **Babylon** became the major power
in **Judah's** world but Judah was inclined to rebel against its authority.
As part of a successful campaign to get Judah to submit properly to
its authority, in 597 and in 587 BC the **Babylonians** transported many
people from Jerusalem to Babylon. They made a special point of trans-
porting people in leadership positions, such as members of the royal
family and the court, priests, and prophets (Ezekiel was one of them).

These people were thus compelled to live in Babylonia for the next fifty years or so. Through the same period, people back in Judah were also under Babylonian authority. So they were not physically in exile, but they were also living *in* the exile as a period of time. A number of books in the Old Testament indicate that one of the issues they are handling is the pressure this experience brings to people.

faithfulness

In English Bibles this Hebrew word (*sedaqah*) is usually translated "righteousness," but it indicates a particular slant on what we might mean by righteousness. It means doing the right thing by the people with whom one is in a relationship, the members of one's community. Thus it is really closer to "faithfulness" than "righteousness."

Greece

In 336 BC Greek forces under Alexander the Great took control of the **Persian** Empire, but after Alexander's death in 323 his empire split up. The largest part, to the north and east of Palestine, was ruled by one of his generals, Seleucus, and his successors. **Judah** was under its control for much of the next two centuries, though it was at the extreme south-western border of this empire and sometimes came under the control of the Ptolemaic Empire in Egypt (ruled by successors of another of Alexander's officers). In 167 the Seleucid ruler Antiochus Epiphanes attempted to ban observance of the Torah and persecuted the faithful community in Jerusalem, but they rebelled and experienced a great deliverance.

Israel, Israelites

Originally, Israel was the new name God gave Abraham's grandson Jacob. Jacob's twelve sons were then forefathers of the twelve clans that comprise the people Israel. In the time of Saul and David these twelve clans became more of a political entity. So Israel was both the people of God and a nation or state like other nations or states. After Solomon's day, this state split into two separate states, **Ephraim** and **Judah**. Because Ephraim was by far the bigger, it often continued to be referred to as Israel. So if one is thinking of the people of God, Judah is part of Israel. If one is thinking politically, Judah isn't part of Israel. Once Ephraim has gone out of existence, then for practical purposes Judah *is* Israel, as the people of God.

Judah, Judahites

One of the twelve sons of Jacob and the clan that traces its ancestry to him, then the dominant clan in the southern of the two states after the time of Solomon. Effectively Judah *was* Israel after the fall of **Ephraim**.

Kaldeans (Chaldeans)

Kaldea was an area southeast of **Babylon** from which the kings who ruled Babylonia came in the time Babylonia ruled **Judah**. Thus the Old Testament refers to the Babylonians as the Kaldeans.

Persia

The third Middle Eastern superpower. Under the leadership of Cyrus the Great, they took control of the **Babylonian** Empire in 539 BC. Isaiah 40–55 sees **Yahweh's** hand in raising up Cyrus as the means of restoring **Judah** after the **exile**. Judah and surrounding peoples such as Samaria, Ammon, and Ashdod were then Persian provinces or colonies. The Persians stayed in power for two centuries until defeated by **Greece**.

Philistia, Philistines

The Philistines were people who came from across the Mediterranean to settle in Canaan at the same time as the Israelites were establishing themselves in Canaan, so that the two peoples formed an accidental pincer movement on the existent inhabitants of the country and became each other's rivals for control of the area.

Remains, Remnant

The Prophets warn that **Yahweh's** chastisement will mean Israel (and other peoples) being cut down so that only small remains or a remnant will survive. But at least some remains of Israel will survive—so the idea of "remains" can become a sign of hope. It can also become a challenge—the few that remain are challenged to become **faithful** remains, a faithful remnant.

Restore

A restorer is a person who is in a position to take action on behalf of someone within his extended family who is in need in order to restore the situation to what it should be. The word overlaps with expressions such as next-of-kin, guardian, and redeemer. "Next-of-kin" indicates the family context that "restorer" presupposes. "Guardian" indicates that the restorer is in a position to be concerned for the person's protection and defense. "Redeemer" indicates having resources that the restorer is prepared to expend on the person's behalf. The Old Testament uses the term to refer to God's relationship with Israel as well as to the action of a human person in relation to another; so it implies that Israel belongs to God's family and that God acts on its behalf in the way a restorer does.

Seleucids, see Greece

Sheol

The most frequent of the Hebrew names for the place where we go when we die. In the New Testament it is called Hades. It isn't a place of punishment or suffering but simply a resting place for everyone, a kind of nonphysical analogue to the tomb as the resting place for our bodies.

Well-being

The Hebrew word *shalom* can suggest peace after there has been conflict, but it often points to a richer notion of fullness of life. The KJV sometimes translates it "welfare," and modern translations use words such as "well-being" or "prosperity." It suggests that everything is going well for you.

Yahweh

In most English Bibles, the word "LORD" often comes in all capitals as does, sometimes, the word "GOD." These actually represent the name of God, Yahweh. In later Old Testament times, Israelites stopped using the name Yahweh and started to refer to Yahweh as "the Lord." There may be two reasons. They wanted other people to recognize that Yahweh was the one true God, but this strange foreign-sounding name could give the impression that Yahweh was just Israel's tribal god. A term such as "the Lord" was one anyone could recognize. In addition, they didn't want to fall foul of the warning in the Ten Commandments about misusing Yahweh's name. Translations into other languages then followed suit and substituted an expression such as "the Lord" for the name Yahweh. The down sides are that this obscures the fact that God wanted to be known by name, that often the text refers to Yahweh and not some other (so-called) god or lord, and that the practice gives the impression that God is much more "lordly" and patriarchal than actually God is. (The form "Jehovah" isn't a proper word but a mixture of the consonants of Yahweh and the vowels of that word for "Lord," to remind people in reading Scripture that they should say "the Lord," not the actual name.)

Yahweh Armies

This title for God usually appears in English Bibles as "the LORD of Hosts," but it is a more puzzling expression than that implies. The word for LORD is actually the name of God, **Yahweh**, and the word for Hosts is the regular Hebrew word for armies; it is the word that appears on the back of Israeli military trucks. So more literally the expression means "Yahweh [of] Armies," which is just as odd in Hebrew as "Goldingay of Armies" would be. Yet in general terms its likely implication is clear; it suggests that Yahweh is the embodiment of or controller of all war-making power, in heaven or on earth.

Zion

The word is an alternative name for the city of Jerusalem. Jerusalem is more a political name; other peoples would refer to the city as "Jerusalem." Zion is more a religious name, a designation of the city that focuses on its being the place where **Yahweh** dwells and is worshiped.

Printed in Great Britain
by Amazon

30526807R00152